YOUR 12 INNER STRENGTHS

A Guide to Your Best Life
Through the Power of Virtues

STACEY A. THOMPSON

First Edition: October 2025

ISBN: 979-8-9995540-0-0 (Paperback)
ISBN: 979-8-9995540-1-7 (Ebook)

Library of Congress Control Number: 2025918833

Cover and interior design by Melissa Williams Design

Published by

THRIVING LIFE
MEDIA

For my mother, Priscilla,
with all my love and gratitude.

~

In loving memory of
my dear friend Kathie Heckler,
Uncle Robert May, and Aunt Ann Rice:
Your remarkable courage, perseverance,
and hope inspired us all.

Cultivate Virtue in your self,
And Virtue will be real.
Cultivate it in the family,
And Virtue will abound.
Cultivate it in the village,
And Virtue will grow.
Cultivate it in the nation,
And Virtue will be abundant.
Cultivate it in the universe,
And Virtue will be everywhere.

—*Tao Te Ching,* Lao Tsu, translated by
Gia-Fu Feng and Jane English

Contents

Introduction

What does it mean to live your best life? You may think it means achieving personal and professional goals, enjoying loving relationships, and finding fulfillment in your work. You might say it's also about growing through challenges, maintaining good health, and pursuing a meaningful calling. No matter how you define it, bringing out the best in you—your inner strengths such as courage, purposefulness, gratitude, and creativity—can help you live your best life.

Yet limiting beliefs and complacency can prevent you from achieving what you instinctively know you can do. To rise above these mental barriers takes strength of heart and mind.

Think for a minute: What would you do if you were braver? What possibilities might open up if you chose to forgive? What could you accomplish if you wholeheartedly committed to something? How would more gratitude and joy affect your life?

I designed this book to guide you in exploring and cultivating 12 inner strengths or virtues—terms I use interchangeably—that can overcome barriers to living your best life.

When you take the helm of your life, guided by these empowering, timeless virtues as your beacon of light, you will navigate life exceptionally! You will live proactively instead of reactively, deepen your relationships, and achieve what matters to you.

You already embody virtue. However, it's natural for people to express particular virtues more strongly than others. For example, you may be naturally compassionate but wish you could be braver.

You achieve goals, yet struggle to handle obstacles. You tend to focus on what's wrong instead of what's right.

As you build your inner strengths—compassion, perseverance, hope, gratitude, and others—they will flow more naturally through your thoughts, choices, and actions. Yet cultivating these strengths requires consistent, thoughtful effort, hard work, and the courage to be uncomfortable.

Henry Ward Beecher, an American Congregationalist clergyman, pointed out, "Our virtues are like crystals hidden in rocks. No man shall find them by any soft ways, but by the hammer and by fire."[1] He reminds us that our virtues, like crystals, may not be easy to find. Fear and self-doubt can keep them buried, so we must dig deep to bring them to light. Through dedication and practice, we become increasingly skilled at unearthing these precious stones or inner strengths. With each strength we reveal, our character deepens, sharpens, and we begin to align with our best self.

Why does this matter? Because a shining character helps us make wiser choices, face challenges with resilience, and build lasting relationships.

The What and Why of Virtue

Virtue, by definition, is the moral excellence of a person. Morally excellent people have a character made up of virtues valued as being "good." They are honest, respectful, and kind, for example. They do the right thing and don't bend to impulses or desires. Instead, they act in accordance with their values and principles. Of course, we're not perfect, and the pull of temptation can be intense. That makes pursuing virtue an even more worthy endeavor! In fact, research shows that these character strengths are universally valued and recognized as the foundation of a moral and thriving life.

Yet, how often do we think to build our "character muscle"? Just like any skill we learn, cultivating virtue takes deliberate practice. As we do, we combat self-absorption, greed, laziness, envy, and the many other vices that diminish our potential. Chiseling out these crystals—these inner strengths—could attract what's missing in our lives. We may have a breakthrough in an area where we're stuck, discover a new purpose, or heal a relationship.

With a habitual disposition of virtue, we naturally become more courageous, grateful, creative, and resilient. We shape our lives to create enduring benefits for ourselves and, consequently, for others.

The opposite of virtue is vice. Vices are behaviors that have negative consequences. Common vices include gluttony (overindulgence in food or drink), arrogance, envy, and greed. But as we know, vices are not easy to overcome.

Swiss psychiatrist Carl Jung said, "Neurosis is a substitute for legitimate suffering."[2] Legitimate suffering comes from trauma, neglect, loss, feelings of inadequacy, and unresolved anger. Facing our pain is difficult work, and it may at times feel easier to escape through self-defeating patterns that can lead to neurosis. But living an inauthentic life—one that is not true to our values, beliefs, or desires—can be even harder to bear. I've faced this struggle in my own life.

In my 20s, I began shopping too much because of persistent anxiety. I used shopping as a crutch for coping with disappointment, insecurity, and sadness. Shopping made me feel better. But the more I shopped, the more shame and guilt I felt. The internal void I was trying to fill with things led to a dysfunctional cycle, lowering my self-esteem and keeping me stuck in mediocrity.

My compulsive shopping came to a head when my therapist asked me to gather up all my recent purchases. I wasn't sure what her motivation was, but I agreed. I pulled out all the clothing, decorations, kitchenware, and more I had recently purchased and placed them on my bed and furniture. My heart sank as I looked at the items sprawled out everywhere. There were so many things, some still with the tags months after I had bought them. At that moment, I realized how deeply unhealthy my behavior was.

Years later, through therapy, courses, and personal development books, I realized that I had been attempting to *soothe* negative feelings rather than learn how to cope with them.

Realizing I had a shopping problem and disliking the person I had become was the first step in healing. I had become acutely aware that excessive shopping was costing me my well-being and potential.

Although my anxiety has not gone away, I've learned to manage it better. I take prescribed medication along with supplements and channel my uneasiness, worry, and fear into healthier activities. Instead of shopping, I focus on creative projects, exercise, watch movies, or spend time with family and friends.

I am also kinder to myself. Instead of asking, *What's wrong with me?* I tell myself, *It's okay—it's just a little anxiety. I will manage it.* Thinking this way helps me embrace my feelings rather than denying them through a bad habit.

Unknowingly, I had applied the virtues of commitment and com-passion—specifically, self-compassion—to my own healing process. I committed to behaviors that supported my well-being rather than harming my life. Self-compassion helped me realize that anxiety wasn't a character flaw but a treatable condition. By strengthening these virtues, I was able to replace my shopping vice with a meaning-ful mission: to inspire and educate people in practicing virtues so they can live their best lives.

Are you facing a challenge? If so, I hope my story encourages you to draw on your inner strengths to help overcome it. When you *consciously apply* virtues to a difficult situation or harmful habit, you *will* create positive change.

Why Cultivate Virtue?

Is your life everything you want it to be? If the answer is "No" or "Not quite," you can use virtues as a personal development tool to help make your life all it can and ought to be.

Here's a sampling of what's possible when you practice virtues:

- **Courage** moves you past fear to fulfill your true potential.

- **Forgiveness** helps you let go of grudges and heal the pain.

- **Gratitude** shifts your perspective and boosts hap-piness.

- **Integrity** keeps you true to yourself and honest with others.

- **Perseverance** enables you to push through obsta-cles and achieve goals.

- **Purpose** guides your decisions and helps you find meaning.

I promise you, the more you make virtue a habit, the more you'll positively change your life. For instance, if you cultivate the virtue of love for your partner by listening more attentively, planning a date night, or regularly saying "I love you," then love grows in your life. Most likely, it's because your partner will feel more loved and return that love. You've not only learned to give your love more, but you've also strengthened your relationship.

With virtue as a source of goodness and strength, you'll bring out your personal best. But it takes repeated virtuous acts—kind acts, courageous acts, honorable acts, and forgiving acts—to truly embody virtue.

As you grow your inner strengths, you'll face challenges, but the journey will reward you unexpectedly. Personal growth can be uncomfortable and even painful, yet always worthwhile.

How to Read This Book

You'll find 12 virtues or inner strengths in this book, one for each month. I have intentionally not labeled the virtues by month, so you can start anywhere. You can begin with a virtue that resonates with you or take a progressive, month-to-month approach. Either way is effective.

Throughout the book are stories of people who emulate virtue. These people have moved past fear to achieve a vision, turned their suffering into service, or created a stronger sense of self. Their experiences reveal the transformative power of cultivating virtues.

Each individual has a different story to tell. They come from diverse backgrounds: some are educated, some are not; some are poor, some are not; some are still living, others have passed; some are famous, while others are not so well known. They include an Olympian swimmer born without lower legs, Holocaust survivors, a spiritual leader, an actor, parents, activists, and more. They are heroes in their own right, some having experienced enormous challenges and devastating circumstances. Still, virtue helped them rise above their obstacles and become role models to many.

As a movie lover, I have included characters from films who exemplify virtue. Movies have a way of creatively illustrating virtue in times of adversity and triumph.

I hope all these stories inspire you on your journey to creating your best life.

At the end of each chapter, you'll find ways to cultivate each virtue and strengthen its presence in your everyday experiences. Some practices are actionable, whereas others are more reflective. I encourage you to keep a journal or notebook while you explore each virtue and complete the practices. You'll experience a sense of accomplishment, and writing things down reinforces your progress while creating a way to reflect later.

If you try just one practice from this book and it helps you, then I've accomplished what I set out to do: to help you experience the meaningful difference that practicing virtues can make. That difference will take many forms, but I take a stand that you will thrive and live purposefully with virtues as your inspiration.

Also, while you read about virtues and put them into practice, be kind to yourself. The goal is *not* to attain perfection. We all make mistakes! We're all susceptible to temptations and impulses. Instead, the goal is to take small steps to create positive change. Whether you write a gratitude letter or take a single step toward a goal, no accomplishment is too small. All of it is there to help you grow over time. But be sure to stretch yourself! No worthy endeavor comes without stepping out of your comfort zone.

Let's Begin

I am deeply grateful that you picked up this book. Your decision to read it tells me you want to access your inner strengths to become the best you can be—and we all have this capacity! As Lao Tsu says in his poem at the beginning of this book, when you cultivate virtue within yourself, it takes root in your life and naturally expands to your family, community, nation, and even the world.

I wish you much success in living your best life through the power of virtues.

CHAPTER 1

Commitment

Commitment is an unshakable devotion to a worthy endeavor,
gracing life with purpose and meaning.

At any point in life, we can start fresh. We can commit or recommit to something we want, something that matters to us. We may already be working on fulfilling a dream—but doing so half-heartedly—or maybe we haven't yet identified a goal that lights us up. Whatever the case, once we commit to something, declaring this promise into existence becomes an elixir for a better life. Our sense of purpose strengthens. We have a clear direction. Success *is* possible.

But as we know all too well, what we pledge to do can be tough to carry out. Life can pull us in too many directions. Days, months, even years go by, and we still haven't written that book, left that unfulfilling job, or had the children we've always wanted. Unforeseen accidents, illnesses, relationship endings, and financial difficulties can get in the way. Fear, procrastination, and ambivalence also present roadblocks to achieving what we want.

Even with these challenges, we can stay true to our commitments through passion, sacrifice, and perseverance.

Committing to What You Want

Committing to something we feel passionate about can make us unstoppable. Take, for example, Jessica Long. She was born in Siberia, Russia with fibular hemimelia, a rare condition that caused missing bones in her lower legs and feet. Jessica's mother, just 16 at the time, feared she couldn't provide the care her daughter needed. After some persuasion, she made the difficult decision to place Jessica in an orphanage with the hopes of adoption.

In 1993, when Jessica was 13 months old, Steve and Beth Long of Baltimore, Maryland, adopted her, along with a boy named Joshua. At 18 months, Jessica underwent a bilateral lower-leg amputation to improve her mobility with prosthetics. The adoption agency had warned the Longs that life would not be easy for Jessica, but Beth responded that while Jessica's life wouldn't be easy, she knew it would be amazing.

Beth and Steve kept their promise. They encouraged Jessica to try gymnastics, rock climbing, and ice skating. Jessica particularly enjoyed swimming, fondly remembering spending time in her grandparents' pool. Pretending to be a mermaid, she felt capable and free in the water.

Swimming became Jessica's passion. Since she excelled at it, she joined her first competitive team at the tender age of 10. Her earliest success came when she won three gold medals at the 2004 Paralympic Games in Athens, Greece, an incredible achievement for a 12-year-old.

Over the years, Jessica faced many trials, including 25 surgeries on her legs, an eating disorder brought on by competition's mental and physical toll, and the lingering pain of abandonment. What helped her heal was scaling back her training schedule and seeing a therapist. Coaching a girls' swim team also helped her find balance and purpose beyond swimming.[1]

At 33, Jessica is a 17-time Paralympic gold medalist, including a gold medal she won in the women's 100-meter butterfly at the 2021 Tokyo Paralympics. She has 30 Paralympic medals, making her one of the most accomplished American Paralympians in history.[2]

Jessica's dedication to her love of swimming and her parents' determination that she have an amazing life became a recipe for greatness.

So often, the passion we feel for our commitments drives their success. Just as Jessica loves swimming, my brother-in-law Carlo Lucatino loves helping those affected by autism and, consequently, has made a positive impact.

Carlo is a hardworking entrepreneur with three children. His oldest son, Giancarlo, has autism. Carlo's passion for helping find a cure for autism has fueled a 15-year commitment to raising money for Autism Speaks, which supports people with autism and their families.

Driven by his values of giving back and spending time with family, he, his wife, and sister-in-law created a bocce tournament that ran for five years. Despite his hectic and demanding schedule, Carlo—along with his team—rallied family, friends, colleagues, and businesses to participate in the tournament.

Over two hundred people sponsored or participated in a joyful and charitable day of bocce. With his sheer enthusiasm for the cause, Carlo increases his donation goal year after year. Through the annual autism walk and bocce tournament, he and his team have raised over $100,000 for Autism Speaks.[3]

Few people would question Jessica's and Carlo's commitment to their passions. This level of conviction—this "all-in" mentality—allowed them to achieve extraordinary results and lasting personal fulfillment.

The What and Why of Commitment

We often describe commitment as an agreement or pledge to support a cause or person and to take action on its/their behalf. Think of marriage, where saying our vows is the action behind our promise. Similarly, we commit to our careers when we show up to work each day, perform well, and express our loyalty to the organization. As parents, we make an enduring commitment to nurture and guide our children.

But why is commitment so important? Committing to a cause we believe is worthy or to a person we love gives our life direction and meaning. We choose not to be at the mercy of our life circumstances but rather the captains of our ships. We dedicate ourselves to a course, so we are now accountable for the destination and for facing each storm with resilience.

Just as we devote ourselves to positive endeavors, we can also commit to harmful ones, such as excessive drinking, remaining in a toxic relationship, or dwelling on negative thoughts. Although we may not recognize these behaviors as commitments, they indeed reveal where our devotions lie. So, it benefits us to recognize both our positive and negative commitments. Because once we're aware of them, we can start to change.

Declaring Your Commitments

Expressing a desire for something comes naturally, but genuinely committing means acting boldly on its behalf. We must take these actions not just when we have time or feel like it but consistently despite our busy schedules and personal comforts.

Here are examples of genuine commitment backed by action:

- I am committed to being the *best parent possible*, so I eat dinner with my kids, ask questions about their day, and do fun things with them.

- I am committed to *better mental and physical health*, so I exercise regularly, eat right, and meditate.

- I am committed to *preserving this beautiful planet*, so I recycle, volunteer for cleanups in my community, and use less plastic.

- I am committed to this *creative project*, so I find time each week to work on it, even if only for an hour.

Personal commitments like these can give you a sense of purpose, an aliveness that opens up new possibilities for an exciting journey ahead. You feel inspired and hopeful when you declare your intent to pursue a dream.

The challenge you face now is whether you'll have the perseverance and grit to fulfill this dream. Once you say, "I want a life I am proud of, so I need to stop drinking," or "I want to paint, write, or play guitar," you have pledged to a specific outcome. By *declaring* and *acting* on your commitment, you have bridged the gap between your current reality and your aspirations.

Practice Declaring a Commitment

Let's identify a commitment that resonates with you. You certainly have a few already, perhaps to your partner, faith, community, and career. Consider deepening an existing commitment or creating a new one that will bring you fulfillment. This commitment doesn't have to be monumental, but it should be meaningful and exciting to you. Ask yourself:

- What matters most to me and why? (Understanding why you are choosing a specific commitment boosts your motivation.)
- Does it excite me enough to dedicate myself to it wholeheartedly?
- Can I adjust my schedule to prioritize this commitment?

Support your commitment with a **SMART goal—one that is Specific, Measurable, Achievable, Realistic, and Time-bound.** For example, if your commitment is to educate and inspire people to live healthier lives, your SMART goal might be:

"I will become a certified wellness coach to gain credibility for my future health coaching business by [month/year]."

This goal is specific and measurable (certification as a clear outcome), achievable and realistic (within your reach), and time-bound (with a set completion date).

Next, create action steps for your SMART goal. Then, identify one step you can take this week to advance your commitment.

Creating a Compelling Vision

Congratulations! You chose a commitment to focus on and took action on its behalf. If you haven't decided on a commitment, don't worry. Your attention is now in this direction, and that focus will help you eventually discover a commitment. Now, ask yourself: What vision is so compelling that it will keep me moving forward with my commitment, no matter what?

Let's say you have a dream of starting your own business. You'll want to create action steps like raising money, talking to people in your industry who have achieved success, writing a business plan, etc. These steps can present potential roadblocks, such as your self-imposed limitations, which may include thoughts of not being good enough or not having enough time to achieve your goal. Criticism from others can also get in the way. In short, you can become stuck in your fears and unable to move forward.

To achieve a commitment or dream, something greater needs to drive you beyond your fears and circumstances. That something is a "compelling vision." A compelling vision is a clear and specific mental picture of your desired outcome that energizes and inspires you enough to take consistent action on its behalf. In other words, your vision connects you to your passion for what you want. When you face fear, discouragement, and even failure, this vision renews your excitement and helps you persevere.

Ken Blanchard and Jesse Lyn Stoner, authors of the international bestseller *Full Steam Ahead! Unleash the Power of Vision in Your Work and Your Life*, define a compelling vision through three essential components: "Knowing who you are [purpose], where you're going [picture of the future], and what will guide your journey [values]."[4] These components work together to empower you in achieving your goal.

They explain that *knowing who you are* means having a clear purpose—one that matters to you and excites you enough to keep going during tough times. The second component, *where you're going*, means having a vivid picture of your desired outcome. Your focus is not on how you'll get there but on the outcome itself. They emphasize that this vision should be proactive rather than reactive and something you want to create, not just something you want to avoid.

The final component, *what will guide your journey*, centers on your values, such as integrity, creativity, kindness, adventure, and courage. These values shape your priorities, actions, and behaviors.

The authors suggest identifying a few core values, ranking them by importance, and consistently upholding them since they form your life's foundation.[5]

Sculptor Michelangelo had a compelling vision. He saw an angel in the marble he was about to carve and wanted to set him free.[6] A vivid picture in his mind's eye propelled him to create the statue of David. Michelangelo took a chisel to the stone, and the realization of his vision began to unfold. Whatever obstacles he encountered, he would not let them overshadow his fierce image of David, a masterpiece of Renaissance sculpture.

Here are more examples of compelling visions:

Martin Luther King, Jr. famously shared his vision at a 1963 rally in Washington, D.C., that one day the United States would truly live up to its founding idea: "We hold these truths to be self-evident, that all men are created equal."[7]

On that sunny day, he boldly expressed a compelling vision of a socially just, free, and nonviolent nation to about 250,000 people. Consequently, he inspired millions to join the Civil Rights Movement.[8]

Karen Armstrong, an acclaimed scholar and bestselling author, made a heartfelt wish during her prizewinning 2008 TED talk. She asked for help creating, launching, and publicizing a Charter for Compassion, inspired by the Golden Rule: "Do unto others as you would have them do unto you." Her vision for a more compassionate world inspired thousands to help turn it into a reality, resulting in the Charter's unveiling in 2009. An organization of the same name emerged to bring compassion's principles to life.[9]

One way the organization carries out its mission is through "Compassionate Communities." Any individual, group, or organization can apply compassion to challenges in their communities such as homelessness and food insecurity. Since 2019, Compassionate Communities have formed in more than 50 countries, and over 121 city governments have become Compassionate Cities.[10]

Alexandra Scott exemplifies how even children can have compelling visions. Before her first birthday, doctors diagnosed Alex with neuroblastoma, a type of childhood cancer. She received a stem cell transplant at four years old. After the transplant, she said to her mother, "When I get out of the hospital, I want to have a lemonade stand."[11] Her vision was to raise money to give to the doctors to help other kids with cancer, inspired by the care she received.

With her brother's help, Alex raised an incredible $2,000 from her first lemonade stand and donated it to her hospital.

Alex's moving story of generosity inspired others worldwide to hold lemonade stands and donate the proceeds to her cause. By the time Alex lost her brave battle with cancer at age eight, she and others had raised over $1 million for cancer research.

Alex's legacy of inspiring generosity lives on through "Alex's Lemonade Stand Foundation for Childhood Cancer." The Foundation has raised over $300 million—and counting—for childhood cancer research in pursuit of a cure.[12]

You can create a compelling vision for your life and call upon it often to rekindle your excitement, especially when obstacles arise.

In contrast, without a vision, circumstances may dictate your life instead of you choosing the path that's right for you. With an ideal picture of who you want to be and what you want your life to be about, you can bring what you want to life.

Practice Creating a Compelling Vision

Imagine yourself in the future, having realized your commitment. Despite roadblocks, you stayed true to what you wanted. How has it impacted your life and others? Hold onto that feeling and create a compelling vision—a clear and specific mental picture of a desired outcome that energizes and inspires you enough to pursue what you want. Refer to this vision when challenges arise or your motivation wanes.

Your compelling vision can be a phrase written in the present tense that describes the best possible outcome. For example, let's say your commitment is to be in the best health of your life. Your compelling vision might be, "I am healthy and strong, having achieved my ideal weight through exercise and managing stress with monthly massages, daily meditation, and weekly yoga classes." Alternatively, if you seek a romantic partner, your vision might be, "I am in a loving relationship with someone who shares my same values and wants in life."

Find a vision that puts a fire in your heart and burns hot enough to help you succeed. And don't be afraid to make it grand! Write it down, review it often, celebrate milestones, and let it motivate you to hit that home run when life throws its curveballs.

Shifting Your Priorities

Do you spend time on what truly matters to you? Think about it for a minute. What matters most to you may not be getting enough—or any—of your attention while days, weeks, and even years pass. Family and career obligations can sideline you from your precious aspirations. "Shoulds" and "musts" take over your life. When you have downtime, you just want to watch a movie, read a good book, or have dinner with a friend. You need an escape to decompress and have some fun!

Many of us say we want something badly, yet a gap exists between what we want and how we actually spend our days. This gap is where living out our commitment stalls. What can help? Realigning our priorities with our commitments so there is no gap.

In his book *Emotional Chaos to Clarity*, Vipassana meditation teacher Phillip Moffitt says that cultivating mindfulness—being present and aware of one's thoughts and actions—can help align priorities with commitments. Moffitt explains that mindfulness clarifies priorities by encouraging reflection through questions like, "Do I have clear priorities? Do I want to set any? Am I living by them?"

By observing their priorities, individuals can see whether their daily lives truly reflect them.[13]

Living by your priorities helps you focus on what means the most to you. Say, for example, you dream of writing a book about a topic you love. You'll need to carve out alone time for this goal, time away from family and friends. They may push back, triggering feelings of guilt that could undermine your efforts.

Shifting priorities to complete the book may mean saying "No" to a friend who wants to go to happy hour, giving up your favorite Netflix show, taking a year off from the bowling league, or delaying a vacation. How else can your dream happen?

Moffitt writes, "Over time, and with consistent practice, you can develop a habit of continual awareness of your priorities. By 'continual' I don't mean that you are mindful of your priorities every single moment of your life but that you periodically check in with your priorities—it could be daily for some and weekly for others—and reappraise them in the context of what's really going on in your life."[14]

Although it can be challenging to say "No" because you feel selfish or don't like letting people down, it's impossible to do it all. Spending time on your dream of becoming a coffee shop owner, accomplished musician, or author is not selfish. Instead, it's your way of honoring what speaks to your heart.

Fortunately, our deepest commitments tend to drive us on a soul level (if we know what we truly desire). So not only are we highly motivated to make them a priority, but the universe rallies behind us as we journey forward.

Patanjali, the Indian sage behind the Yoga Sutras (2nd century BCE), an ancient text on yoga philosophy and practice, described the changes that occur when we commit fully to something:

> When you are inspired by some great purpose, some extraordinary project, all your thoughts break their bonds: Your mind transcends limitations, your consciousness expands in every direction, and you find yourself in a new, great and wonderful world. Dormant forces, faculties, and talents become alive, and you discover yourself to be a greater person by far than you ever dreamed yourself to be.[15]

Have you ever had things happen unexpectedly, seemingly out of nowhere, once you made a commitment? Did resources or people show up in support of your mission? Did you see a book, photo, or poster on your project's topic as if it were calling out to you? You may refer to these occurrences as serendipity or divine intervention. However you refer to them, these are the dormant forces coming alive for "your extraordinary project" or "great purpose."

I experienced some of these forces while writing this book. After I committed to writing the book consistently, instead of sporadically over the years, my mind buzzed with ideas. One day, while at my computer, inspiration struck: a scene from *Willy Wonka and the Chocolate Factory* could beautifully illustrate the virtue of integrity. Later, as I took a break and turned on the TV, *Willy Wonka* appeared!

Another example happened while I was editing the chapter on hope. Music is a muse for me, so I like hearing it in the background as I write. When I glanced at my computer screen to see the name of the beautiful song playing, to my surprise, it was "Hope Has a Place"[16] by Enya.

I interpret these moments as the universe confirming that I am on the right path and that I am precisely where I belong.

In the same way, your commitment flourishes as you adjust your priorities and the universe responds. Your talents burst forth, breaking you out of mediocrity. Your mind opens to new ways of thinking, creating solutions to your obstacles. You become greater than you ever imagined!

Each intentional action—creating a compelling vision, shifting your priorities, and breaking free from limiting beliefs—affirms to the universe, "Yes!" It's a resounding "Yes!" to fulfilling your commitment and being the mighty person you are.

Practice Shifting Your Priorities

Think about how you spend your time. Do you spend most of your hours on obligations and not enough on your treasured desire? To help shift your priorities in favor of your commitment, ask yourself:

- Where can I free up more time for my commit-

ment? Could I wake up earlier, watch less TV, or
take a break from social media?

- Can I eliminate or delay another project?

- How do I effectively communicate my priorities to
  others for potential support?

- Can I save money each week to fund my mission,
  like by cutting back on Starbucks drinks or eating
  out less?

Explore specific ways to adjust your time, energy, and finances
to support your commitment. As you make these adjustments—
whether that means carving out alone time or asking for support—
you may feel guilty. Remind yourself that prioritizing what you want
to improve your life isn't selfish—it's an act of self-care.

Honoring What's Right for You

We can spend so much of our lives committed to what we don't want!
It may sound counterintuitive, but we often stay in jobs we don't like,
unfulfilling relationships, or other situations that no longer serve us.
We might feel stuck and unable to move forward in any direction.
Cartoonist Charles Schulz illustrates this struggle in his March 15,
1981, *Peanuts* comic strip.

Charlie Brown stands outside of Lucy's psychiatric booth.
She leans on her elbow and says, "Maybe I can put it
another way . . ." She props her feet up and continues,
"Life, Charlie Brown, is like a deck chair . . ."

He asks, "Like a what?"

She replies, "Have you ever been on a cruise ship?
Passengers open up these canvas deck chairs so they can
sit in the sun . . ." She points to her left and he looks. She
says, "Some people place their chairs facing the rear of the
ship so they can see where they've been . . ." She points to
her right and he looks. She continues, "Other people face
their chairs forward . . . they want to see where they're
going!" She points to him and asks, "On the cruise ship

of life, Charlie Brown, which way is your deck chair facing?"

She rolls her eyes as he replies, "I've never been able to get one unfolded ..."

Like Charlie Brown, we might find it challenging to "unfold our deck chairs." We neither look back at where we've been nor look ahead to where we are going. We're stuck because of fear, self-doubt, and the comfort of familiarity. Or, life's circumstances are on top of us. We'll deal with it later. But these obstacles often leave us directionless.

Reflecting on what you value and want can help you open your "deck chair" and choose a path. Much easier said than done!

But to stay stuck can be more painful than the self-introspection and facing the truth needed to move forward. Once you understand what's keeping you stuck, you can claim your allegiance: work on or leave the relationship, find the benefits in an unfulfilling job (at least for now), or seek a more meaningful one.

The key is acknowledging what isn't working and honoring what's right for you. Once you've chosen your new path or commitment, the test is to see it through. That entails more than a willingness to act—you must *sacrifice, defend,* and *persevere* for your commitments.

Sacrificing for Your Commitments

Some meaningful endeavors will be painful to achieve—at times, you'll think you can't go on another minute. You'll feel drained, disheartened, and frustrated because you've spent money, time, and effort to make things work. But sacrificing for what matters to us honors our deepest values. Nelson Mandela exemplified extraordinary sacrifice for his compelling vision: freeing South Africans from the injustices of apartheid.

Mandela's vision was evident at the Rivonia Trial, where the South African government accused him and fellow anti-apartheid activists of treason, sabotage, and conspiracy to overthrow the state.[17]

In his acclaimed speech at the trial, he declared his willingness to die for a democratic, free society where all people could live as equals. Two months after his speech, the judge sentenced Mandela to life in prison. He served 27 years.[18]

Nelson Mandela took a brave and unwavering stand for freedom. Through his struggle and leadership, he helped free millions of fellow South Africans from the misery of oppression. He eventually became South Africa's first black president and inspired the world.

Mandela's sacrifice was extreme. For most of us, sacrifice might mean losing relationships or business partnerships. We may have to give up time with family and friends. However, like Mandela, we can navigate our journey with determination and resilience to achieve what matters most to us.

Defending Your Commitments

Saying to someone or a group, "No, I disagree!" is brave, especially if what we say isn't the popular opinion. We might shrink away in self-doubt or fear when faced with opposition. Or, we can speak the truth about our beliefs, risking the potential fallout. The latter takes courage. We must be brave enough to stay true to our commitments without altering or distorting our beliefs and values to avoid the fallout.

People will oppose our views, and when they do, hearing what they have to say and then defending what we believe in—from a kind place—protects our integrity. When people criticize or judge our choices in life, it's tempting to get defensive or feel disheartened. We want to feel validated, respected, and seen for who we are, especially by our loved ones. But if we resist distractions from others' opinions, trust ourselves, and stay true to our path, we will fulfill our purpose.

Computer graphic artist, photographer, and author Zero Dean said it well: "Not everyone will understand your journey. That's fine. It's not *their* journey to make sense of. It's *yours*."[19]

Staying true to our commitments guides us in living our best lives.

Persevering for Your Commitments

Breaking promises to others undermines trust in relationships. Likewise, breaking promises to ourselves weakens self-trust.

Uncertainty, criticism from others, entrenched bad habits, neglected priorities, and numerous other challenges will test our commitments and may derail our progress. Yet, with a deep resolve to persevere, we become unstoppable.

Persisting in our creative passion, dream businesses, or whatever speaks to our authentic selves brings fulfillment. We'll always cherish the decision to honor what feels right for us, even when others try to dissuade us or we face setbacks.

Staying true to our commitments is not just a choice but also a promise to our future selves. Later in life, we will be grateful that we chose to fight for what was right and true for us.

Commitment's Rewards

Deeply committing to something you value matters. By declaring a purpose, you gain self-respect because you have clear priorities that inspire and motivate you. You create a stronger sense of self because you've chosen a path aligned with who you are—your values and passions. You are happier because you are making a valuable contribution to the world.

If you think about your relationships, committing half-heartedly will yield ordinary results. But committing fully to a person creates a deeper, more fulfilling connection.

Beyond personal fulfillment, your commitments elevate your life in extraordinary ways. They give you direction, open up new possibilities, and grace your life with meaning and purpose. You also inspire and touch others. How rewarding!

Taking a stand for what you truly believe in is the most important work you can do in this life.

Practice Honoring What's Right for You

Picture yourself in your elder years, sitting outside on a warm summer night while sipping a cool drink. As you relax, reflect on your life, not with judgment, but with gratitude and peace. You feel a sense of well-being and contentment. Now, take a deep breath and ponder these questions:

- What is one commitment you pursued that brought you joy, purpose, and meaning?

- What sacrifices did you make for this commitment? How did you defend and persevere for it?

- What commitment(s) didn't you pursue that you wish you had?

Be sure to acknowledge the effort you've made to honor your commitments. This exercise might also reveal opportunities that—if embraced now—could help you avoid future regrets.

CHAPTER SUMMARY

Commitment is an unshakable devotion to a worthy endeavor, gracing life with purpose and meaning. We sacrifice, defend, and persevere to honor our commitments and stay true to what's right for us. In doing so, we turn our aspirations into realities and shape the course of our lives.

Complementing virtues: *Loyalty, Perseverance*
Commitment transcends: *Aimlessness, Procrastination*

Remember this . . .

- Commitments give us purpose and vitality. We feel excited and hopeful when we declare our intention to pursue something meaningful. Our choice to fulfill this dream, no matter what, becomes the honorable test before us.

- A compelling vision—a clear and specific mental picture of what we want—energizes and inspires us to uphold our commitments, especially when facing adversity.

- Being aware of our positive and negative commitments helps us shift our priorities and align our precious time and energy with what we want most.

- Honoring our commitments means defending them, making sacrifices, and persevering through challenges. When we take these actions, we may face criticism, envy, self-doubt, and disappointment but the rewards are profound growth and fulfillment.

CHAPTER 2

Love

Love is an enduring and deep affection, expressed through words and actions, bringing us joy, comfort, and strength.

Roman philosopher Cicero once said that gratitude is the parent of all virtues. If so, then love is the most celebrated of all virtues.

Giving and receiving love are life's most sacred gifts. When we love others, we feel deeply connected to them, even as one person. American poet E. E. Cummings expresses this sentiment in the title of his best-known love poem, "[i carry your heart with me(i carry it in]."[1] He begins the poem by describing how he carries another's heart with him, holding it in his own.

Whether this depth of love, as Cummings communicates so well, is for a partner, parent, friend, or pet, we cannot escape the peaks and valleys of the emotion. One moment, we feel euphoric and happy; the next, we feel angry, insecure, or heartbroken. Still, we love.

The What and Why of Love

We can describe love in many ways. It is deep affection, trust, and respect—the kind shared with family and friends. We can define it as nurturing and guidance, like the love between a parent and child. We can also understand it as a romantic bond, a mix of attraction and deep attachment.

No matter its form, love is a profound, life-giving force that unites us all.

So why do we love? Because love is the essence of our being. It moves us to care, support, and uplift one another through the goodness in our hearts. It's a constant source of comfort and security when life changes around us.

Love helps us grow, forgive, and strive to be better people. It challenges us to be self-aware, vulnerable, and willing to trust and sacrifice. Our hearts expand as we learn to be patient, compassionate, loyal, and understanding.

Essentially, love is who we are, and we connect through its power.

Let's take a deeper look at love's true nature.

Love Is Action

The dictionary defines love as a warm personal attachment or deep affection for another, but according to Rabbi David Wolpe, this definition is incomplete. He wrote in a *TIME* article that he became convinced of the one-sidedness of love's meaning after years of speaking with couples and families with relationship challenges. He said, "Love should be seen not as a feeling but as an enacted emotion. To love is to feel and act lovingly."[2]

To illustrate his point, he said women have told him—with visibly bruised faces caused by their husbands—that their husbands love them. He explains that because the women view love as a feeling and not an action, they do not see that if their husbands truly loved them, they would not abuse them.[3]

Wolpe's expansion of love from a feeling to include action makes perfect sense. How can we love others if we aren't respectful of them? If we neglect to show them how much they mean to us? If we don't protect them? Love is offering encouraging words, acting compassionately, and making sacrifices.

The movie *Forrest Gump* beautifully captures Wolpe's belief that love is action. Forrest (Tom Hanks) asks his lifelong love, Jenny (Robin Wright), to marry him. She gently responds, "You don't want to marry me."[4]

Forrest wonders why she doesn't love him. Believing she denies his proposal because he's a simple man with a below-average IQ, he insists, "I'm not a smart man, but I know what love is."[5] He sure does through his actions, repeatedly showing her how much she means to him. He protects her from an abusive boyfriend, rescues her from unwelcome advances at the strip club where she works, and invites her into his home when she gets sick. However, Jenny consistently pushes him away to protect him from her troubled past.

Eventually, as Jenny faces a terminal illness, she seeks refuge with Forrest and embraces his love by marrying him.[6]

Forrest and Jenny's love story reminds us that showing our love is often more impactful than words alone. When people say, "I love you," it gives us a warm, comforting feeling, yet the words can feel hollow without loving actions behind them. Loving actions make people feel validated, cared for, and respected, as Wolpe affirms.

Some ways to show love include:

- Spending quality time with loved ones to deepen connections
- Listening with intention and thoughtfully responding
- Respecting personal boundaries, needs, and wishes
- Cooking a favorite meal, planning a special outing, or giving thoughtful gifts
- Offering support in times of need for comfort and solidarity
- Showing heartfelt gratitude through spoken words or handwritten notes

Expressing love in these ways can deepen even good relationships, helping us move past the mediocrity we often settle into. Still, it takes conscious effort because it's too important to reserve only for holidays, birthdays, or Valentine's Day. Life is fragile. Why wait to show people how much they mean to us? Think of something you can do today to make someone special in your life feel loved.

Love Is Connection

In her book *Love 2.0*, psychologist and positive emotions expert Barbara Fredrickson defines love as "positivity resonance."[7] She explains that positivity resonance arises from micro-moments of social connection characterized by shared positive emotions, biological and behavioral synchrony, and mutual care.

For example, when we laugh with a friend, we share joy, and our biological responses, such as heart rate and brain patterns, synchronize. These moments of connection, Fredrickson explains, reverberate between and among people. She likens positivity resonance to a mirror where people reflect each other's emotions, gestures, biochemistry, and desire to care.

Romantic relationships amplify this mirroring. Partners seemingly melt into one another through mutual respect, devotion, and warmth. But positivity resonance isn't just for friends or partners, Fredrickson adds. It can also exist among strangers and groups.[8]

I personally experienced positivity resonance while volunteering at the 1995 Special Olympics World Summer Games in New Haven, Connecticut.

As part of the volunteer work, we had the honor of watching the opening ceremonies. After Eunice Kennedy, founder of the Special Olympics, spoke, military personnel parachuted out of planes into the middle of the field while patriotic music echoed throughout the stadium.

Seven thousand athletes from 143 countries marched proudly into the arena with colorful country flags as thousands roared with enthusiasm. Unity was present in a way I had never experienced before, bringing me to tears.

Love was also present in our mutual celebration and admiration for the athletes, who pushed themselves to be their best despite intellectual challenges. The social connection among strangers stemming from shared positive emotions and mutual care was unmistakable and deeply moving.

Thinking about love as connection extends its presence everywhere. Recognizing the connective force that love has, along with the power of taking loving action, heightens love in our lives in the most glorious way.

Practice Taking a Loving Action

Express your love by choosing a meaningful action from the list below. Even the smallest loving acts can deepen relationships and bring positivity to everyone involved. Then, reflect on moments in your life marked by a deep connection to reinforce positivity resonance.

Love Is Action

- Write a note of gratitude, telling someone what the relationship means to you.

- Spend time with a loved one, like taking a hike, having coffee, or sharing dinner.

- Truly listen to others by asking thoughtful questions like, "How did that make you feel?" and offering support, such as, "It sounds like you're pulled in too many directions. How can I help?"

- Express affection through encouraging words, a heartfelt text, a voice message, a post-it note, or a simple hug.

Love Is Connection

Reflect on the following questions to deepen your sense of connection:

- When did you last feel a deep connection with someone?

- How can you create more shared moments of connection in your daily interactions?

- Have you ever been part of a group where you felt love was truly present?

By actively showing love and nurturing your connections, you invite more joy, warmth, and positivity into your daily life.

When Love Isn't Enough

Many of us have experienced a relationship where we felt more anguish than happiness. We loved the person deeply, but a personal issue, such as internal struggles or self-destructive behavior, kept them from being emotionally available to us. So even though the love was there, it wasn't enough for that relationship to work.

Of course, many relationships with addiction challenges and emotional struggles can work out with the tremendous love and support of a partner—but only if the other person is *willing* to do the often painful introspection needed to change. In these moments, loving others tests our strength and resilience. We want things to work out but can't force someone to do the work needed to heal. We might try by offering patience, encouragement, and unwavering love, which can lead to heartache. Although love is powerful, people must recognize the harm and pain they may be causing in the relationship and take responsibility to change. No matter how much we care, we can't make that choice for them.

I remember attending a seminar led by an author who wrote about how our thoughts shape our reality. A woman in the audience asked a question about her partner, who was struggling with addiction. The pain in her voice—and on her face—was as raw as it gets. She wanted so badly for their love to work. You could tell how deeply she loved him and how hard she had tried to help him, as she tearfully expressed her frustration that her efforts weren't working.

With the instructor's coaching, she came to realize that her constant rallying behind her partner was, ultimately, fruitless. I don't know what happened to that relationship. It was just a two-hour event, but what stayed with me was her deep and painful struggle.

As much as we may long for love to be enough, sometimes it isn't, especially when it comes at the cost of our self-worth, peace of mind, or happiness. However difficult it may be to walk away—and it can be exceedingly difficult!—we must preserve our well-being. The sadness and disappointment can be excruciating to bear, but having a healthy relationship, where both partners are emotionally present, is what we all deserve.

Ultimately, love can sometimes be messy, confusing, and heartbreaking. Sometimes, we expect too much from people or hope for something that they can't, or are unwilling, to give. To take care of ourselves, we have to ask the hard question: Do I keep trying, or is it time to let go and move forward?

We all struggle with love, even fearing it—because love makes us vulnerable. In the next section, we'll explore this fear.

Love and Fear

Love can stir up a whole lot of emotions, especially fear; fear of rejection, hurt, and failure. The inherent risks of loving someone are enough for us to turn away from it or not give our love fully. It's like we're in a small boat on the open sea susceptible to the waves' ups and downs: some are smooth, while others nearly overturn our boat. Sometimes, we feel like jumping out because the waves seem too high to navigate. Yet, if we stay the course, the reward is deeply satisfying and even life-changing.

Love exposes us to the vulnerability of rejection and loss—a scary but essential part of loving others.

Embracing Vulnerability

We've all felt vulnerable at one point or another—perhaps when we've asked someone out on a date, confessed our love for the first time, or revealed a part of ourselves we dislike to someone. And vulnerability isn't just about love! We might feel vulnerable giving a talk, asking for a raise, disclosing our sexual orientation, navigating dating as a single parent, and sharing mental health issues. Vulnerability can be terrifying!

Surrendering our defenses opens us to people's potential judgment, rejection, criticism, and even poor treatment. Yet, our relationships will be more intimate and fulfilling if we are open and honest.

In her book *Daring Greatly*, research professor and author Brené Brown defines vulnerability as "uncertainty, risk, and emotional exposure."[9] She explains that people see vulnerability as a weakness when, in fact, it takes strength to embrace uncertainty, take a chance, or expose ourselves emotionally. She writes, "Does showing up to be with someone in deep struggle sound like a weakness? Is accepting accountability weak? Is stepping up to the plate after striking out a sign of weakness? NO. Vulnerability sounds like truth and feels like courage. Truth and courage aren't always comfortable, but they're never weakness."[10]

What an empowering shift in perspective! The anxiety we feel when we're about to take an emotional risk becomes a force for bravery rather than a reason to cower away.

So, how can we cultivate vulnerability as a strength? First, we need to recognize why we avoid feeling vulnerable—whether it's because of *false beliefs,* fear of *asking for what we want,* or the discomfort of *honoring our authenticity.*

Uncovering False Beliefs

Mystic poet Rumi eloquently said, "Your task is not to seek for love, but merely to seek and find all the barriers within yourself that you have built against it."[11]

Unknowingly, we can block love through false beliefs like, "I'm not lovable," "I don't deserve love," or "Everyone leaves me." These beliefs often originate in childhood and become so deeply ingrained that we don't recognize how they block love from entering or staying in our lives.

You can uncover these blocks by looking at your relationship behaviors. Are you always looking to please your partner? Do you attract the wrong partners? If so, you may believe you are unlovable. Do you struggle to let a romantic partner get close? Then, you may believe you don't deserve love. If you believe everyone leaves you, you may inadvertently sabotage your relationship, so your partner leaves you first.

Recognizing unhealthy relationship patterns can alert you to the presence of false beliefs. With this awareness, you can take action. You can turn disempowering beliefs into affirmations like, "I am lovable" or "I am worthy of love." Repeating these positive thoughts helps to fade the negative ones. However, deeply ingrained beliefs can be challenging to change. You may benefit from the support of a therapist to explore and overcome beliefs that could be contributing to persistent relationship struggles.

Asking for What You Want

Tamsen Firestone, author of *Daring to Love,* points out that asking for what we want in a relationship cultivates vulnerability, writing, "Asking for what you want is difficult for many people because feelings of shame often accompany wanting or needing something from another person. Shame is a painful, primitive emotion that originates in early childhood from incidents when basic needs were not fulfilled."[12]

Firestone explains that these incidents cause children to feel ashamed of their desire for affection, love, and understanding. As a result, they hide any signs of wanting, fearing humiliation for appearing unloved or unlovable. They carry these fears into adulthood, resisting asking their partner for what they want.[13]

Putting yourself on the line is hard, but it's an emotional victory. As Firestone says, we become stronger when we realize we're no longer helpless children who once felt humiliation and shame. Instead, we're adults who can tolerate disappointment and frustration when our partner rejects our request. If our partner says no, we face a choice: accept their response and move forward or reflect on whether the relationship still meets our needs.

Honoring Your Authenticity

Exposing an imperfection to a partner can feel risky. How will she react when she finds out I'm a recovering alcoholic? What will happen when I tell him about my family? What will she think about my religious beliefs?

As you fear the potential fallout of your openness and push through anyway, you build your capacity to be vulnerable. Regardless of how the conversation goes, you are brave and honest about something that matters to you.

Contorting and adapting yourself to what you think others want to believe about you can undermine self-confidence. Ideally, you want people to accept you for who you are—your heartbreaks, successes, mistakes, past hurts, strengths, and weaknesses. True intimacy happens when you can trust someone to embrace all of who you are with kindness. But if you keep parts of yourself hidden, it prevents your partner from fully knowing you.

As you reveal your truth, you honor and validate the entirety of your beautiful self. Moreover, when you share your humanity, you create a safe space for others to share theirs. There is nothing more beautiful than witnessing people open up about their deepest pain, fears, and desires.

We all feel vulnerable at times. However, thinking of vulnerability in a new way—as a strength, not a weakness—helps us connect more deeply and authentically with others.

Practice Being Vulnerable in Love

Discover how you protect yourself from feeling vulnerable in relationships through these exploratory sentences:

Uncovering False Beliefs

- I might be blocking love from entering or staying in my life by believing I am _____. (To complete the sentence, consider: "What is my biggest fear in relationships?" Examples include fears of being unlovable, not good enough, or abandoned.)

   o Create a positive affirmation to counteract your belief, such as "I am good enough" or "I am worthy of love." Repeat these affirmations daily, but keep in mind that you may also benefit from seeking help from a professional.

Asking for What You Want

- I want from my partner _____, but I resist asking because _____. (For example, if you need more quality time with them, you can say: "I feel disconnected when we don't spend much time together. Could we plan a weekly date night?")

Honoring Your Authenticity

- I want to tell my partner about _____, but I fear they will

_____. (Imagine the conversation going well, with both of you feeling understood and closer. Begin by expressing how much you value the relationship and acknowledging your fear of opening up.)

Recognizing what guards you in relationships allows you to approach vulnerability with self-compassion. Seeking support from a therapist and practicing emotional openness—through affirmations or other intentional acts—can help you build confidence. Take time to reflect on moments of authenticity, celebrating your progress and reinforcing vulnerability as an inner strength.

What Would Love Do Now?

When we face tough decisions and challenging situations in our relationships, asking ourselves one particular question can be an enlightening way to live.

Neale Donald Walsch, author of the *Conversations with God* series, urges us to ask ourselves at crucial points in human relationships, "What would love do now?"[14] This question can guide our words and actions to be more compassionate and thoughtful.

One powerful—though extreme—example of living by this question is the experience of Polish Catholic priest Maximilian Kolbe. He faced a moment when *What would love do now?* came calling.

At a very young age, Father Kolbe pledged to dedicate his life to honor and serve the Blessed Virgin Mary. His life reflected this commitment to extraordinary lengths.

One day in July of 1941, amid the horrors of the Holocaust, a prisoner disappeared from the Auschwitz camp. In retaliation, the camp's cruel commander selected ten men, including Father Kolbe, to die, blaming them for failing to prevent the escape. The men stood assembled in a line, suffering in the heat with no food or water for hours, fearing their fate. Father Kolbe was gravely ill and ready to collapse.

After the head commander had selected two men to die, he chose another, Polish army sergeant Franciszek Gajowniczek. Franciszek begged for his life, crying out that he had a wife and children he would never see again.

Father Kolbe bravely approached the commander, an unheard of act punishable by death. He asked the guard if he could take the man's place, explaining that he had no family and was old and sick. Father Kolbe also said that the younger man could do more work.

The stunned commander surprisingly agreed to his request. Father Kolbe's fate was sealed. The commanders sent him and nine other men to the underground torture cell, where they would die by starvation. The terrible irony was that the prisoner the commander believed had escaped had actually drowned in a camp latrine.

While in the cell, Father Kolbe led the men in prayers and hymns. After ten days, without food or water, he and three others remained alive until a German doctor gave them a lethal injection.[15]

Father Kolbe gave his life for someone else—the ultimate answer to *What would love do now?* He selflessly chose love over fear and acted out of pure compassion.

Similarly, the first responders who charged into the burning World Trade Center towers on September 11, 2001, acted out of love. They did not let danger deter them from their mission to save others but instead answered love's call.

Every day, people live by *What would love do now?*—sometimes risking, even sacrificing, their lives for others.

Everyday Acts of Love

Though the sacrifices of Father Kolbe and the 9/11 first responders are extreme examples of love in action, the question of what love would do now can guide our daily lives.

For example, imagine arguing with your partner over a chronic conflict in your relationship. You feel like they don't hear you. You're frustrated and disappointed by the lack of progress in your conversation. Amid your anger and frustration, it can be difficult to ask yourself *What would love do now?* You'd rather stick with being right. Besides, you feel hurt.

Deep down, though, you want to resolve the conflict because it's causing a divide in your relationship. That's when you might say from love, "I care about how you feel and know how much this means to you, so let's find a way to work through it together." Instead of defending yourself, you extend a gesture of kindness, which diffuses the tension and opens the door for resolution.

Psychologist and researcher John Gottman, founder of the Gottman Institute, studies what makes relationships work. In one study, he examined how couples' reactions—whether loving or distant—contributed to their relationships either thriving or falling apart.

In 1990, he invited 130 newlywed couples to spend the day at a beautiful bed-and-breakfast retreat he had created at the University of Washington. Throughout the day, he watched how these couples interacted while they cooked, ate, cleaned, and hung out together.

Gottman observed that couples made requests, or "bids," for connection. He shared an example of a man who loved birds. One day, the husband saw a goldfinch fly across the yard and asked his wife to look at the beautiful bird outside. Whether she responded to him with interest and support or indifference profoundly affected their marital health.

After following up with the couples six years later, Gottman found that those who eventually divorced had met only three out of ten bids for connection, while those who stayed married had met nine out of ten.[16]

Gottman's research was able to predict whether the couple would last and be happy together, no matter what type of relationship they had: heterosexual or homosexual, with children or without children, rich or poor. Each couple's success depended on whether they brought a spirit of kindness and generosity to the relationship or one of hostility, criticism, and contempt.

Gottman found that kindness makes people feel validated and loved, while hostility and contempt tear couples apart.[17]

His findings may seem logical, even obvious, yet we often overlook the many factors that affect how we communicate. We are having a bad day. The kids might be bickering. Our finances could be weighing us down, or we need alone time. With these everyday stressors, we may dismiss our loved ones unintentionally or react in ways we later regret.

However, as Gottman found, if we want our most precious relationships to thrive, awareness of how we respond to our partner's bids for connection is essential.

To cultivate stronger connections, start by asking yourself these questions:

- Do I listen to loved ones with genuine interest? Do I respond thoughtfully to show that I care?

- Am I attentive to the needs and concerns of my loved ones?

- Do I love people for who they are and not who I want them to be?

- Am I more inclined to encourage and support my loved ones, or to criticize them?

- Do I focus on others' strengths or dwell on their limitations?

Let these questions sink in and help you recognize where you might miss opportunities to show love. You can start with your own family—when challenges come up, you can step back and quietly ask *What would love do now?* Inspired by this question, your kinder words and actions can shape how people respond to you. Their defenses soften. They'll feel heard. They'll feel loved.

Practice Responding with Love

When people hurt us, our instinct is often to react defensively—and for good reason. However, if we choose to view the situation through the lens of love, a shift can occur within us. We begin to see people and situations with more compassion and understanding.

Try this: For one week, whenever you feel criticized, blamed, or find it hard to compromise, pause and ask yourself, *What would love do now?* Let your answer guide your response. Afterward, write down the situations you encounter, describing what happened, how you felt, and any changes in how others responded to you.

Before starting this practice, take a moment to reflect on the people and situations that tend to trigger defensive or angry reactions in you. This awareness will help you recognize patterns and deepen your appreciation for the power of responding with love.

Loving Yourself

How well do you think you know yourself? Do you take the time to understand yourself better? Self-awareness—knowing what you value, what makes you happy, your strengths, your weaknesses, your hopes, and your fears—is the first step to loving yourself more.

When the Greek philosopher Socrates said, "The unexamined life is not worth living,"[18] he emphasized the importance of self-aware-ness for a wise and fulfilling life. Examining your thoughts, behav-iors, and motivations helps you make better choices.

For instance, by recognizing your unique talents and abilities, you can pursue work that you enjoy and has meaning for you.

Acknowledging your emotional triggers and responses can help you create healthier relationships and communicate more effectively. Essentially, gaining deep self-knowledge is an act of self-love.

Embodying Socrates' wisdom, Shannon Kaiser's pursuit of self-love began with deep self-awareness, a journey she explores in her book *The Self-Love Experiment.*

Shannon's life coach gave her an assignment: to love herself more. After more than three decades of struggling with self-accep-tance, Shannon wanted to know what it would be like to feel at peace with herself and her body.

Because of her self-criticism, she made poor relationship choices, overate, overspent, and worked too much. When she wondered what it would feel like to go through a whole day without criticiz-ing herself or thinking she wasn't good enough, she committed to making self-improvements. To find self-love, she recognized that she needed to observe her inner critic and self-destructive beliefs that sab-otaged her happiness.

Shannon endeavored to fall in love with herself—to feel excite-ment for what was possible, feel the devotion to another and the ability to overlook faults.[19]

"This full circle of self-love—falling in love with yourself and then discovering how to make that love last is essential," Shannon writes. "And it's a process that is so very rewarding because suddenly we find that we have discovered a gentler, kinder way to live in the world. One where we are no longer at war with ourselves but are simply celebrating ourselves in a loving light."[20]

How can you celebrate yourself in a "loving light"? Take a moment to think about what may be stopping you from loving yourself. Then think about your talents and skills, quirks and flaws, sense of humor, helpful nature, and story of recovery—whatever makes you authentically you. You are worthy of celebration every day because of the unique and valuable contribution you bring to anyone blessed to know you.

What Self-Love Isn't

Learning to love ourselves is not narcissistic or self-involved. It's the opposite! Loving ourselves means accepting our flaws, failures, and fears with kindness, nonjudgment, and self-forgiveness. This acceptance brings our whole selves into relationships, deepening our connections.

Self-love isn't the same as being selfish. We maintain our sense of worth and integrity by doing what's best for us and communicating our needs.

For example, have you ever accepted an invitation purely because you didn't want to hurt someone's feelings? Or said "yes" to doing someone a favor when you didn't have the time? You then felt depleted and unhappy because you didn't put yourself first.

Placing our needs first may not be easy, but if we don't, we experience inner turmoil that wears on us. How can we give the best of ourselves if we're living with self-contempt or feeling emotionally drained? When we take care of ourselves, we can be emotionally stronger for others and naturally more optimistic.

Lastly, loving ourselves shouldn't depend on external circumstances that may affect our self-respect. That's because self-respect doesn't come from our outside circumstances! When we don't get the job we want, a relationship fails, or we gain weight—we love ourselves anyway. We choose to love and accept ourselves despite whatever happened.

Self-love isn't about reacting by scolding and punishing ourselves when we fail or make a mistake. Still, all too often, we do exactly that. During those times, loving ourselves more is what we need most.

Loving Yourself More

People who practice self-love tend to make good choices in partners and choose careers that are more suited to their values and talents. They stand in their truth and say "No" if a request for their time doesn't work for them. They kindly let others know how they feel and what they need and want in a relationship. They do not tolerate toxic people—people who are mean or unjustly criticize them—even if those people are family. They embrace their past, knowing they did their best with the self-awareness they had at the time. They forgive their mistakes, refusing to let them define who they are in the present.

Certainly, even people who love themselves won't always be perfect in all of the scenarios above, but their heightened sense of self keeps them in touch with what works and doesn't work for them. They respect themselves enough to make choices that reflect this knowledge.

Know in your heart that *you are enough*! You are worthy of all the pleasures and opportunities that life offers.

Maintain your boundaries, express yourself unapologetically, care for yourself, and go after your dreams. Believe in your capabilities and strengths and trust your choices. Let these self-love actions bolster your confidence and commitment to a fulfilling life.

Practice Self-Love

We all define self-love in different ways, whether it's through regular massages, reading romance novels, making dinner plans with friends, taking walks, engaging in creative activities, or quitting a bad habit. Whatever self-love looks like for you, make it a regular practice for your well-being and happiness.

Try this: On a sheet of paper, write, "If I loved myself more, I would_____."

Another way to practice self-love is by challenging and quieting the self-defeating thoughts that undermine your happiness and confidence. Positive affirmations affirm what is best about you and can help enhance your mental and emotional well-being. Here's a step-by-step method of creating positive affirmations:

1. On a sheet of paper, make two columns. Title the

first column "Negative Thoughts" and the second
column "Positive Affirmations."

2. Write down three to five negative thoughts or
   beliefs you have about yourself, such as "I'm not
   good enough" or "I can't possibly do this."

Lastly, write a positive affirmation to counteract each negative
thought, like "I am worthy, and enough just as I am" or "I am smart
and capable."

Keep this sheet handy and repeat the affirmations to yourself or
aloud often, especially when your inner critic emerges.

CHAPTER SUMMARY

Love is an enduring and deep affection, expressed through words and actions, bringing us joy, comfort, and strength. Love's power connects us, uniting hearts and minds, and its positive energy supports us through tough times. With love, we can face fear and suffering more bravely and create inner peace and harmony in our lives.

Complementing virtues: *Kindness, Forgiveness*
Love transcends: *Fear, Suffering*

Remember this ...

- Expressing love through both words and actions can deepen even good relationships, helping us move past the mediocrity we often settle into. Through hardship or celebration, we embrace love's positive presence with both loved ones and strangers.

- We sometimes avoid fully embracing love because of the emotional vulnerability it brings. To overcome this, we can explore and understand our false beliefs, ask for what we want, and honor our authenticity.

- Asking ourselves, *What would love do now?* shifts our perspective. The question guides us to respond with kindness instead of judgment, compassion instead of fear, or understanding instead of anger. As a result, others' defenses soften, and they feel heard and valued.

- Loving all of ourselves—the flawed and best parts—helps us make healthier choices. First, though, we must honestly know ourselves. Once we uncover our talents, skills, strengths, and weaknesses, we can make positive changes.

CHAPTER 3

Perseverance

Perseverance is the will to see things through despite fear, doubt, discouragement, and opposition.

Rain or shine, Maisie DeVore, in her 50s, drove her old pickup truck around Eskridge, Kansas, hunting for returnable aluminum cans. She tirelessly walked the small town's streets and highways day and night, picking up cans and digging for them in trash cans. People saw how driven she was and gave her cans. She worked to the point of exhaustion. Her children discouraged her. The townspeople discouraged her. People called her "Crazy Maisie."[1]

None of that stopped her. Her mission was to fund a community swimming pool with money from deposits because the children needed more summertime activities. That first aluminum can led to hundreds, then thousands, and eventually millions more. Thirty years later, she had raised more than $83,000 from returning the cans!

Maisie also handcrafted blankets and quilts to raffle off. She picked wild berries to make and sell homemade jams and jellies and gathered and sold scrap metal. In all, she raised $100,000. That money, combined with donations from supporters and a grant from the state of Kansas, led to the pool's construction.[2]

When the pool opened in 2001, the town dedicated it to her as

"Maisie's Community Swimming Pool." The town also renamed the highway she walked each day collecting cans in her honor. People now called her "Amazing Maisie."[3]

Many wondered how Maisie stuck with her goal for so long. She said, "You just have to never give up. If you lose sight of your dream, you're sunk. But if you keep that in mind and are really determined to reach a goal, I think you can do it. One way or another."[4]

The What and Why of Perseverance

Maisie is a shining example of perseverance: the will to see things through despite fear, doubt, discouragement, and opposition. She shows us that no matter how tough the circumstances or how long it takes, when we have an unfailing desire to achieve something, we *will*.

Our journey to what we want will undoubtedly be difficult, lonely, and uphill sometimes. But with the mental strength and resilience to succeed, our dreams and potential are not lost.

Mustering the will to push through our personal discomfort means we declare, "I commit to this dream and will do whatever it takes to fulfill it. When times get tough, I will keep going."

A quote often attributed to Harriet Beecher Stowe, the American author and anti-slavery activist, expresses this idea: "When you get into a tight place, and everything goes against you until it seems that you cannot hold on for a minute longer, never give up then, for that is just the place and time when the tide will turn."[5]

She urges us to push forward at that crucial moment when internal and outside forces want to drag us into a pit of self-doubt and disappointment. But we hold onto the rope of hope and resilience, resisting despair and pulling ourselves back up.

Famous people exemplify Stowe's wisdom: Stephen King had his novel *Carrie* rejected 30 times before a publisher accepted it in 1974; Lady Gaga's first record label, Def Jam Recordings, dropped her just three months after signing her; Thomas Edison failed over 1,000 times before inventing the light bulb; and Abraham Lincoln lost multiple elections before he became president.[6]

They each persevered at pivotal moments in their lives. If they had chosen to end it right there at that moment of defeat, such extraordinary talent would have gone to waste. How fortunate we are that they chose to persevere!

With commitment and an unstoppable attitude, you can prevail over setbacks just as they did, and what you want will indeed happen.

What drives people to keep pushing forward despite failure? What motivates them to stay committed to goals that may take years—or even decades—to achieve?

Grit Predicts Success

Along with perseverance, Maisie also had grit! Grit, as defined by University of Pennsylvania psychology professor Angela Duckworth, is "passion and perseverance for very long-term goals."[7] Duckworth found that grit plays a significant role in a person's success.

In a viral TED Talk, Duckworth shares her surprise upon discovering that the brightest students in her New York public school seventh-grade math class did not perform as well as others. These other students, despite their struggles with mathematical concepts, tried harder. She determined that IQ was not the only difference between students who excelled academically and those who did not. Something else was at work.

Fascinated by her observations, Duckworth wanted to understand better what motivates students to learn, so she left teaching to become a research psychologist. She and a research team studied kids and adults in challenging settings to evaluate who was successful and why.

They studied cadets at the prestigious United States Military Academy West Point to see who would make it through and who would not. They evaluated children at the National Spelling Bee competition to see who would advance furthest. They also gauged the success of rookie teachers who worked in tough neighborhoods and salespeople working at private companies. Among these groups, they discovered a "significant predictor of their success" was something they called *grit*.[8]

Duckworth's research reveals that our success depends on our steadfast pursuit of our passion, not just on knowledge or talent. Chris Gardner's journey from hardship to success beautifully exemplifies grit.

Chris lived in San Francisco in the 1980s. He was raising a young child and struggling financially. His inconsistent success as a medical equipment salesperson meant that even though he had a job, his income wasn't enough to pay the bills. His marriage was failing because of the weight of financial pressures.

One day, Chris spotted a sharply dressed man driving a red convertible Ferrari, scanning the area for a parking space. Mesmerized by what the Ferrari represented—not wealth or success, but rather the freedom and options he had lacked growing up—he offered the man his parking space.

When the man pulled in, Chris asked him what his profession was and how he became successful. The man responded that he was a stockbroker at the prestigious brokerage firm Dean Witter Reynolds. He offered to meet with Chris to expand further on the second question.

Not only did the man in the Ferrari inspire Chris, but that moment pushed him to pursue an interview at the firm. Despite lacking trading experience, Chris' dream was to become a stockbroker. He distinguished himself by going the extra mile to stand out. His effort secured him a spot in the competitive Dean Witter Reynolds internship program, where only a small number of candidates ultimately became stockbrokers.

Gardner arrived early to the office, stayed late, and made 200 sales calls per day. He read and studied to learn all he could about the profession. By this time, his wife had left him, and Chris cared for his son alone. The internship was unpaid, so he and his son slept in motels until the money ran out. They slept in homeless shelters (when room was available), train station bathrooms, and on the streets. They relied on soup kitchens for meals, and Chris used his limited funds for his son's daycare so he could work.[9]

Chris did not give in to despair even in the most challenging times. Instead, he lived by the mantra, "Go forward,"[10] inspired by his friend and mentor, Reverend Cecil Williams.

Chris' unbreakable spirit led him to become not just a stockbroker at Dean Witter Reynolds but also a top-performing one.

In 1987, Chris founded Gardner Rich & Company in a modest apartment with just $10,000. By 2006, he sold his small stake in the firm for a multi-million dollar deal and established Christopher

Gardner International Holdings, serving as CEO with offices in New York, Chicago, and San Francisco.[11]

His bestselling memoir, *The Pursuit of Happyness*, inspired the hit movie of the same name, touching many with his message of overcoming adversity through perseverance and resilience.

Maisie and Chris showed incredible grit and a relentless determination to turn their passions into realities. Their stories inspire us to cultivate grit in our own lives in pursuit of success.

With every challenge we face, we have the opportunity to apply grit. But it may not be easy. Life's troubles and setbacks will test our grit.

How can we harness grit in the face of adversity? The first step is understanding what stands in our way.

Practice Reflecting On and Showing Grit

Recognize and celebrate the grit you showed in achieving your goals—your accomplishments are truly commendable! At the same time, take a moment to identify ways to strengthen your grit even further.

- **Reflect on grit:** Recall your greatest accomplishment or an endeavor that required immense effort. What setbacks did you face? How did you demonstrate grit in overcoming them?

- **Add more grit:** Identify a goal you could achieve if you applied more grit. How can you prioritize the goal, practice positive self-talk, revisit your compelling vision, or inspire others to champion your cause?

By reflecting on past successes where you've shown grit—and actively working to strengthen it in the present—you increase your chances of success. Celebrate your accomplishments, keep looking for ways to grow your grit, and remember to be kind to yourself along the way.

What Stops You?

Obstacles like adversity, rejection, criticism, and self-doubt can make us question what we want most. Do we want it badly enough to push through setbacks? Can we bear other people's discouragement or criticism, even when it comes from family and friends?

Despite our sincerest intentions to reach our goals, self-imposed limitations or outside forces can stop us—if we let them. These challenges are natural and shared by many. Now, we'll look closer at the blocks that can stop us from fulfilling our commitments and explore how to move through them.

Adversity

When a cherished relationship doesn't work out, a business venture we've poured our hearts into falls apart, or a job we love is lost, it's natural to feel disheartened and even hopeless. We take these setbacks hard, and rightfully so. We tried our best—maybe we spent precious years of our lives on it—only to have it backfire.

Rationally, we understand we're taking a risk, feeling hopeful, excited, and up for the challenge. We know the reward can be satisfying, even life-changing. But when things don't work out, our emotions take over. We might feel angry at the unfairness, sad about the loss, or defeated by the weight of it all.

Despite the emotional aftermath, we can eventually embrace adversity and learn from it to help us persevere when the next obstacle arises.

Consider Wilma Rudolph's inspiring journey of overcoming a debilitating physical challenge to achieve greatness.

Born in Tennessee, Wilma Rudolph contracted polio at the age of five, which left one leg nearly unusable. She also battled scarlet fever, adding to her health struggles. The doctor fitted Wilma with a metal leg brace, telling her she would never walk again, but her mother affirmed she would. She believed her mother.

Throughout the day, Wilma's siblings and mother massaged her leg. Her mother traveled roughly 100 miles roundtrip for Wilma's leg treatments. Wilma also practiced walking daily in the front yard, sometimes collapsing from exhaustion. She knew deep down that someday she would walk again and even run.

With the attention given to her leg and Wilma's determined spirit, her leg began to heal. She graduated to an orthopedic shoe and eventually could walk without assistance. In high school, Wilma progressed so much that she pursued basketball but then turned to track and field after a chance meeting with Ed Temple, the women's track and field coach at Tennessee State University. He invited her to train with him and the students at the college's summer camp.

At just 16, Wilma competed in her first Olympics, earning a bronze medal in the 4×100-meter relay at the 1956 Melbourne Games. Four years later, the powerful 5'11" sprinter became the first American woman at the Rome Summer Olympics to win three Olympic track and field gold medals.[12]

Once too disabled to walk, Wilma Rudolph became the fastest woman in the world. "Winning is great, sure," she said. "But if you are really going to do something in life, the secret is learning how to lose. Nobody goes undefeated all the time. If you can pick up after a crushing defeat and go on to win again, you are going to be a champion someday."[13]

Wilma Rudolph's approach to overcoming adversity is both inspiring and insightful, suggesting that staying in the fight can turn you into a champion.

Nick Woodman experienced this firsthand when he started a gaming and marketing company called Funbug in 1999. Investors backed him with $3.9 million, but the company failed, and all the money was lost. Nick was so devastated that he took a long surfing trip to clear his mind.

During that trip, he wanted to take videos of himself while surfing but struggled to find a camera that was small and easy to use. That's when inspiration graced him with the idea of creating a camera that could capture video of people doing what they loved.

Nick launched the GoPro camera in 2002 and became a billionaire, a champion in his own right.[14]

Wilma and Nick illustrate that when faced with seemingly insurmountable obstacles or the end of something we hold dear, we can rise again, wiser and stronger. However, it takes the willingness to try and risk again.

Rejection and Criticism

At 19, Andy Andrews lost both of his parents just months apart. Andy struggled financially and became homeless, occasionally sleeping under the Gulf State Park Pier in Alabama. During this dark period, he wondered if life was merely a lottery ticket or if people could steer the future through the choices they make.

In search of answers, he ventured to the library and read over 200 biographies of remarkable figures like George Washington Carver and Anne Frank. He discovered that these people had made choices at crucial points in their lives that led to their success. This knowledge inspired his first book, *The Traveler's Gift: Seven Decisions That Determine Personal Success,* a story about a man's search for meaning and fulfillment through time travel.[15]

When Andy sent his book to publishers, he received rejection after rejection. Fifty-one in total! Determined to share his message with the world, he kept at it. Not only did Andy corral a publisher, but the book also went on to become a *New York Times* bestseller, translated into 40 languages![16]

Andy is now a sought-after speaker, coach, and consultant for Fortune 500 companies and top organizations around the world. He credits his persistence for getting *The Traveler's Gift* published.

"If you're going through a struggle right now, know that there is light at the end of the tunnel. But also know that the majority of the tunnel is long, dark, and scary," he writes in his blog post. "It could be that the only certainty available to you at the moment is the fact that you will persist without exception ... that you will find a way where there is no way."[17]

Here are other examples of people who were rejected or criticized yet still went on to achieve great things:

- In 1922, a man founded Laugh-O-Gram Corporation, which went bankrupt the following year. MGM Studios initially rejected his animated mouse character, and other projects, such as *The Three Little Pigs*, faced similar skepticism. Despite rough starts for *Snow White and the Seven Dwarfs* and *Pinocchio*, Walt Disney persevered. Today, with 22 Oscars, 59 nominations, and a legacy of magical movies and theme parks, Disney's creations have spread happiness to both children and adults.[18]

- A gentleman once faced harsh criticism during an early Hollywood screen test. The studio's verdict was blunt: "Can't act. Can't sing. Balding. Can dance a little." Fred Astaire went on to captivate audiences with his dancing, singing, and acting, becoming one of the most legendary performers in movie history.[19]

- Bullied in high school for having autism, Temple Grandin never let that define her. She pursued her passion for animal welfare and built a groundbreaking career in science. Today, nearly half of all cattle in the United States move through humane livestock facilities designed by Dr. Grandin. She authored the landmark book *Emergence: Labeled Autistic*, one of the first autobiographies to offer a personal perspective on autism. She is a prominent speaker on autism and animal behavior.[20]

Such exceptional talents would have been lost if these pioneers had given up at the first point of rejection or criticism. Their relentless determination to not take things personally, believe in themselves, and draw on willpower and resilience overpowered every impulse to quit.

Self-Doubt

Self-doubt is a debilitating opponent that can steal opportunities, potential, and the chance to fulfill our deepest longings. The voice in our heads says, "I can't do this!" or "I'm not smart enough," or "Who do I think I am?" pulling us into a vortex of vulnerability, shame, and doubt. We fear looking silly or saying the wrong thing, so we hesitate, doubt ourselves, and remain stuck in complacency.

Years ago, I was consumed by doubt at a personal development event where my beloved mentor from afar, Dr. Wayne Dyer, was speaking. Dyer was a spiritual master. Fans called him the "father of motivation."[21] His journeys of healing, as shared in his many books and PBS talks, have deeply inspired me and many others.

Before the workshop began, people gathered in a ballroom with seating for about 200, eager to hear Dyer's talk. He was chatting with people at the back of the room before going on stage. I was coming from the ladies' room and approaching him from behind. I stopped because I thought I might have the exciting chance to meet him. To my surprise, a woman walked away from him, and then he stood alone as if waiting to see if anyone else would approach him.

Now I had the chance to talk to him! But doubt swirled in my head. *What if he walks away as I get closer? I don't know what to say—the words won't come out right. I'll make a fool of myself.*

Then he turned and walked toward the stage, and the moment was lost. I had the chance of a lifetime, and I blew it. I was so disappointed in myself! *Well,* I thought, *maybe I'll have another chance.*

On August 29, 2015, this extraordinary man, a visionary in human potential who inspired millions, passed away at age 75. I felt sadness when he died, as though I had lost a dear friend. He was instrumental in my own growth as a person. I will always regret not seizing the opportunity and missing the chance to meet a man whose work positively affected me.

Yet, this regret taught me to push past self-doubt, especially in matters close to my heart. I realized that not taking advantage of opportunities that resonate with me could mean missing joyful, meaningful experiences. Even though this event may seem small, I now use it as a reminder to take action in spite of self-doubt and to focus on the possibilities that lie beyond it.

Practice Persevering through Obstacles

To tackle the obstacles of adversity, rejection, criticism, and self-doubt, let's apply them to your SMART goal—the specific achievement you're working toward, as outlined in the Commitment chapter.

Start by identifying which of these obstacles are currently hindering your progress. Beside each one, write down potential solutions for overcoming it.

For example, if your SMART goal is to launch a business, self-doubt might stop you from securing your first client. A possible solution could be to research relevant articles, practice your pitch to build confidence, and seek peer support or mentoring.

Or suppose your goal is to write a novel and you fear criticism. Solutions might include enrolling in a writing course, reaching out to another writer for feedback, or committing to learn from criticism instead of avoiding it.

When you brainstorm solutions to your specific obstacles, you'll be better prepared to persevere. Be sure to write in your journal about moments when you've overcome these blocks. Revisit your journal of wins to boost your confidence and remind yourself how far you've come.

Celebrate each victory—whether it's a favorite activity, a dinner out, or a well-earned break. Recognizing your progress fuels the confidence and motivation to keep going.

Being Unstoppable

We typically have the best intentions at the start of a meaningful venture. As time passes, however, daily obligations, hardships, and uncertainty can derail us from our most precious goals. Heck, we have life to deal with!

But to stay on track—especially for the long haul—we need to lean on inner strengths such as *purpose, resilience*, and *belief in ourselves*. Let's look at how these qualities help us keep going when things get tough.

Staying True to Your Purpose

Times of personal crisis can jolt us into trying to make sense of what has happened. We may ask ourselves, "Why?" or, "What did I do?" However, having a worthy purpose can be the guiding light in our darkest times, making us unstoppable.

Linda Lochridge Hoenigsberg shares how her unwavering faith and purpose carried her through life's trying circumstances.

> I was raised in an alcoholic, neglectful home. I didn't understand it then, but my parents had let go of their dreams because of past traumas. They coped with these

traumas by abusing alcohol and prescription drugs. My brother, sister, and I reacted to their neglect the way most children and teens do—we acted out.

When I was 14, the Los Angeles court system deemed me incorrigible and incarcerated me in juvenile hall. A year later, I was kicked out of high school for truancy and suspicion of dealing drugs. At 16, I married my boyfriend. He was five years older than I was and on parole for grand theft auto. He was a burglar, and our friends included pimps and gang members from Watts and East Los Angeles. We had a son together, but by my eighteenth birthday, my husband had abandoned us.

After that, a series of horrible events occurred, and I took drugs to cope with my emotional pain while I was living on the streets. Soon, I entered into a relationship with a man who was addicted to heroin. We had a daughter together, but my partner was abusive, and eventually, I took both my children and ran away. We never saw him again.

In my early 20s, I suffered from serious mental illness and was diagnosed with panic disorder, agoraphobia, and major depression. Within the next few years, both my brother and my father committed suicide, and thoughts of doing the same became my dark companion. I prayed a lot and kept living, sensing God's presence even on the worst days.

As my condition improved, a dream formed in my heart. I wanted to become a psychotherapist and reach out to other people who were hurting. But I was barely functioning myself; I couldn't work or drive a car. Even with continuing troubles like falling down a flight of stairs and breaking my neck, which left me in chronic pain, I knew with God's help, I could do it. So, at 51, I entered college. Four years later, I graduated magna cum laude with a BA in psychology. I was on my way!

The following summer, after acceptance into a university master's program, I learned I had a brain tumor and was told I had one year to live. Even though I was shocked and full of fear, I somehow knew God wasn't finished with me yet. I didn't believe He had brought me all this way just to allow me to die so young. I didn't feel special; I just felt that it wasn't my time.

In a risky, six-hour surgery, a neurosurgeon was able to remove most of the tumor, although he couldn't avoid compromising important nerves. When I came out of the anesthesia, I couldn't walk, and the fatigue was unrelenting. During my first year post-surgery, I was in bed most of the time. Complete recovery would take several years. So, how did I choose to spend my time in bed? I decided to get my master's degree, of course!

Three years later, I graduated with a 4.0 GPA and a diploma. Then came the hardest part: To become a licensed psychotherapist, I needed to get 3,000 hours of counseling under my belt, but I was still suffering from the effects of my brain surgery. Understanding my physical limitations, an agency that treated abused and neglected children hired me. I worked there for two years and helped start their outpatient clinic and a dialectical behavior therapy program that treats people with self-harming behaviors.

Within two years, I received a license and left the agency to pursue my dream of opening a private practice. I rented office space and began working with teenagers and adults. Soon, I had a full practice with a lengthy waitlist, but an enemy was lurking beneath the surface. Eventually, symptoms brought me to the doctor's office, where an MRI confirmed the tumor had grown back, and I would need to have surgery all over again. I packed up my books, said tearful goodbyes to clients, and went home to await another surgery.

As I was healing physically after the second surgery, I noticed an inner healing as well. I felt more grounded, centered, and peaceful. I felt more love and compassion for others. I began to understand God's love for me and how what I was "doing" didn't matter to Him. He just wanted me to love Him with all my heart and love others as well. My parents had died decades earlier, and I was suddenly overwhelmed with a feeling of complete for-giveness for them. Gratitude and acceptance appeared as daily practices in my life as if by decree.

Additionally, my recovery afforded me time to paint with watercolors, work on a book about relationships, dabble in photography, attend a fly-fishing clinic with my husband (a wonderful man), and spend time with my beautiful grandchildren and great-grandchildren. I have come to believe this: No matter what you face or how old you are, it's never too late to become what you might have been. Who you become, the lives you touch, and the lives you allow to touch you are much more important than "what you do."[22]

Linda stayed true to her purpose—her truth—despite unimag-inable adversity. Believing in God's grace and driven by her calling to be a psychotherapist, she succeeded in helping those struggling with emotional and mental health challenges.

Like Linda, we can navigate our unique challenges with perse-verance, resilience, and purpose. Her story invites us to reflect: What purpose ignites my passion enough to carry me through the worst of times? Identifying this purpose can guide our choices, shape our behaviors, and strengthen our actions. Then, when setbacks arise, we can find a way to fulfill our deepest desires.

The Power of Resilience

Life's circumstances were against Charles Hunt from the start. Growing up in Oakland, California, in the 1980s, he faced educa-tional inequities, rampant poverty, high murder rates, and a crack epidemic. His family life was just as hard. His mother abused drugs, and his father was a custodian and a pimp. Despite everything, he knew that his parents loved him as much as he loved them.

Between the ages of seven and ten, Charles experienced trauma that no kid should have to endure. He discovered his mother's boy-friend lying lifeless on the floor from a drug overdose. After that came his father's incarceration and the family's eviction from their home because of his mother's addiction. As a result, his grandmother raised him. One day, she told him that other prisoners had attacked his father, and that he had died. Eventually, Charles's mother was also sent to prison.

With all his hurt, sadness, and solitude, Charles did not fall victim to the pain of his past. He became the first in his family to graduate from college, earning a bachelor's degree and later a master's in business. After two decades in a corporate career, he founded The Audacity Firm, transforming his trauma into his purpose.[23]

Today, Charles is a resilience expert, adjunct professor, and motivational speaker. Through his firm, he strengthens spirits and cultivates resilience in those who share his audacity to succeed. He has taught students and leaders how to build a better future by promoting career readiness, life coaching, and direct hiring opportunities.[24]

How did Charles do it? What made him succeed while others drowned in a sea of despair? Charles credits his mind—his most important resource—for his ability to move through trauma. He recalls the agonizing, harrowing days when he didn't know how he could move forward. What got him through was his belief that tomorrow would be better, even when that belief seemed irrational.

"It's okay to acknowledge that I was a victim. But refuse to own being a victim," he said in his Ted Talk. He believes we can overcome anything with the right outlook and a positive attitude.[25]

Charles's journey from adversity to triumph proves that resilience isn't just about surviving hardships—it's about mastering the positive mindset needed to rise above them.

Believing in Yourself

Time after time, someone—sometimes even ourselves—challenges us to rise above our doubts and fears, to become stronger than we believe ourselves to be. Whether we're presenting our findings to a room of 100 peers, pursuing a long-held business dream, or working on a relationship that's been fading over the years, a choice presents itself.

Do we slither away like a snake and say "No," feeling defeated before taking our first step? Do we smother ourselves with insecure thoughts like "I can't do it" or "I'm not good at that"? Do we listen to the naysayers who tell us, "That's going to be a lot of work" or "You won't be able to raise that kind of money"? Or do we soar above the negative thoughts, ignore the nonbelievers, and go for it anyway?

Erik Weihenmayer chose the latter. After losing his eyesight at age 13 due to a rare eye disease, he made it his mission not to let blindness keep him from living a full, adventurous life.

He discovered rock climbing at a camp for blind teens and soon began challenging himself with bigger mountains. Even though Erik struggled with self-doubt, he remained determined to keep going. When he announced his plan to climb Mount Everest, experienced climbers were skeptical about whether he could succeed. But Erik believed he could do it, and that belief made all the difference.

On May 25, 2001, Erik became the first blind person to reach the summit of Mount Everest.

By the time he turned 34, he had completed all Seven Summits—the highest peaks on each of the seven continents. At the time, fewer than 150 mountaineers had accomplished this remarkable feat.[26]

Unstoppable Vision

You have limitless potential, but unlocking it takes self-discipline, a positive mindset, and an unstoppable attitude. No matter how much you struggle or want to give up, keep moving forward, fueled by a goal that ignites your passion.

Just as Maisie Devore realized her dream of building a town pool in Eskridge, Kansas, and positively affecting her community, you too can achieve your magnificent vision by becoming unstoppable.

Practice Being Unstoppable

To strengthen your perseverance, reflect on *purpose, resilience,* and *belief in yourself* by completing the sentences below.

Staying True to Your Purpose

- To fulfill my purpose, I need to give up_____.
- I will make my purpose a priority by_____.

Cultivating Resilience

- To help get me through a tough time, I believe that_____.

- I can cultivate a positive outlook by

  _____.

Believing in Yourself

- I can fulfill my purpose by believing that I am_____.

- Each day I will embody

  _____ to help me achieve my goal, such as self-discipline, confidence, a positive outlook, or my compelling vision.

As you progress, revisit these sentences to reflect on your growth and new insights, adapting as needed.

CHAPTER SUMMARY

Perseverance is the will to see things through despite fear, doubt, discouragement, and opposition. We achieve great things by harnessing grit, remaining resilient, staying true to our purpose, and believing in ourselves.

> **Complementing virtues:** *Commitment, Determination*
> **Perseverance transcends:** *Adversity, Inertia*

Remember this . . .

- Persevering with passion—grit—is a stronger predictor of success than talent, ability, or intelligence. When we apply grit to our goals, we transform our passions into realities.

- Mental barriers like self-doubt and external obstacles like adversity, criticism, and rejection can hold us back—if we let them. Recognizing them gives us the power to choose our own path despite the challenges.

- To become unstoppable in pursuing our purpose, we must stay true to it, remain resilient, and believe in ourselves. We have limitless potential and the ability to tap into grit, but unlocking it requires self-discipline, a positive mindset, and a compelling vision. No matter how much we struggle or want to give up, we must keep moving forward—driven by a goal that fuels our passion.

CHAPTER 4

Hope

Hope is wishing for something good to happen and taking action to make that good a reality.

Hope can rekindle our dreams and lift our spirits during life's darkest moments. When we think hopeful thoughts, what once felt impossible seems within reach. But hope isn't just about feeling uplifted about something good to come; it's also about taking action to make that good a reality.

Even so, to see our vision through and bring that good into our lives, we must first make hope a conscious choice and continue to choose it—even when things get tough.

In the iconic film *The Shawshank Redemption*, Andy Dufresne (Tim Robbins) brilliantly illustrates the radical difference that having hope can make in our lives.

Andy is a banker sent to Shawshank State Penitentiary for murdering his wife and her lover, a crime he didn't commit. There, he tolerates a sadistic prison guard, abuse by other inmates, and solitary confinement. Andy also endures a tyrannical warden who pulls him into a crooked accounting scheme. Though Andy is smart and skilled, it's his choice to cling to hope over despair that keeps him going. He also makes a steady effort to inspire his prisonmates to adopt a more hopeful outlook.

Driven by hope, Andy executes a complex escape plan, and after nearly two decades in prison, he not only breaks free of the prison but also achieves his life's vision.[1]

Andy's profound words to his best friend Red (Morgan Freeman) emphasized his belief in hope's power to uplift, "Remember, Red, hope is a good thing, maybe the best of things, and no good thing ever dies."[2]

Hope Inspires Your Vision

Hope helped Andy Dufresne get through the horrible prison conditions and gave him hero-like strength to see his plan through to the end. Sure, Andy's story is fictional, but it mirrors the stories of real people throughout history who have done the same. In fact, hope played a crucial role for Amelia Earhart and Sir Edmund Hillary in helping them carry out their visions.

> **Amelia Earhart's** vision was to be the first woman to fly around the world. During her quest, she came up against skepticism, prejudice, and financial troubles.
>
> In 1937, Ameila's plane suffered mechanical issues, which caused her first attempt to circumnavigate the globe fail. She had the plane rebuilt and tried again later that year. On her second attempt, she was 7,000 miles short of the 29,000-mile journey when she lost radio contact over the Pacific Ocean. Sadly, no one ever heard from her again.
>
> Amelia's brave and unwavering vision inspired countless innovators and risk-takers to pursue their dreams against all odds.[3]
>
> **Sir Edmund Hillary** had been passionate about mountain climbing ever since he scaled New Zealand's Southern Alps as a high school student. In 1951, he joined a British expedition and explored the southern flank of Mount Everest, the world's highest mountain at 29,035 feet.

Then, in May of 1953, a team of mountaineers invited Hillary to join their expedition to Everest's summit. As they climbed, some on the team had to turn back, but by late morning, Sir Hillary and Sherpa mountaineer Tenzing Norgay reached the top. They shook hands and embraced in a moment of solidarity and triumph. They had achieved what no one else had done before![4]

Choosing Hope

Hopeful thinking is a deliberate choice. We can choose hope to help us stay optimistic and resilient, even when outside forces attempt to take it away. Like Andy Dufresne, Amelia Earhart, and Sir Edmund Hillary, they chose hope as an ally, which gave them the relentless determination they needed to stay true to their visions.

When we redefine hope as an actionable force, we can push through adversity and turn our visions into reality.

Practice Hopeful Thinking

Think back to the compelling vision you created in the Commitment Chapter. Keep in mind that a compelling vision can boost your hope and help solidify your commitment, especially in challenging times. Let your vision energize you and reignite your hope for what you want to accomplish.

You can reinforce your compelling vision by using words, symbols, pictures, and inspiring quotes. Add them to your journal and put them somewhere you'll see them often—like on your desk, mirror, or fridge.

Remember, there may be days when you feel less hopeful than other days. In those moments, let your compelling vision be your source of strength. It has the power to lift your hope and get you through doubt and fear to help you stay the course.

Hope in Action

Hope is one of the best predictors of a person's success and well-being.[5] Although this may sound surprising, researchers who have studied hope for decades have proven it true.

Charles R. Snyder, the psychologist who developed Hope Theory and a leading figure in positive psychology at the University of Kansas, found that hope influences academic, athletic, and health outcomes. His research shows that students—from grade school through college—with high hope achieve better academic performance than those with low hope, even when intelligence is the same.[6] Why? Because hopeful students set more goals, find multiple ways to achieve them, and push through obstacles.

Snyder's research found that athletes driven by hope notably perform better, especially during high-pressure competitions.[7] The results were valid even with natural athletic ability taken into account.

Similarly, people with high hope cope better with chronic physical pain than those with low hope. Research suggests that hopeful thinking encourages people with pain to find strategies and continually use them to help manage their discomfort.[8]

According to Snyder, hope levels vary, with some people having low hope and others having high hope. Levels vary because we learn hopeful thinking and goal-setting through our interactions with others, which shape our ability to pursue those goals. Plus, according to Hope Theory, hope is based on goal-directed determination and finding pathways to achieve these goals, both of which are influenced by our experiences and relationships.

For example, children who experience neglect or abuse often have lower hope because no one teaches them hopeful thinking. Because goal-directed behavior develops in the context of other people, the abused child's hope diminishes as they learn not to trust these bonds. However, hope can develop later in life, especially through supportive relationships.

Similarly, adults can experience a loss of hope from the death of a loved one, a divorce, or personal trauma.[9] Snyder notes that goal-directed thinking can diminish in these scenarios, lowering our hope. Since people typically pursue goals with their partners, losing them can reduce their sense of direction and motivation.

The more we understand hope's remarkable impact on our lives, the more we can use it to our advantage. But first, what exactly is hope?

The What and Why of Hope

You may think of hope as an expectation or a desire for something good to happen. However, according to authors Casey Gwinn and Chan Hellman, that doesn't fully capture hope's meaning based on the last 20 years of research. In their book *Hope Rising*, the authors challenge us to view hope as an action-oriented concept rather than a mere wish, like saying, "I hope there won't be any traffic" or "I hope I get the job." They explain that these statements are not truly hope because the people saying them have no power over the outcome.

The research-based meaning of hope is action-oriented, distinguishing "hopeful" from "wishful thinking."[10] The authors define hope as "... the belief that your future can be brighter and better than your past and that you actually have a role to play in making it better."[11]

Gwinn and Hellman discuss the pioneering work of Charles R. Snyder, mentioned earlier in this chapter, and his colleagues.

In 1991, Snyder formally introduced Hope Theory, a research-based framework for understanding hope. The theory defines hope through three interactive concepts: goals, pathways or routes to these goals, and the agency or willpower needed to achieve them. Here's a breakdown:

- **Goals** – The foundation of Hope Theory is that our behavior is primarily goal-directed. An unclear or lackluster goal may not motivate us to take action, which makes it harder to create pathways to accomplish it. So, the first step in the Hope Theory is establishing a desirable and personally meaningful goal.

- **Pathways (waypower)** – With high hope and a desirable goal, we'll find it easier to create pathways to its achievement. When obstacles arise, hope encourages us to find alternative ways to move forward instead of giving up. As we make progress, our hope grows stronger.

- **Agency (willpower)** – Agency, or willpower, is the determination to use the pathways designed to

reach our goal. High-hope people have the mental
energy to begin and persist in pursuing a goal,
even when obstacles like doubt and fear appear.
Willpower also increases with the other's encouragement to achieve our goal.[12]

Andy Dufresne's story illustrates Hope Theory in action. His
desirable and personally meaningful goal was to live in Zihuatanejo,
a beautiful seaside town in Mexico. He'd open up a small hotel on
the beach and refurbish a boat to take his guests out charter fishing.
Even trapped within prison walls, with no prospect of parole in sight,
he maintained relentless hope for his future. He knew that he was
wrongly imprisoned and didn't deserve to be there. He may have
been a bad husband, as he admitted to Red, but he was not a mur-
derer.

Andy's pathway became the tunnel he painstakingly chiseled out
with a small rock hammer that Red had smuggled into the prison.
Over 19 years, Andy stayed motivated by hope and his compelling
vision, covering up the hole in the wall with pin-up posters (also
from Red) until he could crawl to freedom. Part of Andy's plan was
to expose the warden's illegal activities and amass the money needed
for his new life, so he used his role as the warden's financial advisor
as another pathway to his vision.

While Andy's hope rose as he identified and used pathways to
achieve his goal, his agency (willpower) grew. As he told Red, "I
guess it comes down to a simple choice, really. Get busy living, or get
busy dying."[13]

Andy's brave words and actions helped earn him the respect and
support of his fellow prisoners, further increasing his will. He captivated and won them over with his hopeful spirit, a disposition he
maintained not just as an emotion but also as an actionable way of
life.

We can apply the Hope Theory as an effective method for achieving any goal.

Let's say you want to open a pastry shop inspired by your passion
for baking. You've set an exciting, fulfilling goal propelling you
forward.

Next, you outline pathways like consulting a successful bakery owner and researching shop locations.

Lastly, you show willpower by following the bakery owner's advice and exploring rental costs for your desired location. Every action boosts your hope. High hope empowers you to overcome setbacks like high rental costs or time constraints.

Your journey of setting a desired, meaningful goal, creating pathways, and persistently working to achieve it despite obstacles shows that hope thrives on active participation, not merely wishful thinking. Hope diminishes when any element of Hope Theory is missing, such as pathways to achieve your goal. All elements must work in unison to sustain hope.

With Hope Theory on your side, you're far more likely to achieve your goals—no matter what hurdles come your way.

Staying Hopeful

What happens to hope when we face setbacks? How do we sustain hope, especially when the outlook is grim? Barriers to hope are also part of Snyder's Hope Theory, as they inevitably come up whenever we strive to reach a meaningful goal. Barriers can decrease our motivation if we don't have high hope. As mentioned before, Dr. Snyder found that high-hope people excel at creating alternative paths to their goals.

Let's try this: Take a moment to close your eyes and think about a goal you want to achieve. Think about how you plan to get there. You'll see that if these ways are viable to you and the goal means something to you, your hope begins to rise. You'll feel better, more capable, and more confident as it does.

Now, think of a potential obstacle to achieving your goal. For instance, if your goal is to buy a new home, a low credit score might make that more difficult. You can choose to have this problem deflate your energy or focus on how hopeful you feel about attaining your goal. Hope increases your willpower, enabling you to explore ways to improve your credit score, like reducing credit card balances and regularly reviewing the credit report for errors.

Whenever barriers come up, we can start thinking about creating new routes or pathways to move forward and stay on track.

Practice the Hope Theory

Do your dreams seem to elude you? The Hope Theory's three tenets—goals, pathways, and willpower—can be your roadmap to their fulfillment. First, write down a specific goal that supports your dream or use the SMART goal you created in the first chapter.

Next, list the pathways to reach that goal, and start acting on them. Each action taken will give rise to your hope.

Lastly, to build your willpower needed to reach your destination, you can revisit your compelling vision, recite positive phrases, and stay physically strong through exercise and getting enough sleep. Also, seek encouragement and support from your family and friends, or a support group, as this will raise your hope too.

When we cultivate hope in achieving our goals, we'll be more likely to find alternative pathways and the will to persist when obstacles arise.

Keeping Hope Alive

Even with the Hope Theory guiding you to keep hope alive and reach your goals, maintaining hope is still challenging, particularly when situations seem hopeless. Anyone who has faced an addiction, the loss of a loved one, unemployment, a devastating accident, or a cancer diagnosis may have trouble staying hopeful.

Still, oncologist Jerome Groopman, in *The Anatomy of Hope*, observes how hopeful thinking helped his patients endure invasive treatment, even when the odds of a cure were against them.[14]

Groopman shares the moving story of his 67-year-old patient, Barbara, a resilient woman who battled breast cancer. After enduring treatment, Barbara discovered a hard swelling over one of her lower ribs. She underwent a series of X-rays and scans.

When Groopman reviewed the test results with her, he gently explained that she had tumor deposits in her ribs, pelvis, and spine, along with three tumors in her liver. He told her the cancer was aggressive, so he wanted to treat it aggressively.

Barbara expressed her desire to live as long as possible but with quality of life. Because the breast cancer had metastasized, his goal was remission, and treatment was palliative since there was no cure.

To Groopman's surprise, Barbara was calm, in control, and accepting despite the treatment's uncertainty and limitations. He said she approached each difficult conversation with realistic expectations, frankly expressing her wishes.[15]

Groopman said Barbara's hope was "real and undying."[16] He believed that the meaning she found in her life—faith in God and precious relationships with loved ones—sustained her hope during her illness and until the end of her life. Rather than focusing on her suffering or its reasons, she focused on purpose and meaning, which made all the difference in how she lived out her days.

Not everyone can access this kind of hope when faced with a prognosis like Barbara's. Understandably, some of us react with anger, sadness, or depression. How we react to devastating news is deeply personal. However, in times of crisis, we can turn our attention to the special meaning that our lives have for others, the joy we've brought into their lives, and the meaningful work we've accomplished. These reflections can be just what we need to keep our hope alive and ease our suffering.

Hope and Meaning

Austrian psychiatrist and Holocaust survivor Viktor Frankl wrote about finding meaning amid a hopeless situation in his 1946 classic book, *Man's Search for Meaning*. His memoir describes the enormous suffering he and other prisoners endured in a Nazi prison camp during World War II. Along with the inhumane conditions and cruelty of their captors, each prisoner felt an unbearable longing for family and home.

Frankl observed that, despite the despair of looming death, prisoners who found meaning in fulfilling a future goal had a higher chance of survival. The goal could be reuniting with a loved one, completing an unfinished work, or contributing something that mattered. With this aim, they found hope and with it came the inner strength to better endure the cruelty around them.

In contrast, prisoners who felt hopeless about the future faced mental and physical deterioration. Without a sense of purpose, they could not summon the will to keep going.

Frankl himself found meaning in the hope of seeing his wife again. He imagined her in vivid detail, speaking with her in his mind.

He also dreamed of one day lecturing students about the psychological experience of prison camps. These future goals gave him hope and, consequently, the will to live.[17]

After the camp's liberation, Frankl developed Logotherapy, a psychological theory inspired by his experiences and observations of fellow prisoners. His theory suggests that finding personal meaning in suffering can sustain our hope even in our worst moments. He identifies three sources of this meaning: finding purpose in work or completing tasks, embracing life and love fully, and adopting a chosen attitude in response to unavoidable pain.[18]

Reflecting on the third source—our attitude toward suffering—Frankl writes: "Everything can be taken from a man but one thing: the last of the human freedoms—to choose one's attitude in any given set of circumstances, to choose one's own way."[19]

To illustrate this concept, he shares the story of an older doctor who sought help from him for severe depression after losing his wife. Frankl asked the doctor what would have happened if he had died first. The doctor replied that his wife would have suffered terribly. Frankl then pointed out that, by outliving her, he had spared her that pain. The doctor shook Frankl's hand and left the office.[20]

Frankl had helped the doctor see that there was meaning in his staying behind and bearing the suffering—a perspective he could not have grasped for himself while consumed with grief. With Frankl's help, the doctor chose to change his attitude, and his depression was relieved.

What's so compelling about Frankl's Logotherapy is how it emphasizes that we can find meaning even in life's darkest moments—and that meaning can instill hope within us. Even when anger, disappointment, or despair consumes us, shifting our focus to meaning and purpose can rekindle our hope.

Hope's Promise

Hope lightened the pioneers' load as they traveled across North America to settle in a new land. The hope of a freed people drove a president to abolish slavery. Hope keeps us pursuing a job or relationship after months, even years, of disappointment. The hope of easing suffering drives scientists to search for a cure. Hope for justice strengthens us to fight for our most cherished causes. Hope empow-

ers us with a sense of control over our destinies. Hope quietly promises a better future.

Practice Keeping Hope Alive

What situation could you view with greater hope? Could you see
a problem or painful life circumstance in a more hopeful way? Use
hope as a tool to shift your perspective during difficult times or when
facing unpleasant emotions. In other words, if you are feeling down
about something, think about how you could view the situation more
hopefully.

Here are ways to help keep hope alive:

- **Reflect on your life's impact:** How have you positively influenced others? Think back to moments
  when you made a difference—whether through
  volunteer work, offering a new perspective, or
  simply brightening someone's day with a kind
  gesture.

- **Seek joy:** Pursue activities that bring you happiness
  and fulfillment. List five things that lift your spirits,
  no matter how small, and incorporate one or two
  into your week. Doing this can create a spark of
  hope for what's ahead.

- **Connect with loved ones:** Knowing we are not
  alone in what we are going through can strengthen
  our hope. So, reach out to family and friends to
  say hello or set up a time to catch up and remind
  yourself that people love and care for you.

- **Embrace purpose:** Identify and engage with what
  gives your life meaning. Whether volunteering, a
  hobby, or a project, find ways to do what matters
  most to you, sparking your hope.

Take a moment to reflect on how you can apply these ideas to
your own life to find hope when things feel uncertain or overwhelm-

ing. Remember, hope can be a limitless source of strength if you choose it when you need it most.

The Gifts of Hope

Life can be so cruel at times. The question becomes, "How can I possibly live with this?" Remarkably, even when people's worlds shatter in an instant, they manage to catch a glimmer of hope that makes a future possible. Christopher Reeve experienced precisely that.

Best known for his role as Superman, Christopher shared in his autobiography, *Still Me*, how hope helped him navigate the devastating horseback riding accident in 1995 that left him paralyzed from the neck down. He initially told his wife, Dana, that he thought dying would be better than burdening his family.

She responded, "I am only going to say this once: I will support whatever you want to do because this is your life and your decision. But I want you to know that I'll be with you for the long haul, no matter what. You're still you. And I love you."[21]

The "depth of her love and commitment,"[22] Christopher wrote, not only saved his life but gave him the strength to pursue a meaningful and productive one.

During his grueling rehabilitation, Christopher often felt fear, self-pity, and despair. Once a revered actor, a pilot who had twice flown solo across the Atlantic Ocean, and a sports enthusiast, he was now utterly dependent on others. He focused on how he could still be a good father and husband, get back to creative work, and possibly be helpful to other people.

In rehab, Christopher met fellow patients facing similar mental and physical struggles. Their challenges, along with his interest in scientific research and his desire to fund its progress, inspired him to advocate for people with spinal cord injuries. He strongly believed that he and others like him could regain mobility and even walk again.

Christopher's compelling vision motivated him to establish a foundation through which he raised funds tirelessly by giving speeches, lobbying, and organizing fundraisers.[23]

In 1996, he became chair of the American Paralysis Association (APA) and founded the Christopher Reeve Foundation. By 1999, the two organizations merged and were renamed the Christopher Reeve Paralysis Foundation.

Sadly, in 2004, at age 52, Christopher Reeve died of heart failure. After Dana's passing in 2006, the Foundation was renamed the Christopher & Dana Reeve Foundation.[24]

The Foundation has invested over $140 million in research to improve the quality of life for people living with spinal cord injuries.[25]

Giving Hope to Others

Christopher Reeve's extraordinary story reminds us that choosing hope can not only transform our own lives but also positively influence those around us. Like Reeve, we can spark hope in others by sharing our stories of resilience to help them discover pathways that can lead to healing and renewed purpose.

These pathways—whether through charitable foundations, community support groups, or simple acts of kindness—extend hope, encouragement, and support to even more people.

Even a few compassionate words can ignite hope. Dana Reeve's loving support lifted Christopher from despair and helped guide him toward a brighter future.

Hope is a precious gift we can offer others, inspiring them to rise above their difficulties and doubts to see what's possible. Never underestimate the profound impact your words or actions can have in renewing someone's hope.

Hopeful words gave her the confidence to pursue a job better suited to her talents. Hope gave him the courage to start a business that helps others thrive. Hope kept her spirits up as she coped with a chronic illness. What a joy it is to give people hope and change lives!

Practice Giving Hope

Can you help someone feel more hopeful? For instance, a loved one may feel discouraged because they can't find a job or are going through a breakup. Sending a note of encouragement or inviting them over for coffee can lift their spirits! The idea is to help them feel hopeful through your supportive words and kind actions.

Afterward, write about what you said or did to give them hope.

How did they react to your encouraging words and actions? How did you feel when you helped them regain hope to move forward?

Writing about your experience can help you reflect more deeply on the power of offering your hope to others, which you can return to in the future to remind yourself that your words and actions matter.

CHAPTER SUMMARY

Hope is wishing for something good to happen and taking action to make that good a reality. Setting meaningful goals, creating pathways to reach them, and staying motivated through challenges all increase our hope and chances for success. With higher hope, we can more effectively pursue and accomplish our dreams. Hope calls us to rise above doubt and difficulty to see what's possible.

Complementing virtues: *Faith, Courage*
Hope transcends: *Despair, Frustration*

Remember this . . .

- Hope keeps our visions alive in our hearts. Through persistent, hopeful thinking, we can achieve what once seemed impossible and inspire others to do the same.

- Hope is action-oriented, built on a scientific trilogy: goals, pathways, and willpower. When the steps we take toward our goals don't work out, hope diminishes. But when we find new pathways, hope rises again. We need all three elements to maintain high hope—and the higher our hope, the more likely we are to succeed.

- As Viktor Frankl said, shifting our perspective in times of suffering—finding meaning in our pain— can turn adversity into triumph. With a purpose to our pain, we begin to live empowering life stories.

- Giving hope to others is a rare kind of superpower. It can pull someone from the depths of despair and give them the strength to forge a new, exciting path.

CHAPTER 5

Integrity

Integrity aligns words and actions with both moral and ethical principles, reflected in doing the right thing, keeping promises, and living honestly.

One summer afternoon, I was at the community pool with my 11-year-old goddaughter, Ella, and her sister. We had been in the pool for about an hour, and I was ready to leave. "Let's go now," I said to Ella. Well, she wasn't ready. No surprise.

"Just another five minutes?" she asked eagerly.

It was getting late, but being the softy that I am, I said, "Sure. Five more minutes, but that's it." Then, thinking she wouldn't notice, I got out of the pool. Of course, when she had said "five minutes," she meant having me stay in the pool *with* her for another five minutes.

When we finally left the pool, Ella was quiet. "Are you mad at me?" I asked as we got into the car.

"I'm not mad—I'm more *disappointed*," she quietly said.

Ugh, she's calling me out on my word, I thought. I was humbled and impressed by her frankness. No matter how much I wanted to leave, I had made a promise, and while it seemed insignificant in the grand scheme of things, it wasn't to her. I failed to keep a promise, and she noticed.

My experience with Ella underscored a universal truth: not keeping our promises can trigger negative responses from others. Unlike Ella, many people keep quiet, silently harboring resentment or mistrust over hurtful or disappointing actions. We might stop getting invited places or not hear as much from the person we let down.

Most of us would agree that when people don't do what they say they will, especially when it happens consistently, they show a lack of integrity. In this way, integrity becomes a key measure of a person's character, even the first sign of good character.

Keeping Your Promises

You have seen what integrity looks like in people: you can rely on them, trust that they'll do the right thing, and know they'll care for your children. They admit their mistakes and don't shy away from responsibility. Their actions align with their promises.

Yet, upholding integrity is not always easy. Life often presents situations where the right choice isn't always clear.

Consider these scenarios:

- You see your best friend's spouse in a restaurant with another person, having an intimate exchange. Do you tell your friend?

- A family member asks you to cover for them by going along with a lie about where they were. Do you agree to it?

- A colleague slips office supplies into her tote bag to take home, violating company policy. Do you say something to management?

- You find several hundred dollars in a company parking lot, far from a car. Do you turn it into Lost & Found?

- A cashier misses an item at checkout and gives it to you free. Do you go back and let her know?

How we respond to these situations reflects our values, principles, and beliefs. For some, the answers to all or some of these questions may be clear. For others, how to respond may fall into more of a gray area. Regardless of how we respond, consequences—external, internal, or both—still exist.

With each action we take, we weigh these consequences, and how we choose can affect our lives. If we distort the truth, conceal information, or avoid doing what's right, we end up living behind a facade, constantly worried about being exposed. This is the high price of compromising our integrity.

We may see this in our personal lives and in public life—when politicians, newscasters, and corporate leaders make poor choices, their reputations crumble. Their refusal to admit their mistakes further diminishes our respect for them.

Then the opposite is true. People make choices grounded in integrity, such as a business leader valuing safety over profit, a politician rejecting a bribe, or a friend honoring a dinner commitment over a free concert ticket. They display strong character and earn trust and admiration from others.

The What and Why of Integrity

The *Oxford English Dictionary* defines integrity as "the quality of being honest and having strong moral principles" and "the state of being whole and not divided." In other words, integrity is telling the truth, even when it's difficult, as in life-altering decisions, uncomfortable conversations, and moments with high consequences.

Integrity also means being honest in *all* situations. For example, a person of integrity is consistent in their thoughts, feelings, and actions and bases their behavior on moral principles—no matter the circumstances.

This consistency is identified as the core component of integrity by So-Young Kang, founder of the award-winning Awaken Group—a firm known for its innovative business consulting.[1]

Kang cites the example of a manager who, after having a bad day and arguing with someone just before a meeting, still remains consistent in behavior, actions, values, and words. Before entering the room, the manager decides to stay calm and in control of her emotions, as if no argument had happened. But that's not all. Her integrity shines through not just in the office, but also at home, in the community, and with family and friends. People recognize her as a leader who can be trusted and relied upon when needed.[2]

In his book *Integrity*, psychologist and leadership expert Henry Cloud explores the concept of a whole (or complete) self, aligning with the *Oxford English Dictionary's* second definition of integrity as being whole and undivided. Cloud explains that having integrity means being whole and fully functional in all aspects of one's character and actions, essentially "running on all cylinders."[3]

We can liken Cloud's description of integrity— the wholeness of character needed to be a person of integrity—to that of an aircraft. A pilot must have all the aircraft's components working together to fly people safely to their destination.

A crack in any component weakens the plane and compromises its integrity, threatening the pilot's mission. Just as a plane must have all of its mechanical parts solidly integrated to make it structurally sound, so do people, as Cloud says, need to have an integrated character—i.e., all of their character aspects working together—to be maximally effective.

Cloud identifies six key aspects of character that support integrity: the ability to build trust, face reality, achieve results, resolve problems, grow potential, and expand perspective. Cultivating these aspects empowers us to achieve wholeness and enhance effectiveness in all areas of life.[4]

Cloud believes that developing these character aspects leads to positive outcomes. However, he emphasizes that it's not about excelling in every area since we all have weaknesses. Instead, it's about growing in these areas to capitalize on our talents and gifts and to bring about the best possible results.

To illustrate this concept, he highlights a brilliant designer whose potential falls short because she struggles with meeting project deadlines. Or, a talented engineer's career stalls because he has difficulties with teamwork and communication.

"Strengths turn into weaknesses without the other parts of a person to balance them out,"[5] Cloud affirms.

The ideal, then, is to achieve wholeness of character so we can reach our full potential and thrive. However, external forces such as self-interests, confusing situations, the desire to please others, and temptations can knock us off-balance.

Integrity Matters

We see the damage that a lack of integrity can cause. Dishonest politicians undermine the confidence of those they pledge to serve. Some financial institutions extended risky loans to borrowers who couldn't afford them, and when many of those loans defaulted, they helped trigger the 2008 financial crisis. As a result, countless people lost their jobs, homes, and life savings. Sports figures we idolize cheat with performance-enhancing drugs, crushing their fans. The lies, deceits, and betrayals can sometimes be shocking and even tough to bear.

People acting purely out of self-interest disheartens the rest of us. Their self-centeredness comes at a huge cost to themselves and those around them, eroding our society's moral fabric.

The same holds true in our personal lives—if we aren't honest with our family, friends, and co-workers, our relationships suffer, sometimes beyond repair. That's why integrity is so important—people rely on it to build trust and ensure reliability in relationships.

The 1971 film *Willy Wonka and the Chocolate Factory* cleverly illustrates why integrity matters. In the story, five lucky children find golden tickets hidden inside Wonka chocolate bars, granting them a tour of Willy Wonka's (Gene Wilder) mysterious factory. Each child is allowed to bring a chaperone, and all are promised a lifetime supply of chocolate if they follow the rules. During the tour, their character is put to the test in subtle but revealing ways.

As Wonka shows the children and their chaperones around his wondrous factory, the children display unattractive qualities, such as greed, gluttony, and pride, leading to their elimination from the tour. However, Charlie (Peter Ostrum), the good-hearted protagonist, stands out by resisting various temptations along the way, with only one slipup: his Grandpa Joe (Jack Albertson) encourages him to drink the "Fizzy-Lifting Drink." Charlie hesitates. He knows it's wrong according to Wonka's rules but drinks it anyway.

After the factory tour, Willy Wonka, Grandpa Joe, and Charlie gather in Wonka's office. With irritation in his voice, Wonka announces to them that Charlie will not receive the lifetime supply of chocolate because he broke the rules.

Upset and angry by Wonka's decision, Grandpa Joe walks toward the door to leave, with Charlie following. He whispers to Charlie that they are finished there and reveals his plan to get even by selling Wonka's "Everlasting Gobstopper" to his rival.

But in a moment of moral clarity, Charlie turns back and quietly approaches Wonka. With Wonka's back turned, Charlie gently places the gobstopper on the desk beside him, interrupting Wonka's writing. This act of integrity prompts Wonka to whisper to himself, "So shines a good deed in a weary world."[6]

Wonka turns to Charlie, who is about to leave, and enthusiastically reveals that the entire tour was a test of character! He apologizes for his anger and says that Charlie's honesty has proven him worthy of not only a lifetime supply of chocolate but the inheritance of the entire chocolate factory![7]

The film wonderfully illustrates how people appreciate and reward our integrity. We may not receive an entire chocolate factory, but we might receive a promotion or a raise based on our strong work ethic. Our relationships thrive because we've earned our loved ones' trust and loyalty. We're highly respected, so we have influence. Integrity shapes our world for the better.

Yet, we are not perfect. We certainly all have moments where we act in ways we're not proud of. Let's explore how we might lose our integrity and why that happens.

Practice Assessing Your Integrity

Take a moment to assess your integrity by asking yourself the questions below. As you answer, try to honest without judgment. Be compassionate and forgiving of yourself. Notice any areas where your integrity might need strengthening.

- Do I keep my promises to others and myself?
- Am I being dishonest with anyone in my life?
- Do people see me as someone they can trust?
- Where am I not whole and complete in my character? In other words, what qualities—tenacity, authenticity, self-discipline, truthfulness, and transcendence—might I lack that keep me from bringing

my talents and gifts into the world? These aspects contribute to the wholeness of our character.

- Do I bring all of myself—my skills, talents, and best qualities—to situations and projects?

When you think about how you might lose your integrity, you can take action to preserve your reputation, gain trust and respect from others, and find inner peace.

Uncovering Self-Betrayals

How often have you said "Yes" to an invitation when you really wanted to say "No"? You may have agreed to the request because it caught you by surprise or because you would have felt bad refusing. But saying "Yes" gave away your time, time needed for yourself or perhaps your family.

Agreeing to do something when you don't want to is one way you betray yourself. Other forms of self-betrayal include:

- Not honoring what feels right for you out of fear of judgment, criticism, or rejection
- Putting off what you truly want in life because of your obligations
- Letting a remark slide even when it hurts your feelings
- Committing to something important to you and not following through
- Staying in a relationship or a job that no longer works for you

You may have experienced one or more of these scenarios. Alternatively, you may have been on the receiving end of someone who has behaved this way, and that behavior hurt or disappointed you.

To stay true to ourselves—to have personal integrity—means to uphold our values, moral principles, and desires regardless of outside influences. However, it can be tough to always do what's right for us. People may feel slighted, threatened, or critical of our decisions. Perhaps we feel ashamed of something we did in the past and hide it from the people we love. That happens.

Yet, when others courageously share their truths, like confessing past mistakes and personal struggles, we can't help but admire and praise their raw honesty.

Being true to ourselves—aligning our thoughts and actions to what we value, want, or need—is just as important as being true to others.

The Self-Saboteurs

What prevents us from being more faithful to ourselves? According to Kelley Kosow, Master Integrative Life Coach and CEO of The Ford Institute, it's the "Integrity Snatchers." She identifies them as *shame, shadow, fear, your story, playing the role of the victim, wanting,* and *people who empower your helplessness.*[8]

As Kosow explains, *shame* stems from our limiting beliefs like "I'm not worthy" or "I'm not lovable," often rooted in childhood experiences. Feeling undeserving or incapable blocks our path to what we desire. For instance, if we believe we're not good enough, we might shy away from taking risks that could better our lives. Our *shame* causes us to disown the qualities we dislike about ourselves, creating a *shadow* of them. By hiding these disliked parts, we deny our true selves.

Additionally, *fear* of judgment, rejection, or embarrassment around our shadow qualities drives our behaviors. Simplifying this idea, we may avoid pursuing opportunities or expressing ourselves authentically because we fear criticism or failure.

Kosow asserts that our thoughts, beliefs, and fears collectively form what she calls *your story.* "Life is always on top of me" or "I'll never have what I want" can become the narrative we play out in our lives. These disempowering stories often lead us to *playing the role of the victim,* as we often blame others for our lot in life. By blaming others, we evade taking responsibility for our story and its impact on our lives.

Moreover, *wanting* things and people at the cost of our integrity comes from fear or lack. For example, if we desire a relationship so desperately that we overlook mistreatment, we compromise our self-respect. Consequently, we become more helpless and dependent on others.

Lastly, *people who empower our helplessness* may seduce us with their words to remedy feelings of helplessness. Watch out for these people! Kosow says they make us doubt that we can achieve what we want or make us think we cannot live without them. Our confidence suffers because of this powerlessness.[9]

"Integrity Snatchers diminish your sense of self and erode your self-trust. They are not 'bad' or 'wrong.' They are not something to be gotten rid of since they are part of our humanity, and if you are human you won't be able to get rid of them," Kosow writes. "But the important thing is to become aware of them and to understand that when left unattended, Integrity Snatchers will keep you from making the highest choices for yourself and going for the life of your dreams."[10]

Take a moment to reflect on instances in your life where Integrity Snatchers may have influenced your decisions or behaviors. How can you identify and lessen these influences to protect your integrity in the future?

Preserving our personal integrity means honoring our needs and desires and trusting our decisions. By doing so, we can realize our magnificent potential.

The Courage of Integrity

Lisa Nichols is a stellar example of how personal integrity is not only a way to achieve extraordinary results but a massive act of self-love.

Living in Inglewood, California, Lisa was a single mother in her 20s receiving governmental assistance. One day, she needed to buy diapers for her son, but she only had about $11 in the bank. So, she wrapped her baby in a towel for two days. While looking at her son, Lisa experienced a life-changing shift, which she later put into these words: "I was willing to completely die to any form of me that I had been so that I could birth the woman that I was becoming."[11] Lisa knew at her core that the person she was being wasn't working for her.

Determined to be a more empowered person, she sought out successful people to teach her about money. One of her daily commitments became to invest cash in herself.

Lisa worked nine-hour days but didn't have the degree she needed to keep her job permanently. So, she stopped eating out and no longer got her hair and nails done. After work, she spent five and a half hours at night with her son beside her, working on herself. With her paycheck in hand every two weeks, she wrote a check to herself and, on the memo line, noted that she was supporting her dream.

Eventually, Lisa got a second job to save more money. She bought an older, less expensive car and moved into an apartment with a roommate. She also challenged herself to increase her savings by 5 percent with each paycheck she received.

She never looked at the bank statements because, just as money had "burned in her mother's pocket," as she put it at the time, she thought the same was true for her.

Three-and-a-half years later, she walked into a Wells Fargo branch to see how much she had accumulated in her account. When the teller passed the slip of paper to her, Lisa thought she had the wrong person's account and asked the teller to check again. The teller assured her that, yes, she was the right person. *Lisa had $62,500 in her account!*

She turned to her five-year-old son, Jelani, and assured him their lives would change. He asked if they could finally go to McDonald's.[12]

Today, Lisa is the founder of Motivating the Masses, a multi-million-dollar organization that is a testament to her personal growth and transformation. The organization helps clients develop the strategies, motivations, and accountability essential to the success of their business and personal lives. Through her work, Lisa is inspiring others to achieve their aspirations, just as she did. She has authored seven best-selling books and has won numerous awards.[13]

Lisa's personal integrity was courageous. Not only did she become the person of her dreams, but her life lessons also molded her into an extraordinary leader, inspiring others to rise to their potential, no matter the hurdles.

When we become our highest selves, we often become unrecognizable to others. We are making choices aligning with our authentic selves, which means shifting priorities and making personal sacrifices—just as Lisa did.

We also risk disapproval from our loved ones, and we create

more demand for ourselves as we grow, both of which can be uncomfortable.

The journey toward self-actualization can be challenging, but it's one of the most meaningful ways we honor ourselves and create a more fulfilling life.

Practice Uncovering Self-Betrayals

Think about how you might betray yourself, such as postponing what you want, letting a hurtful remark slip by, failing to follow through with your commitments, or staying in unfulfilling jobs or relationships. Journaling about how you betray yourself can help uncover patterns and gain deeper insights into your actions.

Next, consider what has made you fall out of integrity with yourself. Is it fear of judgment, criticism, or rejection? Or perhaps it's because of shame, self-limiting beliefs, or a lack of confidence. Knowing how and why you lose your integrity can make you less likely to betray yourself.

Recognizing self-betrayal is the first step to living a life that truly reflects what you want, making your dreams more attainable.

Living Honestly

Living honestly is keeping our promises and doing what's right, even when it's hard. We may falter along the way. When we do, all we can do is be truthful with others and do our best to make things right if we can.

Honesty has many facets. Beyond keeping our promises and doing what's right, it also includes telling the whole truth, resisting life's temptations, standing by our values, and being impeccable with our words. Let's explore each one of these facets next.

Telling the Whole Truth

A Special Forces team is conducting a training exercise and needs to cross a large, fenced-in farmer's field with a huge bull in it. The team leader goes up to the farmer and asks him if his bull is dangerous. The farmer answers, "My bull wouldn't hurt a fly."

The team proceeds to open the gate and start across the field. They're not even a quarter of the way across when the bull bellows and charges the team. The team turns and sprints back to the gate, barely escaping the furious, charging bull. Panting, the team leader, runs up to the farmer and gasps, "Why did you tell us that the bull wasn't dangerous?"

"Not my bull," replies the farmer.[14]

Omitting critical facts, as the farmer did, is a form of dishonesty because others don't have all the information they need to make the best choices for themselves.

Even so, we may have our reasons for not telling someone the whole truth. We might fear the person's reaction, for example, or feel guilty because we shouldn't have done what we did. Maybe we think we are protecting someone from getting hurt.

Consider this scenario: You went to the coffee shop, yet excluded that you bumped into an old flame and had coffee together. If your partner eventually learns about this meeting, they may feel let down and question why you chose to keep that part a secret. However, fully disclosing your experience ensures you avoid the pitfalls of deceit that can diminish trust in relationships.

Many of us have faced similar situations where it wasn't worth telling our partner because it was perfectly innocent but the problem is leaving things out can feel dishonest, even if that wasn't our intention. Over time, the guilt, anxiety, or defensiveness can weigh on us. So telling the whole truth is generally the best path to take.

Resisting Life's Temptations

Life is full of temptations: overeating, excessive spending, laziness, and even infidelity, to name a few. Indulging in these behaviors can lead to health issues, financial debt, unmet goals, and broken relationships. Yet, temptation's seductive pull of immediate gratification can often outweigh the potential negative fallout.

For instance, we might overeat to comfort ourselves when feeling stressed. An affair may seem exciting if we feel neglected or unappreciated by our partner. We sometimes rationalize these choices to ease our guilt. This can only make us feel worse, because deep down we know those rationalizations don't hold up. Of course, we all have our "guilty pleasures," and when enjoyed in moderation and without harming ourselves or others, they are simply a pleasurable part of life.

Ultimately, preserving our integrity takes effort. Who doesn't know how hard it is to resist the lure of putting off a difficult project in favor of watching a movie or scrolling through videos? Staying true to what's best for us can be a constant challenge! But with each win, we safeguard our self-worth, our relationships, and our chances of reaching cherished goals.

Standing by Your Values

Nowhere is there more attention paid to the virtue of integrity than in leadership. We expect people in the highest positions to have correspondingly high ethical and moral standards. Unfortunately, this is not always the case. Greed and self-interest drive the actions of some leaders, devastating both organizations and their employees.

Conversely, leaders who value truthfulness and honor create unparalleled trust and rapport throughout the enterprise and beyond. People will follow them into battle, help them launch companies, and journey with them to faraway places for a worthy cause.

However, sharing values is not always easy for some, whereas for others it's clear, as Meg Whitman demonstrates.

Meg was CEO of eBay in 1999 when a system outage disrupted services, leaving thousands of eBay community members unhappy. Exhausted senior staffers were discussing what to do about the service agreement with eBay sellers. The agreement stated that if a seller's auctions ended at the time of an outage, eBay would be responsible for refunding the seller's fees. However, not only did the service disruption affect auctions set to end during the outage, but *all* eBay auctions.

With two million active accounts, eBay would have to pay almost $5 million to reimburse sellers. That would be enough to make eBay's stock plunge.

When Whitman overheard the senior staffers talking about this tricky issue, she popped her head into the conference room. She writes in a TODAY books article, "Listening to the conversation, it was clear to me that some voices in the group were trying to rationalize the smaller refund. 'What is the right thing to do here?' I asked, and then I left the room."[15]

Rajiv Dutta from her finance group later told her that the debate ended on the spot. They agreed that all sellers whose auctions were active when the outage occurred would receive a refund of listing fees. Moreover, if the service goes down for more than two hours in the future, the company will refund the fees.[16]

Meg Whitman was clear about what she valued: doing the right thing. She honored not just the words but also the spirit of the company policy. Since we are all leaders within our spheres of influence, sharing our values builds credibility and trust with others.

Knowing what matters to you brings clarity, helping you choose actions that work for you rather than against you. If you don't live by your values, your life may not go in the direction you want, or you may find yourself overly influenced by societal values. Consistently aligning your actions and words with what you value and believe helps you lead an authentic life.

Why does living an authentic life matter? Because you'll feel more confident, choices become clearer, and you attract opportunities that align with who you truly are.

Being Impeccable with Your Words

Words have the power to inspire or crush us, as Don Miguel Ruiz discusses in his best-selling book *The Four Agreements*. Based on ancient Toltec wisdom, the book's first agreement is "Be impeccable with your word."[17] Ruiz writes:

> The word is the most powerful tool you have as a human; it is the tool of magic. But like a sword with two edges, your word can create the most beautiful dream, or your word can destroy everything around you. One edge is the misuse of the word, which creates a living hell. The other edge is the impeccability of the word, which will only create beauty, love, and heaven on earth.[18]

Being mindful of what we say to people is an act of integrity. When we speak out of anger, jealousy, disgust, or impatience, people become defensive, hurt, and may even stop listening. We achieve what we don't want from the conversation: diminished understanding. However, it can be hard to handle our emotions when triggered.

Surely, someone said something to you that you've never forgotten, whether it was good or bad. Perhaps the words were from an authority figure like a teacher, parent, or supervisor. Years later, you remember the words as if it were yesterday. You may not have pursued a dream because of those words. Or, you took a certain career path because someone said you had a talent for it. The lasting impact of another's words can be that significant!

A single sentence changed Gabe Sonnier's life. He was the janitor at Port Barre Elementary in Louisiana. One day, Principal Westley Jones privately told him, "I'd rather see you grading papers than picking them up."[19]

Gabe recalled in a CBS News interview that those words affected him deeply because he never had anyone believe in him that much. Inspired by the principal's words, Gabe started pursuing a teaching degree at 39 while working as the school's janitor.

Shortly after graduating college, he got his first teaching job at the school. But Gabe didn't stop there. He furthered his education by earning a master's degree and ultimately became the principal of the school he had cleaned for 27 years.[20]

Had the principal not said those sincere words to Gabe, he might still be living beneath his potential. Instead, those words changed his life. They became the "magic words" Ruiz describes.

Words have enormous power—they can discourage, humiliate, and hurt. Yet, as Gabe's story illustrates, they can also encourage, heal, and transform us.

Practice Living Honestly

Explore the ways that you can stay true to your integrity—telling the whole truth, resisting life's temptations, standing by your values, and being impeccable with your words—by completing the sentences below.

Telling the Whole Truth

- If I were my partner, boss, colleague, parent, child, or friend, I would want to hear the whole truth from me about_____.

- I don't tell the whole truth to my partner, boss, colleague, parent, child, or friend because_____.

Resisting Life's Temptations

- I am regularly tempted to_____.

- I am feeling this temptation because_____.

- If I give in to this temptation, I will cause_____.

Standing by Your Values

- What I value most is_____.

- When I don't stick to my values, I feel _____.

- I can start upholding my values by_____.

Being Impeccable with Your Words

- I can speak more honestly about_____.

- If I choose my words more carefully, I would_____.

Exploring honesty's role in your life can give you insightful reflections that helps understand yourself better, gain clarity on your choices, and make positive changes.

CHAPTER SUMMARY

Integrity aligns words and actions with moral and ethical principles, reflected in doing the right thing, keeping promises, and living honestly. Embracing integrity cultivates trust, respect, and authenticity, encouraging us to uphold our values, especially in difficult moments. Living with integrity rewards us with self-respect, confidence, inner peace, and meaningful influence on others.

Complementing virtues: *Honesty, Respect*
Integrity transcends: *Temptation, Deceit*

Remember this . . .

- Keeping promises is a key measure of our character. Not doing what we say we'll do diminishes the trust in our relationships. Conversely, following through on our promises boosts our reliability and strengthens relationships.

- Living with personal integrity—honoring the commitments we make to ourselves and doing what feels right for us—leads to a more authentic life. Staying true to our values and desires, even when outside influences push against them, is a powerful act of self-love.

- Telling the whole truth, resisting life's temptations, standing by our values, and being impeccable with our word is living with honesty. Honest living means we never have to manage the chaos our deceptions can cause. Making the right choices can be difficult, but it is worthwhile because we'll have a clear conscience.

CHAPTER 6

Creativity

Creativity is bringing ideas to life, solving problems unconventionally, and making unique connections that enrich our lives with joy and purpose.

All creation begins in our imagination. With a mental image, we travel to faraway places, immerse ourselves in exciting situations, and sculpt our destinies.

Think about this: when you were young, did you imagine you were a superhero, famous musician or sports player, movie star, or inventor? You had no rules or structure around what you could think up; the world was your playground. You could be anyone and do anything through the power of your mind.

Children have this incredible ability to use their imagination, morphing themselves into other beings and using everyday objects to invent exciting scenarios. Creativity sparks and enlarges as children express themselves through their beautiful minds.

As we grow older, we may not exercise our imagination as much. Obligations leave us little time for wandering thoughts. We're focused on reality. But when we realize the power of our imagination to create the life we want and who we want to be, it's a gateway to all that's possible. Neville Goddard had a robust recipe for manifesting through our thoughts.

Goddard, a 20th-century philosopher of the New Thought or mind-healing movement, believed that we could transform our mental states into our daily experiences. Goddard taught this belief, crediting not just our thoughts but also our feelings as the *secret* to manifesting anything we want. He explains that to manifest a desire, we must vividly imagine it as already present in our lives. But Goddard takes it further by saying we must immerse ourselves in the *feelings of the wish fulfilled* as mental practice.[1] Our repetitive positive feelings of the wish fulfilled bring that wish into existence.

Consider John, who unknowingly applied Goddard's principles. As a child, John dreamed of becoming a marine explorer and deep-sea diver like his hero Jacques Cousteau. He faithfully watched the popular 1960s TV series *The Undersea World of Jacques Cousteau*. John imagined himself as Cousteau exploring beautiful creatures in the depths of the sea. Each time he thought about the treasures beneath the ocean, he felt uplifted and inspired.

In his late 20s, after studying marine technology for years, John started a commercial diving business. Cousteau's adventures undoubtedly influenced John's career choice. John felt consistently excited about following in his hero's footsteps.

Goddard would say the secret to John's realization of his dream to be like Cousteau was his intense emotional connection to the outcome—as if it was already here.

When we use our imagination in the way Goddard describes, we can become who we want to be, rewrite old narratives, and shape the future of our dreams.

The What and Why of Creativity

Imagination plays a vital role in bringing our desires to life. But it takes the act of creativity to make what we want a reality.

Typically, we associate creativity with turning an idea into reality, solving a problem with unconventional thinking, or making connections between unrelated things. We use our intelligence, skills, and motivation to realize our visions. No wonder creativity feels so satisfying!

American existential psychologist Rollo May explores the gratifying aspects of creativity. He defines it as our intense engagement with the world, heightening awareness and enriching thoughts, senses, and memory.

May asserts that joy accompanies this high level of awareness as individuals actualize their full potential through creativity. In this way, creativity becomes a powerful tool for personal growth.[2]

Indian spiritual guru Osho describes creativity in the context of religion, writing, "The creative person is one who brings something from the unknown into the world of the known, who brings something from God into the world, who helps God to utter something—who becomes a hollow bamboo and allows God to flow through him."[3]

Creativity can certainly feel like divine intervention. An artist experiences a frenzy of inspiration, painting for hours and neglecting to eat or sleep. The brush moves with ease across the canvas, and the artist feels blissful, as Rollo May describes.

Psychologist Mihaly Csikszentmihalyi describes these blissful feelings—or even ecstasy—as arising from a mental state called "flow,"[4] where time and space have disappeared and nothing else matters.

Conversely, the creative process can be grueling and lonely. A divine force or muse might not visit us for days, months, or even years. "Flow" doesn't happen—instead, the creative process is like squeezing the last bit of toothpaste out of a near-empty tube. We've run dry and don't know how or where to get more!

But with any steadfast commitment to a creative endeavor, we're willing to work through the most excruciating blocks. We can step away from the project, call on our muses, or simply give patience to the process. Easier said than done, perhaps, but how else can we accomplish anything worthwhile?

Creativity, whether it surges or stifles, is a rewarding expression of our individuality and a source of enormous pleasure.

The Creative Self

We channel our creativity through art, music, gardening, engineering, cooking, photography, and writing, not only for our benefit but also for others' benefit. For instance, a musician's mastery of the instrument brings applause of joy. The engineer's solution to a problem creates an easier way of doing something. The scientists' discovery leads to a more effective treatment of a disease. Creating changes lives and improves our world.

But how do we find our creative selves? For some, creativity comes naturally. Passion can also fuel our creativity, and some feel "called" to pursue a purpose. One thing is for sure: When our creative selves emerge, the journey of self-discovery and growth begins.

American psychologist Abraham Maslow brilliantly captured the enormity of our creative nature: "A musician must make music, an artist must paint, a poet must write, if he is to be ultimately at peace with himself. What a man can be, he must be."[5]

Self-actualization, the full and most beautiful expression of ourselves where we are using our skills and talents, takes guts, though. We become vulnerable to potential judgment, criticism, and rejection. But holding back our gifts denies who we are. When we convey our individual brilliance, we make exquisite contributions to others.

Practice Discovering Creativity

Reflect on the role creativity plays in your life. Do you wish you could be more creative? How do you express your creativity? Would you like to share your creativity with others in a meaningful way? Complete these sentences to explore your creative nature:

- I can become more creative by_____ (for example, taking risks or experimenting with new ideas).

- I express my creativity through_____ (for example, cooking, writing stories, or planting flowers)

- I am not as creative as I could be because I_____ (for example, fear judgment, criticism, or failure)

- I can experience the state of "flow" when I_____ (for example, draw for sheer pleasure, play the guitar for hours, or work on a jigsaw puzzle)

Flow describes feelings of joy—even ecstasy—in which time and space have disappeared, and nothing else seems to matter.

- I share my creativity through_____
(for example, my website, social media, an Etsy shop, or problem-solving for clients)

- Creativity gives me meaning by allowing me to_____ (for example, express my emotions, turn my pain into beauty, explore my inner self, or make a meaningful impact on others)

Through this exercise, you may uncover your creative potential and find ways to share it with others.

Creativity's Benefits

Finding a smarter way to do something or solving a complex problem is valued for its efficiency and innovation, but most of all for the difference these solutions can make in people's lives.

Take, for example, the innovative work of architect Ginger Krieg Dosier. She came up with a new way to create a brick using a smaller carbon footprint. (Traditional brick manufacturing releases vast amounts of carbon into the air.) Inspired by seashells and their structural efficiency, Dosier worked with scientists and microbiologists to develop a material strong enough to build houses and commercial properties.[6]

Dosier, the visionary co-founder of Biomason, harnessed the power of marine ecosystems to reduce carbon emissions in building material production. Biomason aims to end the world's dependence on carbon-emitting construction materials.[7]

Many people have innovated over centuries, sometimes out of dire necessity. Consider the Apollo 13 mission in April 1970, a dramatic example of creativity under pressure.

Two days into its journey and halfway to the Moon, one of the Apollo 13's oxygen tanks exploded. The loss of oxygen caused the fuel cells—which generated the electrical power needed to create breathing oxygen and water—to shut down. With resources diminishing and a four-day trip home ahead, the three astronauts moved into the lunar module (LM), a spacecraft designed for short trips between the command module and the moon.

The move came with a new challenge: the LM was designed to support two astronauts, not three, therefore the lithium hydroxide (LiOH) used to remove carbon dioxide from the air was not adequate. Additionally, the LM's lithium hydroxide (LiOH) supply, crucial for removing carbon dioxide, was insufficient for the crew size and mission length.

In a race against time, the astronauts had to adapt the LiOH canisters from the command service module (CSM) to fit the LM's system. However, the CSM's canisters were not a perfect match. As NASA described, mission control engineers had to fit a "square peg in a round hole."[8]

Under extreme duress, with rising carbon dioxide levels in the LM, mission control instructed the astronauts to build an improvised CO_2 filter using cardboard, duct tape, plastic bags, and a spacesuit hose. The design worked and saved the crew! NASA later hailed the mission as their finest hour.[9]

Ginger Krieg Dosier and the Apollo 13 team show us the universal benefits of creativity, from driving innovation to solving challenging problems. Their stories remind us of the resilience, hope, and determination that come along with creativity to shape meaningful solutions.

More of Creativity's Benefits

Creativity has so much to offer us! Sylvia Duckworth, an award-winning teacher and enthusiast of sketchnoting (or visual notetaking with sketches), expands even further on how creativity enriches our lives. Here are her insights:

1. Creativity is multi-disciplinary (spreading beyond the arts to science, technology, engineering, business, and education).

2. Creativity allows you to express yourself.

3. Creativity promotes thinking and problem-solving.

4. Creativity reduces stress and anxiety.

5. Creativity allows you to enter your happy zone and have fun!

6. Creativity gives you a sense of purpose.

7. Creativity leads to feelings of accomplishment and pride.

8. Creativity can link you to others with the same passion.

9. Creativity improves your ability to focus.

10. Creativity promotes risk-taking and iteration.

11. Creativity is a prerequisite for innovation.

12. Creativity encourages us to be life-long learners.[10]

Which of Duckworth's creativity benefits above resonate most with you? Reflecting on these can highlight the vast potential creativity offers in our lives.

That said, recognizing what holds us back from pursuing creative endeavors is paramount. Let's explore how to overcome these blocks to help unleash our full creative potential.

Practice Problem-Solving with Creativity

Identify a challenge in life, whether it's related to a relationship, finances, or work. Now, look at the problem from different perspectives to spark creativity. Ask yourself: What unconventional approach have I not tried? How would I solve this if there were no limitations? A shift in perspective can be just what's needed to help you with the issue!

For example, if you're unhappy with your job but want to figure out ways to make the best of it until you find another one, you can start a side hustle, focus on what's good about the job, or go to lunch regularly with a colleague. You can also brainstorm creative solutions with your partner, family, or friends.

See if you can come up with three to five solutions. Then, choose the one(s) that best help you cope with your current job or other challenging situations.

Blocks to Your Creativity

At age 24, Sergei Rachmaninoff, the brilliant Russian composer and pianist, premiered his first symphony in 1897. The performance was poor due in part to the conductor, Alexander Glazunov's leadership. Some speculated that Glazunov might have been drunk. The critics' response was brutal. For three years, Rachmaninoff fell into a depression, suffered from writer's block, and stopped composing.

At the urging of family and friends, Rachmaninoff saw a doctor who used hypnotherapy to unlock his creativity and find the courage to compose again. In 1901, he premiered his *Piano Concerto No. 2*, which became a famous and beloved classical composition. The praise he received restored his reputation and confidence as a composer.[11]

Criticism, along with self-doubt, perfectionism, and fear of rejection or failure, can paralyze on our creative journey. Do any of these statements sound familiar to you?

- "My family won't approve."
- "I don't have enough time."
- "My friends will think I'm crazy."
- "I'm not talented enough to do this."
- "People will want more from me once I..."
- "What if I fail?"
- "I can't start until I..."
- "I'm too old."

Self-defeating thoughts like these can keep our extraordinary talents and skills hidden from the world. However, they also present us with opportunities for growth and self-discovery. Knowing how to handle blocks when they arise is crucial for our fulfillment! Below are two common blocks: fear and the belief that we're not creative, which can stifle creative potential.

Fear

In *The War of Art,* author Steven Pressfield says, "Most of us have two lives. The life we live, and the unlived life within us. Between the two stands Resistance."[12] He explains that we experience resistance as fear, which prevents us from achieving our deepest aspirations and our soul's purpose. He adds that the more meaningful the pursuit is to us, the stronger our fear. But fear is a good thing because it tells us what we need to do.[13]

Pressfield zeros in on our internal struggle with the things we care most about in the world. We can want something so badly, yet think, "Who am I to do this?" or "I don't have what it takes." The thing we feel a deep connection to—that calling to do something bigger than ourselves—is what we seem to resist the most. We hold it precious in our hearts, we're protective of it, and we will defend it until the very end, yet we don't begin to make it a reality. We're stuck between what we're settling for and what's possible, which can be intensely uncomfortable because we know we can *do* and *be* more.

Think about what forces such as fear of success, criticism, and failure are holding you back. Once you figure out what stops you, tackle them head-on with small, manageable steps.

For example, if fear of criticism holds you back, share your work with someone you trust and use their feedback to learn and grow. If self-doubt is your barrier, write down your achievements to remind yourself of your abilities and boost confidence.

Remember, you can overcome any resistance that stands in the way of the life you want to live. But you'll need to act on your ambitions, seek support, and consistently remind yourself of your talents, strengths, and capabilities.

Thinking You're Not Creative

Have you ever been stunned by the complexity of someone's creation? You may have thought, "How the heck did they do that?" Or maybe the simplicity of a brilliant idea made you wonder, "Why didn't *I* think of that?"

Creativity feels unnatural to some people—they feel like they weren't born with it. They follow the myth that creativity is only for the talented, the gifted, and the geniuses among us. Yet, according to Sir Ken Robinson, a global authority on creativity and education, being human means we all have immense creative capacities. Our challenge is to develop them.[14]

In Robinson's book, *Out of Our Minds*, he writes, "If someone tells you they can't read or write, you don't assume they are not capable of it, just that they haven't learned how. It is the same with creativity. When people say they are not creative, I just assume they have not learned how. I also assume that they can."[15]

Psychologist Robert Epstein shares Robinson's belief that anyone can learn and develop creativity. He offers these four skills as effective ways to do so:

1. **Keep a creative idea log** in a notebook or digital recorder.

2. **Pursue challenging tasks** without obvious solutions, such as designing a complex puzzle.

3. **Expand your knowledge** by taking classes or reading extensively.

4. **Immerse yourself in stimulating experiences and people,** like visiting museums, attending the opera, and dining with diverse and interesting people.[16]

To strengthen these skills above, Epstein gave 74 Orange County, California employees games and exercises. Eight months after the training, the employees generated 55 percent more ideas than before, resulting in over $600,000 in new revenue. They also ingeniously cut company costs by approximately $3.5 million![17]

Whether these employees thought they were creative or not didn't matter because they thrived when tasked with being creative.

Imagine the transformative effects if other cities and corporations rolled out this creativity initiative. What breakthroughs could they achieve?

We can conquer doubts about our creative abilities by thinking unconventionally, harvesting new ideas, and daring to explore the unknown. However, because routine and habit can stifle creativity, we must practice getting our creative juices flowing.

Practice Unblocking Your Creativity

What keeps you from pursuing a creative project or exploring a great idea? Is it fear of rejection, judgment, criticism, failure, or even success?

For instance, if rejection is hindering your progress, don't take it personally—learn from it and keep moving forward. Maybe you fear failure, so you keep procrastinating on a project. Think about how you'll feel if you never complete it. Set small goals to build confidence, celebrate successes, and view fear as a challenge to overcome.

Write down any fears you have around your creativity. Then, in your journal, explore how these fears might be preventing you from doing the work you feel called to do. You can even seek advice on how to work through these blocks from family, friends, or a creativity coach.

Sparking Creativity

Imagine you're a monk in the late 1400s, sitting down for a cup of hot soup in the new dining hall of a monastery in the heart of Milan, Italy. On the north wall is a mural—*The Last Supper*. Utterly transfixed by the painting, you notice how exquisitely it captures the moment Jesus announces that one of his 12 apostles will betray him. The painting vividly portrays the Apostles' turmoil—from shock to disbelief to sorrow. What an extraordinary narrative to behold!

Leonardo da Vinci, the brilliant mind behind this captivating scene of human emotion, faced technical challenges in his work. Traditional fresco painting, popular at the time, required quick and uninterrupted application on fresh plaster. To take more time with the finer details and achieve better color blending, da Vinci developed a new technique that used a mix of oil and tempera (a fast-drying paint traditionally made with egg yolk) applied to plaster. Although the method ultimately failed, leading to peeling paint over the years, he broke new artistic ground with his masterpiece.

From 1980 to 1999, a major restoration helped preserve and enhance *The Last Supper,* though very little of da Vinci's original paint remains.[18]

To this day, people admire da Vinci's Renaissance-era art: the

Mona Lisa, Saint John the Baptist, The Last Supper, and his famous drawing, *The Vitruvian Man.* He was also brilliant in other disciplines, such as sculpture, architecture, engineering, anatomy, and aeronautics.

What made da Vinci so creative? His intense curiosity, wild imagination, commitment to gaining knowledge, and ability to think differently.

But da Vinci left many of his works unfinished, often shifting to new experiments and inventions.[19] Despite distractions, da Vinci's commitment to his talents led to the creation of some of the world's most treasured artworks.

We can spark creativity by emulating da Vinci's vivid imagination, childlike curiosity, sharp observational skills, and passion for knowledge. Like him, we must be willing to explore the unknown through bold ideas, innovative thinking, and experiments like his flying machines and studies on solar power. We'll also need to work hard and remain resilient and adaptable in our creative endeavors. All these things can inspire our own creativity—just as they did da Vinci's.

To cultivate creativity, we can use specific tactics: acting on inspiration, adopting a beginner's mind, writing morning pages, exploring the unknown, and changing our environment, as we'll explore next.

Acting on Inspiration

When people are creatively inspired, it's transparent to all. A musician becomes one with his instrument. An actor's raw emotions show all over her face. An engineer beams with delight at a new product he created. The magic of inspiration has captured them.

Indeed, we don't just feel inspiration—it can transform us. As New York Times columnist and author David Brooks beautifully writes:

> Inspiration is always more active than mere appreciation. There's a thrilling feeling of elevation, a burst of energy, an awareness of enlarged possibilities. The person in the grip of inspiration has received, as if by magic, some new perception, some holistic understanding, along with the feeling that she is capable of more than she thought.[20]

Brooks's notion that inspiration elevates and expands our awareness and abilities might suggest a spiritual quality. Italian composer Giacomo Puccini expressed a similar belief when he said, "The music of this opera [*Madame Butterfly*] was dictated to me by God. I was merely instrumental in getting it on paper and communicating it to the public."[21]

That *is* what inspiration can feel like—as if it comes from a divine source out of nowhere, challenging logic, choosing us to deliver a special message to others.

With its origin from the Latin *inspirare*, which means "to breathe into," inspiration is defined by *Merriam-Webster Online* as "a divine influence or action on a person believed to qualify him or her to receive and communicate sacred revelation." This kind of influence can come in a flash—a brilliant idea pops into our head, or we suddenly understand something that changes how we see the world. It's a refreshing, even exhilarating, feeling that can strike anywhere: in the shower, while driving, during a conversation, or while reading a book. We just need to pay attention so as not to let inspiration escape!

Consider Paul McCartney. In the autumn of 1968, he was going through tough times. The Beatles were having problems, and he was drinking and staying out too late.

One night, his mother, Mary, who had passed away 10 years earlier, came to him in a dream. With a comforting reassurance, she said to him, "Let it be."

Paul woke up the next morning feeling inspired by her wise words to let things go and move forward. He went straight to the piano and created the lyrics for one of the Beatles' biggest hits, "Let It Be."[22]

Cultivate a "Beginner's Mind"

Brothers Tom and David Kelley, founders of the IDEO design firm and authors of *Creative Confidence*, suggest building creative confidence by adopting a "beginner's mind" or "rediscovering the familiar."[23] They explain that seeing something as if for the first time opens us to new ideas.

The Kelley brothers, also founders of Stanford's Hasso Plattner Institute of Design (a.k.a. the "d.school"), teach both students and professionals to view the ordinary with fresh eyes. In one exercise, they asked a group of executives to drop their preconceived notions about airports and observe how people line up to check in, interact with airline representatives, and retrieve their bags from the carousel. The executives left the airport noticing things they hadn't before, such as safety rituals people perform, travelers arriving four hours early, or moms paying bills before boarding.[24]

"By adopting the eyes of a traveler and a beginner's mindset, you will notice a lot of details that you normally might have overlooked. You put aside assumptions and are fully immersed in the world around you. In this receptive mode, you're ready to start actively searching out inspiration,"[25] explain the Kelleys.

Try looking at everyday experiences with fresh eyes because the more you do, the more ideas and insights start to flow.

Write "Morning Pages"

Artist and author of *The Artist's Way,* Julia Cameron suggests a simple yet powerful method to tap into creativity called "morning pages." She defines them as three pages of stream-of-consciousness writing, done by hand with pen and paper first thing in the morning. This "mind dump" technique, as she calls it, involves unedited, unfiltered writing to clear out the negative, trivial, and distracting thoughts cluttering your mind.

Cameron emphasizes that these writings aren't intended to be clever, shared with others, or even read by you for eight weeks. Their purpose is to silence your inner critic, clear your mind of mental noise, and access deeper wisdom—all to awaken your creativity.[26]

Explore the Unknown

We tend to stick with what's familiar, but routine and habit can squash creativity. So, explore new activities that inspire, thrill, or even scare you! Enroll in a workshop, try pickleball, golf, or Tai Chi, learn a new language to prepare for that dream trip, or dive into writing, photography, gardening, or drawing.

When you step out of your comfort zone, you can gain new perspectives and expand your creativity.

Change Your Environment

Since our surroundings play an important role in the creative process, design your working and living area in a way that inspires you. Fill it with meaningful photographs, motivating quotes, artwork, or special artifacts you love. Think about the colors that make you feel peaceful, happy, or energized.

You can even switch up your environment entirely! If you typically write or draw at home, venture somewhere new to write or draw, like a coffee shop, a beach, or even a hotel.

Practice Sparking Creativity

Creativity is not just for the talented and the gifted but a strength we can all develop and enhance with practice.

Choose one (or more!) of these practices—cultivate a "beginner's mind," write "morning pages," explore the unknown, or change your environment—to spark your creativity. Try to stick to the practice regularly (writing "morning pages" can be especially helpful) because as you develop the habit, your creativity expands.

Try one of these practices for thirty days and see how it affects your creativity. Boosting your creativity creates opportunities for more joy and purpose.

CHAPTER SUMMARY

Creativity is bringing ideas to life, solving problems unconventionally, and making unique connections that enrich our lives with joy and purpose. It empowers us to express ourselves through artistic endeavors, technological innovations, scientific discoveries, and more. Our creations allow us to share our authentic selves and reshape the world around us.

> **Complementing virtues:** *Joy, Purposefulness*
> **Creativity transcends:** *Ordinary, Complacency*

Remember this . . .

- Creativity entails exploring the limitless nature of our imagination. When we do, we can turn possibility into reality through creation. We also make unique and meaningful contributions through this self-expression.

- Creativity isn't just about making our mark on the world. It offers valuable personal benefits, including a sense of purpose, improved focus, reduced stress and anxiety, and encouragement of life-long learning.

- Blocks to our creativity—like fear and the belief that we're not creative—can stop us before we start. Becoming aware of these fears can help us embrace innovative thinking and commit to realizing our visions.

- To spark creativity, we can tap into our imagination, childlike curiosity, and observation skills. Acting on inspiration, cultivating a "beginner's mind," writing "morning pages," exploring the unknown, and changing our environments all help kindle the creative flame.

CHAPTER 7

Compassion

Compassion is recognizing suffering and acting to relieve it through kindness and generosity.

Detective Jack Mook, a tough-minded, no-nonsense 22-year veteran of the Pittsburgh police department, faced a challenging case he simply couldn't turn away from. While volunteering at a gym to teach underprivileged kids how to box, he met 15-year-old Josh and his 11-year-old brother Jessee. Jack formed a special bond with the boys and became concerned when they stopped coming to the gym.

When Jack finally found Josh, he learned that the boys' foster parents were severely abusing and neglecting them. "They have had it as worse as any other kid that's ever lived in the city of Pittsburgh, living-conditions-wise, and that just . . . I had enough of it,"[1] Jack said in a CBS News interview. He didn't want the boys to suffer and have their lives turn out badly. So, Jack decided to become their foster parent. This was quite an adjustment for him. He cooked healthy meals, helped with homework, and became a dedicated, caring father to the happy boys.

Two years later, Jack legally adopted Jessee and Josh. Not long after, he married a woman with three kids of her own. Jack, once a committed bachelor, found joy in his loving family of seven—beyond what he ever could have imagined.[2]

The What and Why of Compassion

Jack's story is a stellar example of compassion in its true form: recognizing the suffering of others and acting to relieve that suffering. While Jack felt empathy—an awareness and understanding of others' emotions—he went a step further by showing compassion through his actions to help the boys. Although compassion may begin with empathy, it's expressed when people are distressed. For example, if a friend loses his job, we ask him to meet us for coffee and offer encouragement and support. Kindness, then, becomes the outward expression—the manifestation—of compassion.

Sometimes, our biases or judgments can get in the way of our being more compassionate.

His Holiness the Dalai Lama, the spiritual leader of Tibetan Buddhism, believes that to accomplish genuine compassion, we must cultivate equanimity. Equanimity is the mental composure and calm needed to rise above feelings of discrimination and partiality toward others. He explains that to cultivate equanimity, we must understand that we *all* aspire to be happy and free of suffering.[3]

Thinking in this way helps us let go of ideas of superiority or inferiority. As a result, we become more compassionate toward all human beings, even those we may dislike.

Pema Chödrön, also a Tibetan Buddhist, shares the Dalai Lama's sentiment: "Compassion is not a relationship between the healer and the wounded. It's a relationship between equals. Only when we know our own darkness well can we be present with the darkness of others. Compassion becomes real when we recognize our shared humanity."[4]

Yet, it's challenging to feel compassion equally for our friends and for those we dislike. People hurt us; they are disrespectful, even cruel. How can we feel any compassion for them? Then again, if we don't, what can that cost us? You've heard of instances where family members have a falling out. Hurt feelings, anger, or resentment keeps them from talking to each other for years, sometimes for a lifetime. But if families could set aside their pride and recognize each other as equals in our shared human wants and needs, they could begin to heal their relationships.

Not everyone responds with compassion to others' suffering—whether friend, stranger, or foe. Some may ignore another's pain out of fear, apathy, or discomfort. Others may react with anger such as if a homeless person asks them for money. They think the person should get a job and stop bothering other people. Nevertheless, we can build our compassion when we start to see that we all have the same emotions, struggles, and desires for happiness.

What Compassion Is Not

Some people might view compassion more as a gentle emotion than a powerful one.

Author and storyteller Oriah Mountain Dreamer writes, "Having compassion does not mean indiscriminately accepting or going along with others' actions regardless of the consequences to us or the world. It is about being able to say no where we need to without putting the other out of our hearts, without making the other less of a fellow human being."[5] She reminds us that sometimes, the most compassionate thing to do is to say no to someone.

One example that comes to mind is when a loved one is abusing drugs. We see the depth of pain as he asks us for money, and though he doesn't say it, we fear it's for the drugs he so desperately wants. We say "No" even though his suffering breaks our hearts. We feel deeply for what he is going through and do not see him as lesser. Instead, we see a person unable to overcome his past wounds, using drugs as an escape.

Compassion doesn't mean being a pushover. On the contrary, it means showing kindness while standing firm in our beliefs and values. True compassion is not for the faint of heart.

Think about the emotional strength it takes for a hospice worker to care for dying patients while also comforting the patient's loved ones. Or a veterinarian tasked with euthanizing animals to relieve their suffering. Without the compassionate actions of people like these, the misery of our circumstances would be even tougher to bear.

Selfless people like this remind us how compassionate acts can be incredibly challenging—yet vitally needed.

Practice "Lovingkindness" Meditation

Made popular in the West by meditation teacher and author Sharon Salzberg, lovingkindness meditation (known as "metta bhavana" in the Pali language) is an ancient Buddhist practice. The lovingkindness meditation is a practice where we silently repeat phrases of love and goodwill for ourselves and then for others. The meditation is intended to cultivate compassion, reduce anxiety and negative emotions, and support emotional well-being.

First, think of three or four meaningful phrases that reflect outcomes you want for yourself, beginning with the words "May I." For instance, you want more happiness, peace, wisdom, and health. Create the phrases with these outcomes in mind (see the below example).

Now, sit comfortably with your eyes closed and take some deep breaths. Gently repeat these sample phrases below to yourself at least three times. Try to connect with the feeling behind the words as you wish yourself well.

"May I be happy."

"May I be at peace."

"May I be wise."

"May I feel healthy and strong."

Next, send the same loving, compassionate intentions to a partner, friend, family member, or difficult person by replacing the "I" in your phrases with "you" (e.g., "May you be happy"). Visualize the person is in front of you while you say these kind words. Embrace any negative feelings you have and let them pass gently through you.[6]

After you meditate, take a few moments to reflect on what you noticed during your practice. Was any part of it challenging? Was it easier to send compassionate intentions to yourself or others?

The lovingkindness meditation can be a powerful way to develop more compassion for yourself and others.

A Courageous, Open Heart

"Birdfoot's Grampa," a poem by author and storyteller Joseph Bruchac, begins with a grandfather and his grandson, Birdfoot, driving down a rainy country road. Noticing small, leaping toads in the road, the grandfather pulls the car over repeatedly to collect and place them safely in the roadside grass. He wants to do what's right for the toads, even if it means getting wet and dirty himself.

The grandson, however, wants to go about their business. They've already stopped two dozen times! Thinking about how his grandfather can't possibly save all the toads, the boy grows more and more impatient, distancing himself from the toads' plight. He tells his grandfather to get back in the car because they have places to go. The grandfather smiles widely says the toads are going places too.[7]

Being mindful of living beings' suffering is the first step to being compassionate. We must, however, have an open heart and the strength of heart not to turn away, even when we're uncomfortable or uncertain—whether it's stopping for tiny toads on a rainy road or validating someone's pain and letting them know they're not alone.

For those who may turn away, so many act with kindness. While having lunch at a restaurant, a man overhears a woman telling her companion that she received a difficult diagnosis. He feels drawn to show kindness by anonymously paying for their meal. She selflessly donates her kidney to a stranger. He rescues someone from a burning car. They don't let fear of judgment, criticism, or rejection stand in their way. They *feel compelled* to help. They *have* to help.

Compassion connects us with others in extraordinary ways that are heartwarming to witness.

I had the pleasure of seeing the power of compassion and fellowship while attending a Baptist church for the first time with my husband's family in Tennessee. While the music played softly during prayer time, I noticed a man walk to the front of the church and kneel on the altar's large platform to pray.

After a short time, another man walked up and knelt beside him. A moment later, he placed his arm around the one who had been praying. At first, I wasn't sure why that man joined him until more people did the same. They came to the altar with heavy hearts to pray, while others knelt with them, offering quiet comfort.

And so it is—people at their finest.

Blocks to an Open Heart

Compassion takes courage and an open heart. The compassionate acts of others can move us to tears, yet we may doubt our own ability to extend such kindness.

We admire people for their bravery when doing extraordinary acts of kindness. Of course, no one is perfect, but recognizing what holds us back from being more compassionate—lack of mindfulness, fear of judgment, criticism and rejection sensitivity, stress and exhaustion, and self-preoccupation—helps us cultivate more compassion.

Let's explore these barriers to compassion.

Lack of Mindfulness

To show compassion, we first need to recognize someone else's suffering. Birdfoot was so preoccupied with the places he and his grandfather needed to go that he wasn't aware of the toads' predicament. If he had been, he might have understood his grandfather's quest to help them and even helped too. Awareness of our surroundings, the people in them, and the circumstances we find ourselves in can help foster compassion.

In the past, we might not have helped someone in need. We may have passed by for various reasons, such as lack of time, feeling stressed, or even fear of rejection. Later, we wished we had helped. If we had been more mindful of the situation instead of in our heads, we might have acted. Of course, there were times when we did lend a helping hand and felt so glad we did.

Ultimately, mindfulness helps open our hearts to the struggles of others.

Fear of Judgment

When we judge others by appearance, age, gender, lifestyle, or skin color, we shut down any potential for valuable connections and meaningful experiences. Judgment tends to alienate us from other people. But we can choose to replace judgment with compassion.

My sister-in-law Melody, an ICU nurse at our local hospital, exemplifies choosing compassion over judgment. Day after day, she faces the full range of human suffering, from patients detoxing from drugs to those still battling complications from COVID-19. Her goal is to alleviate her patients' suffering no matter how much money they have, what color their skin, their religion, or their political views. As she puts it, healthcare is the "great equalizer" because all patients are treated with the same dignity and care.

What a gift Melody is to her ICU patients! She remains steadfast beside her patients, defending their needs and offering hope amidst their anguish. Melody sees beyond people's circumstances, reminding us that true compassion rises above judgment.

While judgment is essential for making choices, such as deciding whether to marry someone or accept a job offer—it's important to distinguish between healthy judgment and critical judgment.

Critical judgment builds barriers, such as labeling people or pointing out their shortcomings silently or aloud. In contrast, choosing compassion over judgment opens the door to meaningful friendships, strong partnerships, and loving relationships.

Criticism and Rejection Sensitivity

People closest to us may not always approve of our generous acts. They might think our decision to support a charity is financially irresponsible or that our plans to volunteer in a foreign country are unsafe. Of course, we value their opinions and good intentions, but we must not let their criticism stop us from pursuing compassionate work and rewarding experiences.

Rejection may stop us as well. Suppose your friend receives a diagnosis of a chronic illness. You struggle to find comforting words, fearing you'll say something foolish or insensitive, so you avoid the topic entirely. Similarly, you notice an opportunity to help an elderly man struggling to cross the street. You hesitate out of fear he will reject your help as an intrusion on his independence.

Even if our efforts to help aren't always welcomed, it's still important that we try. Many others need and would appreciate our help.

Recognizing that criticism and rejection are natural parts of being openhearted helps us to move beyond them. In doing so, we can show kindness in situations where it's needed most.

Stress and Exhaustion

Often, we're just too worn out to help anyone. When we come home from a hard day's work, all we can do is eat dinner and prepare for the next day. Our feelings of stress and exhaustion can weigh heavy on us to the point where handling daily life is overwhelming.

When we feel drained, it can be harder to be present for others. According to psychologist Tara Cousineau, author of *The Kindness Cure*, this isn't just a personal issue. She explains, "Chronic stress is the most significant modern-day ailment in developed countries, and it's connected to so many maladies. When you are disillusioned, afraid, or feeling threatened or unsafe, it's hard to engage your kindness instinct. You can become exhausted, indifferent, and uncaring—all states that cause you distress."[8]

To help combat stress, Cousineau encourages people to practice kindness to boost their well-being. She suggests asking ourselves, "How can I bring kindness to this moment?" whether toward others or ourselves. She also recommends setting a daily intention to be kind, especially to someone we don't know well, and keeping a kindness diary. As our notes of kind acts accumulate, we begin to feel better.[9]

Self-Preoccupation

Have you ever talked with someone who seemed more focused on themselves than on truly listening to you? People who consistently behave this way are often so preoccupied with their own wants and thoughts that it's difficult for them to be present for the suffering of others.

Social media can kill our empathy. Some social media users view people as avatars in the abyss, making criticizing and ridiculing them easy. Apathy and self-involvement—both potential side effects of social media—lessen our chances of taking compassionate action.

Yet, while social media may diminish compassion, it also helps us interact easily and share talents, skills, and positive messages.

We can use social media to foster goodwill by paying compliments, responding kindly to posts, sharing inspiring stories, expressing gratitude, and supporting causes.

Compassion's Overwhelm

For all the blocks that can get in the way, compassion is still our most natural response to another's misery. Yet, it's understandable that always being compassionate may be overwhelming. Compassion asks us to open our hearts where our instinct may be to close them off.

Recognizing the potential for overwhelm, we may need to set boundaries when we find ourselves overextending or when others begin to take our kindness for granted.

Striking a balance between giving too much and showing healthy compassion protects our well-being and sustains our generosity.

Practice Unlocking Compassion

Recall the common blocks to your compassion discussed in this chapter— lack of mindfulness, fear of judgment, criticism and rejection sensitivity, stress and exhaustion, and self-preoccupation.

Now, think of an example where one or more of these blocks prevented you from feeling compassion. For example, have you argued with a loved one and found yourself focused on your side of the story and your feelings (self-absorption or fear of judgment block)? Perhaps you could have listened better, cared more about their feelings, or tried to understand how stressed or overwhelmed they might have been.

Catching your resistance to compassion can lead to kinder choices later, resolving conflicts and improving mental health.

Compassion's Power

Our compassionate actions have so many rewards! Not only does our mental outlook improve when we are compassionate, but our physical health improves as well. As we orient ourselves to people's suffering and act to relieve it, we gain life-changing benefits. Let's explore these benefits more closely.

Happiness Increases

Have you ever wondered why helping others feels so good? The answer lies within our brains.

Neuropsychologist Jordan Grafman exposed a direct link between giving and pleasure. He led a brain-imaging study where parts of the volunteers' brains (the pleasure centers) lit up when they thought about donating money to a charity rather than keeping it for themselves. These same pleasure centers are the ones activated when people think about sex and money.[10]

Social services leader and volunteerism expert Allan Luks refers to this feel-good response to helping others as the "Helper's High."[11] We release endorphins (the pleasure hormone) when we help others. The charitable activity lifts our mood, giving us a real and natural "high."

Health Improves

Researchers Steven Cole and Barbara Fredrickson found that a compassionate lifestyle has a surprisingly positive impact on our immune system.[12] They studied 80 adults who described themselves as "very happy." Some adults' happiness stemmed from a "hedonic" lifestyle characterized by self-gratification, while others found their happiness through a "eudaimonic" lifestyle based on meaning and purpose.

Cole and Fredrickson revealed a stark contrast in health outcomes between the two lifestyles. Adults who pursued a hedonic lifestyle showed higher levels of cellular inflammation, a marker associated with increased risks for cancer and other diseases. Conversely, adults who found meaning and purpose in their lives or had a sense of contribution to society showed lower levels of cellular inflammation.[13]

Their findings suggest that seeking ways to be compassionate—something that naturally brings meaning and purpose—can be deeply beneficial, not only giving us a natural high but also improving our physical health.

Purpose Blooms

Along with greater happiness and health, compassion also gives us a sense of purpose. We take the focus away from ourselves by supporting loved ones, giving time to causes we believe in, and being mindful of our words and actions. Even the smallest interactions, like opening the door for someone, letting a driver merge into traffic, or simply saying hello, can make us feel helpful and connected.

By helping others, we build stronger, more meaningful bonds. We can profoundly affect and even change others' lives. What could be more gratifying? Years later, we recall the times when we helped people and, in doing so, feel uplifted and proud once more.

I remember a time when I was boarding a plane to Washington, D.C., and a young woman, about 19 years old, stood crying at the door of the plane, unable to board because of her fear of flying. I looked back at her and asked the flight attendant if she could sit beside me. She agreed, and thankfully, the seat next to mine was available.

When the girl sat down, I began talking with her—asking her where she was from and where she was going. She told me she had just graduated high school and was joining the military. I thought to myself, what a brave young woman, to be completely on her own and taking this admirable leap into service to our country.

As the plane began to rev up for takeoff, she was visibly anxious, so I asked if I could hold her hand. She said yes. She seemed comforted by this—and so was I, as I don't like flying either. We talked through takeoff and continued the conversation for much of the flight. She thanked me before we parted ways, and to this day, I'm so glad I was able to support her during such a pivotal moment in her life.

I share this story not to boast, but to show that compassion doesn't always look dramatic or heroic—it often shows up in quiet, simple ways that can make us feel good and purposeful.

Receivers of Kindness

We've all been on the receiving end of kindness that lifted our spirits during tough times. That kindness could have been an encouraging word, a compliment, or a helpful hand. Whatever it was, at the time, the person making the caring gesture might not have known the potential impact of their good deed. In fact, sometimes, a person's big-heartedness changes the course of another person's life. Marcus Engel experienced that fate.

Eighteen-year-old college freshman Marcus and his three friends were on their way back from a hockey game when a drunk driver broadsided them at twice the speed limit. The force of the blow sent Marcus flying out of the vehicle. He lay face down on the concrete, permanently blinded. Every bone in his face was crushed.

While Marcus endured excruciating pain and hallucinations in the hospital, a 20-year-old patient care tech named Jennifer kept reassuring him, saying, "I'm here." Her gentle and supportive words made him feel safe and not alone during a dark and scary time.

Enduring a two-year recovery that included 300 hours of facial reconstructive surgeries, Marcus was profoundly moved by the compassion shown by his healthcare providers—especially Jennifer's compassionate words. So much so that he started the "I'm Here Movement," which advocates for empathy in healthcare worldwide.[14]

Through speaking, writing, and consulting, he spreads the importance of human presence as the cornerstone of compassionate care.

Marcus's journey led him to earn a Master's in Narrative Medicine from Columbia University. He also married and became a father of three.[15]

Our compassionate acts can create a ripple effect, where the initial good deed spreads to others in unimaginable ways. Jennifer's caring words to Marcus may have positively affected countless patients as he shared his story with healthcare workers. As a result, healthcare workers are likely to become mindful of how even small acts of compassion can make a significant difference in patient care.

Practice Compassionate Action

Keep track of your compassionate acts for a week. Write down even the actions you think are more of an obligation or a routine, such as tucking your child into bed, picking up your partner's dry cleaning, or listening attentively to a friend's problem. You'll be surprised at the amount of kindness you extend daily!

Now, challenge yourself to do one random act of kindness, something you don't normally do. Here are some ideas:

- Write a thank-you note to someone who has helped you recently.
- Pay for someone behind you at the drive-through.

- Say good morning or hello to passersby.
- Volunteer or donate to a worthy cause.
- Mentor someone in your area of expertise.
- Forgive a person who has hurt you.
- Call someone you haven't talked to in a while.

Notice how these compassionate acts made you feel. Did they increase your happiness or reduce your stress? Next, think about the impact your kindness had on others. Lastly, challenge yourself to do intentional, kind acts beyond a week.

Self-Compassion

How might we think differently about our flaws? "The Cracked Pot" is an Asian-Indian folktale with a simple yet powerful message about the value of our imperfections. Storyteller and musician Mary Dessein retells the story in the anthology *The Healing Heart ~ Communities*:

> A water-bearer carries two large pots on a yoke across his shoulders up the hill from the river to his master's house each day. One has a crack and leaks half its water out each day before arriving at the house. The other pot is perfect and always delivers a full portion of water after the long walk from the river.
>
> Finally, after years of arriving half-empty and feeling guilty, the cracked pot apologizes to the water-bearer: "I'm sorry that I couldn't accomplish what the perfect pot did." The water-bearer says, "What do you have to apologize for?"
>
> The cracked pot replies, "After all this time, I still only deliver half my load of water. I make more work for you because of my flaw." The man smiles and tells the pot, "Take note of all the lovely flowers growing on the side of the path where I carried you. The flowers grew so lovely because of the water you leaked. There are no

flowers on the perfect pot's side. You are both perfect in your own way."[16]

Have you ever felt shame or guilt about your limitations? Maybe you lack coordination, tend to procrastinate, seek constant validation or feel socially inadequate. You compare yourself to others, wondering why you are not as capable, which brings you down.

Like the Cracked Pot, you may see your flaws as burdens and not strengths. But if you learn to embrace them, improving where you can, your imperfections can become part of your strength.

Trevor McDonald shares how, through self-compassion, he fully accepted himself—flaws and all—and overcame unworthiness and self-doubt.

> I struggled all my life with ADHD (Attention Deficit Hyperactivity Disorder). I was convinced I wasn't "normal" and not "good enough." After many years of self-hatred and episodes of hopelessness over something I couldn't change, I turned to taking a shot of alcohol to calm myself down. That shot eventually turned into three . . . then four . . . and thus, when I was 16, my alcohol addiction began. I used alcohol as a coping mechanism— it felt good to be numb and ignore my insecurities.
>
> When I was 22, I suffered from severe alcohol poisoning and a drug overdose that almost killed me. After that, my doctor suggested I enter an addiction recovery program, and I quickly agreed. I'd always known I needed to become sober, but I'd never wanted to acknowledge it as a tangible issue.
>
> Initially, I thought the recovery methods were tedious. But over time, I opened up in group therapy, stopped lying to my therapist, and learned that many everyday people just like me were also screaming on the inside. I submitted to the mandatory doctor check-ups and removed every trigger that made me want to drink. I tried to be nice to myself without cringing.
>
> What ultimately healed me, though, was accepting that I couldn't change things that were out of my control,

like my ADHD. I learned that I could never run away from thoughts and emotions. I embraced honesty and stopped believing I could fix myself with substances. I also regained the dignity and self-respect to rewire the harmful perceptions I held about myself.

I understand now that I could have avoided substance addiction by being kinder to myself and using positive affirmations instead of cruel ones. I could have stopped lying to myself and poured the shot down the drain. But then I wouldn't have the perspective I need to potentially influence someone else to stop and think about how they talk to themselves. I now know that one hateful remark you say to yourself, like "I'm not good enough" or "I'm a failure," can become a series of many debilitating beliefs that create destructive feelings and hopelessness.[17]

Trevor came to understand that judging himself for things beyond his control—like his ADHD—only deepened his pain. However, by practicing self-compassion, he found not only the hope to become sober but also the strength to rebuild his sense of worth.

Self-Kindness Matters

Kristin Neff, Ph.D., a pioneer in the study of self-compassion, found that being more self-compassionate promotes well-being and contentment. In her book *Self-Compassion: The Proven Power of Being Kind to Yourself*, she identifies three components of self-compassion: self-kindness, common humanity, and mindfulness. She notes that people must combine them to experience true self-compassion.[18]

With the first component, *self-kindness*, Neff recommends that instead of being judgmental and critical of ourselves, we treat ourselves as our friends would treat us. For example, if a friend confided in us about a recent failure, we wouldn't say, "You should have known better!" or "You're just not capable." Instead, we would offer kind, encouraging words. That's what we need to do for ourselves, too.

Common humanity, the second component, acknowledges that we all experience loneliness, disappointment, failure, and sadness. So, rather than feeling isolated by our suffering or personal inadequacies, we realize we are not alone. We understand that other people are going through the same things, feeling the same feelings, and bearing similar circumstances. Our common humanity helps us overcome self-loathing because we realize that we are not different from other people in our experience of life.

Lastly, Neff describes *mindfulness,* the third component, as the simple acknowledgment that we *are* suffering. We often fail to recognize that we are! Instead of suppressing or exaggerating our negative thoughts and emotions—that can cause stress, exhaustion, and feeling overwhelmed—we step back to observe thoughts and emotions without judgment. Then, we can feel self-compassion when we need it most.

The Beauty in Our Imperfections

Through Neff's self-kindness, common humanity, and mindfulness, we can see the beauty in our imperfections. Harshly judging or criticizing ourselves can keep us stuck in anxiety, discouragement and self-doubt. By recognizing the emotional harm we may be causing ourselves, we can begin to practice self-compassion to build our confidence, resilience and deepen our life satisfaction.

Practice Self-Compassion

Take a moment to explore your own "cracks"— those imperfections or areas of self-doubt you've struggled with or felt defined by. What parts of yourself have you judged harshly? What would it look like to respond to those parts with kindness instead of criticism?

Here are some ways you can begin practicing self-compassion:

- Choose a kinder inner dialogue, using more supportive and encouraging words.
- Remind yourself that everyone struggles sometimes—you are not alone.
- Referred to as lovingkindness earlier in text, consider changing for consistency.
- Allow yourself to feel negative emotions without denying or judging them.

- Take care of yourself through movement, rest, and nourishment.

- Pursue activities that make you happy and that matter to you.

Now, take it a step further by reflecting on one aspect of yourself you dislike. How might your perceived flaw have contributed to the beauty of your journey? Try exploring these questions in your journal: What is the flaw, how has it affected you, and what hidden strengths might it carry?

Self-compassion takes discipline, but it can be a rewarding and life-changing practice.

CHAPTER SUMMARY

Compassion is recognizing suffering and acting to relieve it through kindness and generosity. When we recognize our shared humanity, we're less likely to judge or criticize others, ultimately forming deep and even unexpected connections. Cultivating compassion enhances our relationships, reduces stress, and increases happiness.

Complementing virtues: *Caring, Understanding*
Compassion transcends: *Suffering, Judgment*

Remember this . . .

- To feel and build genuine compassion for others, we must see one another as equals, united in our desire for happiness and freedom from suffering.

- Our willingness to witness the suffering of others and not turn away, but rather act, is a strength. Certain blocks, however—like a lack of mindfulness, a tendency to judge one another, fear of criticism and rejection, stress and exhaustion, and self-preoccupation—can get in the way. Still, compassion is our most natural response to another's misery.

- When we express compassion and kindness to others, our happiness increases, our health improves, and we create authentic connections with others.

- Harshly judging or criticizing ourselves can keep us stuck in anxiety, discouragement, and self-doubt. But by recognizing the harm we may be doing, and practicing self-compassion, we can overcome challenges, heal, and unlock our potential.

CHAPTER 8

Courage

Courage is the strength to face challenges, take risks, and endure fear, driven by the belief that the reward outweighs the discomfort.

Wesley Autrey, a 51-year-old construction worker and Navy veteran, stood on the 137th Street platform with his two young daughters, waiting for the subway train. Nearby, a 20-year-old man collapsed to the ground, convulsing from a seizure. Wesley and others rushed to help him up. The man got up and looked fine, so the bystanders walked away. Then, just as they turned, he stumbled toward the edge of the platform and fell onto the tracks, landing between the rails.

Seeing the headlights of an oncoming train, Wesley made a split decision to help the stranger. He sprang off the train platform onto the tracks and threw himself on top of the man, holding him down. They lay flat between the two rails in a space about 21 inches deep. Five cars screeched and rumbled over them until the train stopped just an inch above them. When Wesley shouted that they were both okay, panicked screams became cheers and applause.[1]

Many would say that Wesley acted with Herculean courage; some would say he was foolish. Wesley felt that he had acted in good conscience, telling the *New York Times*, "I don't feel like I did something spectacular; I just saw someone who needed help. I did what I felt was right."[2]

The What and Why of Courage

At one time or another, brave souls like Wesley—and professionals whose jobs put them in danger every day—have feared for their safety. But they push through fear anyway because they believe in the power of their actions to make a difference.

Even with fear's mighty grip, we can break its hold on us to do extraordinary things.

American novelist Anaïs Nin said it well, "Life shrinks or expands in proportion to one's courage."[3] She suggests that the quality of our lives directly relates to the risks and challenges we take. So, pushing through our fear of rejection, change, or loss, we take a stand for what's on the other side—a creative project, a fulfilling career, or a healthier relationship.

On the other hand, fear can make our lives smaller, limiting our experiences. Facing our fears builds courage, and that courage makes our lives richer.

Years ago, I was talking to a co-worker, Teri, about someone leaving the company where we worked. I mentioned the saying, "The grass isn't always greener on the other side." I'll never forget her response: "Well, at least they're mowing it."

"How true!" I thought. We want something different from what we have, but we're not guaranteed the outcome we want. But challenging ourselves to be bigger, better people gives us confidence and vitality. And that's huge!

Although our courage doesn't always deliver what we expected, if we hadn't taken the risk, we might regret it forever. Until we start mowing, we won't know what we're missing!

Fundamentally, courage is a desirable and admired virtue. We can accomplish great things with it, like pursuing our treasured dreams despite discomfort and uncertainty.

Consider legends like Neil Armstrong, Mahatma Gandhi, and Harriet Tubman, who each changed the world through various kinds of courage. Astronaut Neil Armstrong's physical courage led him to walk on the moon, an extraordinary feat for humanity. Mahatma

Gandhi demonstrated moral courage by using nonviolent resistance to challenge British rule in India. He inspired global movements for justice and civil rights. American anti-slavery advocate Harriet Tubman showed both physical and moral bravery. She repeatedly risked her life to lead enslaved people to freedom, defying slavery's injustices.[4]

Most of us will experience these kinds of courage—physical, moral, and emotional—in our lifetime. They are an inevitable part of our living fully. Let's explore them further, specifically moral and emotional courage.

Kinds of Courage

Physical courage, like facing danger or trying a new sport, is straight-forward and easily recognized. However, moral and emotional courage can be more complex. For example, societal pressures and fear of judgment can make it difficult for us to stand up for what's right. When we witness something we know is not right, it takes moral courage to say, "That's wrong!"

Sometimes, we need emotional courage to confront someone about a deeply personal issue. We struggle with the bravery it takes to open ourselves up to honest, even painful conversations.

Understanding these two kinds of courage better can help us handle challenging situations more effectively.

Moral Courage

Moral courage means standing up for what's right—for justice—even when it comes with adverse consequences. These consequences could include criticism, social exclusion and even tangible losses like careers. Yet, morally courageous people are committed to certain principles and ethical standards; they value them and are not willing to overlook these standards, even at great personal cost.

Wendy Addison bravely challenged unethical behaviors in her workplace that clashed with her morals. The Giraffe Heroes Project, an organization that honors individuals who boldly take risks to serve the common good, recognized her actions. The organization gave permission to share Wendy's story.

Wendy worked as treasurer for one of the largest and most powerful companies in South Africa in 2000. She never wanted to be a whistleblower, but she could not stand by while the two heads of the company were defrauding investors. She took a huge personal risk by making an anonymous phone call to the South African Revenue Service to report what was happening.

Within weeks of her report, the company ceased operations, and the courts convicted the executives of fraud. Sentenced to seven years in prison, they served just 19 months.

But even before the trial, Wendy's name went public. At the time, South Africa did not offer protection for exposing illegal or unethical activity, so after the court summoned Wendy to testify, she faced death threats. The situation became so bad that she and her 12-year-old son left South Africa and moved to England. However, people knew her as South Africa's notorious whistleblower, which scared off potential employers.

After years on welfare, Wendy returned to South Africa in 2005 but was unable to get paid for her work or obtain legal help. She eventually moved back to England for good, where she found the perfect job as a member of the Corruption Research Group at Surrey University.[5]

In 2014, Wendy founded SpeakOut SpeakUp to promote workplace transparency and open dialogue. The organization uses innovative training methods, including virtual reality, to focus on courageous conversations, earning worldwide recognition.[6]

Wendy showed extraordinary courage in exposing corruption, even though it came at the cost of her safety, career, and home. Her story challenges us to ask: What are you willing to risk to do what's right? Moral courage may come with pain but it can lead to the greater good.

Emotional Courage

Emotional courage is sharing our innermost feelings and desires, even when doing so might be uncomfortable or painful. With emotional courage, we can achieve intimacy and gain a deeper understanding of our relationships.

In her book *The Gifts of Imperfection*, Brené Brown points out that emotional courage connects to the original meaning of courage, which was about speaking from your heart. She explains that this meaning vastly differs from today's definition of courage, which is more about heroism.[7]

"Heroics is important and we certainly need heroes, but I think we've lost touch with the idea that speaking honestly and openly about who we are, about what we're feeling, and about our experiences (good and bad) is the definition of courage." She adds, "Heroics is often about putting our life on the line. Ordinary courage is about putting our *vulnerability* on the line."[8]

To share our struggles, flaws, talents, needs, and dreams is as raw and risky as it gets—we open ourselves up to potential rejection, criticism, judgment, hurt, and loss. Anticipating a potentially undesirable outcome of our courage can be agonizing and downright scary. Consider these typically challenging scenarios:

- Telling our partner what we need, like more time, more romance, or more appreciation.
- Asking for a raise or promotion
- Forgiving someone or asking for forgiveness
- Speaking with a friend about their addiction
- Publicizing creative work such as music, writing, art, or filmmaking

In the above scenarios, pushing our vulnerability off for another day may be tempting. However, if we have the guts to put ourselves on the line, we've expressed what's true for us. Not being true to ourselves can take a psychological toll by diminishing our self-respect and self-confidence. Even when the outcome is not so desirable, when we act courageously, we've honored our personal integrity.

Comedic actor Jim Carrey faced a particularly discouraging moment at age 15. At his first stand-up show at a comedy club in Toronto, he had such a bad experience with people's negative outbursts that he stayed away from performing for two years. Fortunately, Carrey bounced back from the criticism and became a big Hollywood star. He showed us that emotional courage can lead to great things.[9]

We need emotional courage most in our relationships. Many of us long to feel more appreciated, loved, or valued by our partners.

However, expressing those needs can trigger fears of our partners becoming defensive or, worse, indifferent. But does their reaction matter more than being true to ourselves? Even if the conversation doesn't go well, we've still honored our needs and desires. Now, we can more confidently choose our next steps. If it goes well, we'll feel so much better that we took the courageous step needed to improve our relationships.

We can reap huge rewards by bravely sharing our needs, stories, talents, or passionate advocacies. We affect our lives and the lives of others in the most meaningful and beautiful ways.

Our discussion about physical, moral, and emotional courage leads us to a question: What stops us from being brave?

Practice the Kinds of Courage

Choose one type of courage from the list below to begin practicing. Start with small actions and gradually work your way up to bigger ones.

Physical

- Is there a physical challenge you'd like to take on—like dance lessons, running a 5K race, playing golf, or starting a workout program? If so, set some goals for how you will fulfill the challenge. These goals can be researching training options, finding a partner to join you, or learning more about it through books or online resources.

Moral

- Has someone ever challenged your values? If so, are you willing to take a brave stance to stand up for them? Reflecting on this, how would you approach a similar situation differently?

Emotional

- Ask for what you want at work, such as a raise, promotion, or more vacation time. In a relation-

ship, ask for what you need such as more attention, affection, or honest communication. When
you express your needs clearly and confidently,
your manager or partner is more likely to respect
and fulfill your request—if willing and able.

Although you might feel uncomfortable working on these areas
of courage, the more you push through your fear, the more your confidence and bravery will grow.

Embracing Your Fears

Life takes a lot of courage. We face threats of natural disasters, mass
shootings, health crises, and job losses that can keep us on edge. Fear
of failure, rejection, the unknown, or making a mistake can hold us
back. We've all felt the dread and anxiety of fear, but events beyond
our control are inevitable. We have to keep going like a punctured
raft fighting to stay afloat. We must survive or withdraw from the
world and never leave our homes.

Even though fear is unpleasant, it's natural and helps guide us
away from danger. However, when fear becomes excessive or irrational, it stops us from taking chances, exploring new opportunities,
and advancing in life. Consistently doing what scares us helps build
our courage muscle and keeps us from playing too small in life.

Fighting the Beast

Mark Twain once said, "Courage is resistance to fear, mastery of
fear—not absence of fear."[10]

Mastering fear is tricky, though. When we're afraid, we experience
the "fight-or-flight" response, which is the body's physical reaction
to a perceived threat. Our heart races, our muscles tighten, and our
breathing accelerates. Feeling this way can stop us right in our tracks.
Yet many of us still take action, determined to conquer the fierce beast.
What surely helps is valuing more what lies on the other side of our
fears: doing the right thing, overcoming our psychological demons,
physically surviving, or accomplishing something meaningful.

Zen master and global spiritual teacher Thich Nhat Hanh offers valuable insight into mastering fear through mindfulness. He suggests that instead of suppressing our fears, we should acknowledge them gently, without judgment, and seek to understand their roots. By identifying whether our anxiety stems from past childhood events or current situations, we can release it and embrace a more fulfilling life.[11]

"We may think that if we ignore our fears, they'll go away. But if we bury worries and anxieties in our consciousness, they continue to affect us and bring us more sorrow," says Hanh. "We are very afraid of being powerless. But we have the power to look deeply at our fears, and then fear cannot control us."[12]

Public speaking can be terrifying for many of us. We fear making a fool of ourselves. Our hearts race, and our hands and voices get shaky. Now, we fear the audience will notice our physical symptoms. That thought makes it even worse. But as Hanh says, instead of pushing the fear down, we become mindful of it and why it's happening. We recognize that our fear is rooted in irrational assumptions: We might imagine being criticized or judged by others. With this awareness, it helps us regain our emotional composure.

Arguing with loved ones often stirs up deep-seated fears, such as rejection and abandonment. These fears often stem from our experiences. By understanding the roots of our fears through self-discovery or professional help, we can respond to conflicts calmly and clearly, helping to diffuse emotionally charged situations.

Fear can be reactionary, making mindfulness difficult. Yet, if we learn to pause in those fearful moments, we can work through them and move forward.

Accessing Your Inner Hero

In *The Wizard of Oz*, Dorothy (Judy Garland) travels down the yellow brick road to the Emerald City to meet the Great Wizard of Oz (Frank Morgan). When a tornado whisks her away from her home in Kansas to a mysterious land, she desperately wants to return and hopes the Wizard can help. Along the way, she meets the Scarecrow (Ray Bolger), who wishes he had a brain; the Cowardly Lion (Bert Lahr), who longs for courage; and the Tin Man (Jack Haley), who desperately wants a heart. So, the three join Dorothy to see if the Wizard can grant their wishes.

Once in Emerald City, the Wizard awards the Lion with a medal of valor for the bravery he showed throughout the journey to Oz. He honors the Scarecrow with a degree in "Thinkology" for his intelligence and presents the Tin Man with a heart-shaped clock for his compassion. With these symbols of recognition and encouragement, they acknowledge that they already possess the qualities they seek—courage, intellect, and compassion.

With the Good Witch Glinda's guidance, Dorothy's realization gives her the power to return home—the power she had all along. She acknowledges that while she believed her heart's desires were elsewhere, they were always with her family and home.[13]

The movie so cleverly shows us that we can bring out traits latent within us to become heroes in our own stories. However, bringing these traits out isn't always easy, because we often carry false beliefs that we're not courageous, not smart enough, or not worthy.

By realizing the power we have to shed these false beliefs to bring out the best in us, we can become the people we are fully capable of being and want to be. To change our lives is to change our beliefs, and that power lies within all of us.

The Courage to Choose

Making any tough decision—whether in a split second or over time—calls for courage that can reward us immeasurably! Changing careers can bring greater job fulfillment because we are using our talents more. Ending an unfulfilling relationship can lead to a more intimate, satisfying connection. Relocating to a new city can provide exciting opportunities. Pursuing a creative passion gives us purpose.

But the key lies in our willingness to let go of fear. Like a chick breaking through its shell, we must leave our comfortable environment to grow. In these moments, we have to believe in our inner wisdom and capabilities to thrive. We all have this internal strength, and when we look back on the courage we've shown in our lives, we can be proud, knowing we've honored ourselves.

Practice Accessing Your Inner Hero

Think of three fears you'd like to overcome. They are personal to you, so acknowledge them without judgment. Let's explore those fears with the following exercise.

Create four columns on a sheet of paper or in your journal. Label the first column "My fear"; the second, "Why am I stuck?"; the third, "The prize or reward"; and the fourth, "Action steps." Complete each column to identify your fears (below are some common examples), explore what's keeping you stuck, and clarify what you truly want. Then, begin to conquer your fear by taking one action step.

My fear	Why am I stuck?	The prize or reward	Action steps
Speaking in public	I will make a fool out of myself. People will think I don't know what I am talking about.	Educating and inspiring people with a message I'm passionate about and want to spread.	Contact a podcast host who might be interested in sharing what I have to say with their audience.
Flying	I might die in a fiery plane crash.	An unforgettable trip to Paris, a dream fulfilled that I've had since I was a young adult.	Learn about how a plane flies, common noises, and facts about turbulence.
Rejection	I'll be embarrassed and hurt because it's happened to me before. I'll find out that I am not lovable after all.	A date with a person that I have had a crush on for years.	Practice how I'll ask the person out, making what I say short and sweet, i.e., "Want to go for coffee sometime?"

Courage Is Personal

Courage lives in all of us. From the little boy who stands up to the school bully to a single woman searching for love year after year to a middle-aged man who changes careers, these individuals show personal courage.

Positive psychologist Robert Biswas-Diener explores the concept of personal courage in his book, *The Courage Quotient.* He talks about how researchers distinguish between general courage and personal courage. They see *general courage* as what most people think of as bravery, such as saving a life, fending off a wild animal, or speaking out for an unpopular cause. In contrast, *personal courage* involves tackling something that feels scary, even if others don't see it as scary. He uses the example of people who are afraid to fly. They show personal courage when they bravely board a plane, whereas others view it as routine.[14]

He further elaborates on the concept when he says, "And herein lies one of the great insights about courage: we all have the capacity to be brave in the realm of personal courage. It is here—in the context of personal courage—that we can say with confidence that courage can indeed be learned."[15]

Biswas-Diener suggests that we can learn courage by observing people who embody excellence. Understanding the how behind people's courage can help us learn from them and potentially apply it in our lives, as we'll explore below.

Courage as a Skill

Captain Chesley Sullenberger embodies excellence. After an American Airlines plane suffered multiple bird strikes, Sullenberger safely landed on New York's Hudson River. He called upon his continuous preparation, training, and more than 30 years of experience. Because of his skill, he saved all 155 people on board![16]

We admire people like him—people who methodically and calmly carry out their responsibilities for those they pledged to serve, even in terrifying situations. They give the best of themselves. They are committed to excellence, and when the pressure's on, their unwavering dedication to their work and principles fuels their courage to accomplish the mission. Here are other people who exemplify excellence:

- **Polish social worker Irena Sendler** risked her life to save 2,500 Jewish children by smuggling them out of the Warsaw Ghetto during World War II. She refused, even under torture, to divulge the names of the children or of the people who had helped her, displaying extraordinary moral strength.[17]

- **Terry Fox, a Canadian advocate for cancer research,** took on the incredible challenge of running over 3,300 miles on an artificial leg, raising over $24 million. Because of his determination and inspiring achievements, the annual Terry Fox Run has contributed, to date, over $850 million to cancer research![18]

- **Victoria Soto, an elementary teacher** in Sandy Hook, Connecticut, made a valiant attempt to protect her students while they were hiding by telling the gunman they weren't in the classroom. She selflessly gave her life, standing by her principles and duty to keep the children safe.[19]

- **Mathematician and scientist Mary Jackson** broke through gender and racial barriers to become NASA's first Black female aerospace engineer. Her commitment to equality led her to revolutionize NASA's recruitment, hiring, and promotion of women.[20]

- **The Unknown Protester, also known as "Tank Man,"** bravely halted a column of army tanks by standing in front of them. His defiant act, captured the day after the deadly government crackdown on human rights protesters in Beijing's Tiananmen Square, was a testament to the power of one.[21]

The examples above are of heroes—ordinary people making extraordinary choices involving risk and personal sacrifice. They chose to be brave at that moment, like Victoria Soto, or over time, like Irena Sendler. In each case, the same motivations were there: a steadfast commitment to a higher ideal, loyalty to their values and moral principles, and a concern for the well-being of others. These commitments embody their excellence, which gave them the courage to do what they believed was right and to act in service of their purpose.

Cultivating Personal Courage

You can probably think of a time when you valued something enough to endure your fear. But how can you find the courage to achieve what you want *every day*? Recognizing how often you are brave is the first step. And you are braver than you might think! You may have asked for a raise or forgiven a friend who hurt you. You might be managing a chronic illness or weathering financial challenges. Maybe you stood up to someone mistreating you or someone you know. All are courageous acts!

Acknowledging and celebrating your daily acts of courage is the first step in building bravery. As you do, you'll gain the confidence to take bolder steps—expanding your life in ways you might not have imagined.

Practice Personal Courage

Keep taking small action steps to move through the fears you identified in the last practice. Tell yourself that you have what it takes! Nothing can stop you if you believe in yourself and your abilities.

When you experience uncomfortable emotions, understand that feeling this way is positive because it means you are stretching beyond your comfort zone. Journaling, physical activity, speaking to a friend, and practicing deep breathing can all help you cope with fear more effectively.

Also, remember, your fears are personal, so try not to judge them as lesser than anyone else's. What matters is that you overcame a fear to feel a sense of fulfillment, renewed confidence, and self-respect.

CHAPTER SUMMARY

Courage is the strength to face challenges, take risks, and endure fear, driven by the belief that the reward outweighs the discomfort. Courage can mean doing what's right despite criticism or opposition, standing up for ourselves, and pursuing what we want. While our bravery may make us vulnerable, its benefits include greater vitality, fulfillment, and helps us realize our truest potential.

Complementing virtues: *Integrity, Confidence*
Courage transcends: *Complacency, Self-Doubt*

Remember this . . .

- We all have a built-in capacity to express physical, moral, and emotional courage. Physical courage is our willingness to confront danger, pain, or adversity—sometimes at the risk of personal harm. Moral courage means defending what is just and right despite potential consequences, while emotional courage involves sharing our innermost feelings and desires, even when it's difficult. Our courage transcends the ordinary. We feel most alive and fulfilled when we honor what is true and right for us.

- Embracing our fears is our most challenging yet most rewarding job. Overcoming self-oppression means placing greater value on what's on the other side of our dread, anxiety, or feelings of overwhelm. Understanding the root of our fear helps loosen its hold on us.

- Courage is personal. What feels courageous for one person might be easy for another. To cultivate personal courage, we must first acknowledge how often we *are* brave. Realizing how capable we are allows us to continue to build our courage muscle, one brave act at a time.

CHAPTER 9

Forgiveness

Forgiveness is letting go of anger, hurt, and resentment over harm to improve well-being and fulfill potential.

People forgive the most horrific offenses. How do they pardon pure evil? Isn't it tough enough to forgive people who betray us, lie to us, or steal our property? Yet, people find a way to break free from the chains of rage, pain, and grief.

One such person is Immaculée Ilibagiza. In 1994, she was a 22-year-old university student visiting her family for Easter. They were Tutsis living in the Hutu-majority country of Rwanda. Hutus had massacred approximately 800,000 to 1 million people—primarily Tutsis—in what became the Rwandan genocide. That number would come to include Immaculée's parents and two brothers. Thankfully, a third brother was studying abroad. She told her astonishing story of survival and spiritual transformation in her book, *Left to Tell*.[1]

During Immaculée's Easter visit, her father sent her to stay with a local pastor because it was safer. The pastor hid her and seven other women in a 3x4-foot bathroom behind a wardrobe. The killers lurked outside, so the women constantly feared for their lives. They didn't move much, ate sporadically, and kept quiet.

One night, Immaculée heard the screams of an infant close to the house. She believed the Hutus had killed the mother and left the baby to die. The baby screamed all night, with cries fading in the morning and then silence by the evening. Immaculée prayed to God, asking Him to receive the baby's soul.

For days, she had recited the Lord's Prayer but struggled when it came to the part of forgiving the sins of others. With a heart full of anger and resentment, she could not comprehend how to forgive the killers who, by now, may have slaughtered her family and friends. Then, she asked God how she could possibly forgive such cruelty against an innocent child.[2]

She writes:

> I heard His answer as clearly as if we'd been sitting in the same room chatting: *You are all my children . . . and the baby is with Me now.* It was such a simple sentence, but it was the answer to the prayers I'd been lost in for days. . . . In God's eyes, the killers were part of His family, deserving of love and forgiveness. I knew that I couldn't ask God to love me if I were unwilling to love His children. At that moment, I prayed for the killers, for their sins to be forgiven.[3]

Immaculée's willingness to open herself up to God's infinite love was a turning point for her. As she asked that He forgive the killers' sins, she moved closer to forgiving them herself. Her anger slowly dissolved, and she slept peacefully that night for the first time since entering the bathroom.

Azim Khamisa's story is another one of unfathomable pain transforming into hope through radical forgiveness.

On January 21, 1995, Tariq Khamisa—Azim's son and a 20-year-old college student—was delivering pizza to a house in San Diego when 14-year-old gang member Tony Hicks attempted to rob Tariq. When Tariq resisted, under the orders of an older gang member, Tony shot and killed him.

Although Azim's grief was overwhelming at times, he recognized that there were "victims on both ends of the gun,"[4] and so began his forgiveness journey.

Not long after, Azim contacted Ples Felix, Tony's grandfather and guardian, and they became friends.

In October 1995, Azim and Ples founded the Tariq Khamisa Foundation (TKF) in honor of Tariq. The organization's mission is to end youth violence. They began visiting schools to talk to students about the realities of gangs, violence, and revenge and the importance of making the right choices.

Five years after losing his son, Azim found the courage to visit Tony in prison. To Azim's surprise, Tony was exceptionally composed for a 19-year-old. After asking Tony about his son's last words, they shared a long, painful gaze. Tony expressed deep remorse and fully accepted responsibility for his actions.

In a StoryCorps interview, Azim said that in that moment, he realized the spark within Tony was no different from his own. It was then that he forgave Tony. Azim's stride was bouncier when he walked out of the prison than when he walked in, as he said to StoryCorps.[5]

In 2019, 39-year-old Tony was released from prison. He now works as a plumber and serves on the board of the Tariq Khamisa Foundation. Each year, he speaks to thousands of at-risk young people to help them avoid making the same mistakes he made.[6]

Immaculée and Azim looked beyond the killers' actions, extending them compassion and mercy. They prove that forgiveness is possible, even amid unthinkable tragedies. Indeed, they felt unbearable anguish and the desire for justice. However, in time, they chose to forgive, which freed them of hate, bitterness, and resentment.

Their extraordinary stories show us that through forgiveness we can heal, start fresh, and make meaningful contributions. In our lives, forgiveness may mean letting go of a partner's betrayal, a family member's criticism, or a friend's misunderstanding. Yet, the essence of forgiveness, the ability to forgive the wrong to release ourselves of negative emotions, remains consistent, whether it addresses monumental offenses or daily grievances.

Practice Reflecting on Forgiveness

Forgiveness can profoundly change your life, though it can involve navigating complex emotions. Consider a situation when you found it difficult to forgive someone, whether it was a minor disagreement or a deep hurt. Revisit the specific event now, explore your thoughts with the following questions, and consider writing your answers in your journal.

- Do you feel anger, resentment, sadness, or perhaps a combination of these emotions and others?

- Were you able to forgive the person who hurt you? If so, describe the reasoning behind your decision. If you didn't forgive, what might be holding you back?

- What impact has your decision to forgive or not forgive had on your life?

By expressing and exploring the complex emotions and insights that arise from your experience of forgiveness or lack thereof, you can better understand yourself, your relationships, and your interactions with others.

Unraveling Forgiveness

Forgiving those who hurt us is a divine gesture. We show compassion even when it seems impossible to do so. If we don't forgive, we remain shackled to the past and tied to the offender, which can rob us of happiness and even our potential.

However, forgiveness deeply challenges us. We can obsess about wanting revenge, the what-ifs, and injustice done. Yet, forgiveness is the key to releasing this cycle of negative emotions and moving forward.

Ultimately, embracing this matter of the heart called "forgiveness" is in our best interest. So, then, what do we need to know about it?

The What and Why of Forgiveness

Forgiveness expert Fred Luskin and author of *Forgive for Good,* describes forgiveness as "... the feeling of peace that emerges as you take your hurt less personally, take responsibility for how you feel, and become a hero instead of a victim in the story you tell."[7]

He points out that we often create a "grievance story"[8] because of a painful event. The story forms when we make what happened to us exceedingly personal rather than seeing it as something that just happened. We revisit the hurtful event in the same manner each time, and gradually, it becomes a narrative. That story keeps us looping in one perspective.

Luskin notes that learning to forgive helps us regain control over our thoughts and feelings, reducing feelings of helplessness. Our hostile thoughts transform into hopeful ones, paving the way for a new, more empowering story—a hero story. He explains that a victim story says, "Look at what life did to me! I'll never recover," while a hero story says, "Look at what life did to me, and look how well I've coped with it."[9] The hero story is about resilience and healing.

Another way to understand forgiveness is to understand what it isn't. Scientist and psychologist Joan Borysenko says, "Forgiveness is not the misguided act of condoning irresponsible, hurtful behavior. Nor is it a superficial turning of the other cheek that leaves us feeling victimized and martyred. Rather, it is the finishing of old business that allows us to experience the present, free of contamination from the past."[10]

So forgiveness is *not* about ignoring or condoning the harm done. Nor does it mean that we must reconcile or rejoin a relationship, as Luskin affirms. Instead, forgiving liberates us from the burden of negative feelings that affect our emotional well-being.

Why Is Forgiving So Hard?

We know that forgiveness is good for us. Then why is it so hard to do? Feeling rejected, hurt, or abandoned triggers our defenses. We may blame the other person. We feel angry and may even hate the person for what they did. We see no reason to forgive, nor do we want to, ever.

These intense emotions keep us from forgiving. Here are other reasons:

- **We want revenge** – Wanting to punish the wrong-doer can be a natural response. We want them to suffer as we did. Of course, legal action is justified when we are victims of a crime, but simply wanting payback brings out the worst in us, keeping us angry and ruminating in toxic emotions.

- **We fear vulnerability** – Anger and hate can be strong armor, seemingly protecting us from further hurt. If we forgive, we might think we open ourselves up again to possible mistreatment. But not forgiving can block our life's flow of goodness, trust, and love.

- **We want an apology** – We are waiting for the person to admit the wrongdoing and say sorry. Though it might help us forgive, waiting for someone to apologize could take a lifetime.

- **We are right** – Even if we are right about what happened, it can still leave us feeling stuck. Our insistence on being right can stop us from truly hearing someone else's side. We don't have to give up what we believe, but listening to the other person's perspective is essential to move forward together, if possible.

Forgiving is not easy. It takes a willingness to be vulnerable. You risk the person not apologizing to you or, worse yet, acting as if there's nothing to forgive. On the other hand, you might witness the other person's relief as you extend your mercy. Then, both of you could begin to heal.

Although the outcome of your forgiveness is uncertain, what matters is that you chose to forgive. You took a stand for your healing and inner peace.

Keeping Our Hearts Open

A single jarring event can bring us to our knees. In these moments, forgiveness can open our hearts again to life's possibilities.

Susyn Reeve, author and transformational heart healing coach, experienced such an event—an unexpected breakup. In her book, *Heart Healing*, she talks about the heartbreak she experienced and her path to forgiveness.

When Susyn's boyfriend sent her an email during his trip to China telling her that he wanted to end their relationship, she was heart-broken. But as time passed, she decided not to let the ending of one love story close off her heart to future love. So, she chose to look at the relationship as "a gift that opened my heart to Love more boldly than ever before."[11]

"When heartbreak or unmet expectations occur in the present, unhealed wounds of the past are triggered ... Clearly, a present situation like this [the unexpected breakup] can be exaggerated by the wounds of the past. We use the older circumstances of the broken-heartedness as evidence that 'No matter what I do, I'm not going to be happy' or 'It's not safe to trust and open my heart to someone,'" Reeve says.[12]

She realized that the breakup had reopened an old wound: the feeling of being unloved that she hadn't yet healed. Instead of ignoring it, she opened her heart to how this belief affected her now. Reeve embraced her feelings and released her attachment to them, which helped her forgive her former lover.

"Forgiveness is the act of courageously freeing our hearts and minds from the emotional and spiritual wounds that result in often repeated pain and suffering and block the flow of Love in our lives," Reeve writes. "Each act of forgiveness allows you to deepen and expand your capacity to be, give, and receive Love."[13]

Knowing When to Forgive

How can we tell when we need to forgive? According to Reeve, some clear signs that we need to forgive are "anytime you feel resentment or regret toward yourself or another," "when you are plagued by a circumstance from the past," "when you believe you are right and someone else is wrong," and "when misery, suffering, and complaining have taken up permanent residence in your being."[14]

Staying attuned to our feelings and behaviors can be difficult, but doing that work helps us know when to forgive. Let's say someone close to you betrays your trust. Because of the hurt you feel, you emotionally distance yourself from them. That emotional distance may linger, affecting the relationship, until you're able to release your pain through forgiveness.

Not forgiving those who hurt us puts us in a prison of toxic feelings. Our hearts harden, and over time, we experience the psychological and perhaps physical toll of not forgiving. Of course, forgiveness doesn't mean excusing mistreatment or sacrificing our self-respect. We *always* have a choice to do what's best for us: to forgive a person's behavior and give them another chance or to forgive and move on from the relationship.

Once we acknowledge the need to forgive, each of us follows a different timetable for forgiving someone. For some, forgiveness is an arduous process that may take years. Others may achieve it in months or even days. The key is to be patient and kind to ourselves during this emotional challenge. Remember, even the smallest steps move us closer to healing and inner peace. So, be gentle with yourself—you're doing your best.

Mahatma Gandhi wisely said, "The weak can never forgive. Forgiveness is the attribute of the strong."[15] Forgiveness is an act of extending mercy and compassion to someone and a beautiful reflection of inner strength.

Practice Reflecting On Forgiveness

Forgiving is a decisive step toward personal growth and emotional freedom. To begin this journey, think about someone who you might want to forgive. You might already know who that person is or have to dig deeper. Digging deeper might mean asking if you hold any resentment or anger in a relationship but are hiding or denying those feelings.

Start by answering these questions:

- Am I feeling anger, sadness, resentment, or a desire for retribution? (Describe in your journal how that person hurt you and your feelings then and now).

- Do I often complain about the offender?

- How might the pain be affecting my physical and mental health?

- Is my lack of forgiveness limiting what is possible for me?

As you answer these questions, be brutally honest with yourself. This self-reflection is a powerful tool that can help you understand your feelings and the need for forgiveness. Allow your answers to flow freely with curiosity and strength.

Thinking about your feelings toward someone you need to forgive may trigger a range of emotions, from anger to sadness. If you need help processing these emotions, counseling, support groups, or additional readings could be beneficial.

Forgiving Yourself

Does something you said or did in the past still trouble you? So much so that you continue to judge and punish yourself? You may feel tremendous guilt over what happened. We often recognize the need to forgive others, yet we don't feel deserving of a pardon.

Rick Hanson, a psychologist and senior fellow of the Greater Good Science Center at UC Berkeley, says that we can be too harsh on ourselves for past mistakes. We tend to blow things out of proportion or focus on our faults, which traps us in guilt, shame, and remorse.

Hanson believes these feelings should teach us not to repeat our mistakes. However, we often use them to punish ourselves. He says self-forgiveness involves owning our flaws with remorse, making amends, and finding peace.[16]

Forgiving ourselves, however, can be deeply personal and challenging whether we're struggling with a breakup, a mistake at work, a lost dream, or the pain of having hurt someone. One woman's story highlights the struggles and insights of self-forgiveness following a tragic accident.

One morning in Perth, Australia, 17-year-old Kelly Connor was driving to her telephone exchange job. While climbing a steep hill, she noticed a taxi on her right, waiting to merge into her lane. Fearing it might pull out in front of her, she kept her eye on it while steadily accelerating. Suddenly, an older woman appeared in the crosswalk, and although Kelly slammed on the brakes, she couldn't avoid colliding with her.

On The Forgiveness Project's website, Kelly described how, when she learned Margaret Healey, 77, had died from her injuries, she felt alienated from the world—a feeling that lasted for years.

Two weeks after the accident, Margaret Healey's brother visited

Kelly's parents. He told them his family didn't blame Kelly and believed Margaret would have felt the same. Despite his forgiveness, Kelly couldn't shake her guilt and shame, especially because the police officer had protected her by falsely reporting she had been driving 35 mph instead of the actual 45 mph.

Still haunted by guilt four years later, Kelly went to the police station to admit she had lied about her speed. The senior police officer would not take her statement, saying, "Putting you in jail would turn a disaster into a tragedy."[17]

For nearly 20 years, Kelly never spoke about the accident, wrestling with remorse to the point of attempting suicide. She avoided relationships for years but eventually married and had a daughter, Meegan, who gave her a renewed will to live. When her daughter turned two, Kelly left her husband, bringing Meegan with her.

A few years later, Kelly read a book on creative visualization that started her journey of self-forgiveness. She imagined what her life would have been like if she hadn't caused Margaret Healey's death. She realized that Margaret's death had shaped who she was, yet she still struggled with self-forgiveness and the idea of being grateful for her own life.

Kelly had kept the accident a secret from Meegan, but fearing it could harm their lives, she finally told her 14-year-old daughter what happened. Her daughter's acceptance became the catalyst for Kelly to face her past.

In 2001, when asked to write a book about her experience, Kelly agreed.[18]

"Going public terrified me, but I knew I had to do it to help others who were traumatised by the guilt of causing a death. The book was a great success, and the letters started flooding in," she said. "The first person to contact me was a woman whose young daughter had been killed as she stepped out onto the road, and her mother wrote, 'every day for the last ten years, I've worried about the driver.' In that moment, I suddenly realised that people had been more forgiving of me than I ever realised."[19]

Considering Kelly's realization, the timeless words of the 13th-century Persian poet and mystic Rumi resonate: "The wound is the place where the light enters you."[20]

Our emotional wounds can teach us resilience, compassion,

patience, and forgiveness. That is, if we are willing to face them and the effect they may be having on our lives.

Through self-forgiveness, we can find solace in our darkest moments. How do we achieve this? First, we must understand that we can forgive ourselves, no matter how monumental the mistake or tragic the circumstance. We all have regrets, and when we dwell on them, it's a call for self-compassion.

If you have not forgiven yourself for something in the past, create a plan for your healing. You may make amends with the person you hurt, write yourself a forgiveness letter (see next practice), practice self-compassion, or seek guidance from a therapist.

Remember to be gentle with yourself. Everyone makes mistakes and does things they feel bad about and regret. What's essential is to forgive yourself so you can stop the unnecessary suffering and live in peace.

Practice Self-Forgiveness

What is something you did or said that you've never forgiven yourself for? As part of your healing, write yourself a heartfelt letter of forgiveness.

Find a quiet, private place to write. Let the words flow from a place of support and understanding rather than self-loathing. Use encouraging, kind words like a friend would say to you. Self-compassion is vital in this process.

In your letter, include what you've learned about yourself and how you've grown since the event. Express gratitude for all the good in yourself and your life.

If you need help getting started, here is a prompt: "Dear [Your Name], I want to talk about [the past action or event] that I've struggled to forgive. It's time to release this emotional pain, and here's why..."

Once you complete the letter, keep it or throw it away—do whatever helps you heal best. You could also try a self-forgiveness ritual, like lighting a candle, walking in nature, or sharing your journey with a trusted friend. Embrace these rituals to help guide you in self-forgiveness and healing.

Lastly, remember to be gentle with yourself. Everyone makes mistakes. What's important is that you learn from them, let go, and forgive yourself—freeing you from the psychological weight of guilt, shame, and regret.

What's Possible with Forgiveness

Forgiving others who have wronged us can cost us mentally and physically, but it also serves as a catalyst for a brighter future. In *The Book of Forgiving*, Desmond Tutu and his daughter, Mpho Tutu, explore how forgiveness affects our present and future. They affirm:

> Without forgiveness, we remain tethered to the person who harmed us. We are bound with chains of bitterness, tied together, trapped. Until we can forgive the person who harmed us, that person will hold the keys to our happiness; that person will be our jailer. When we forgive, we take back control of our own fate and our own feelings. We become our own liberators. We don't forgive to help the other person. We don't forgive for others. We forgive for ourselves.[21]

As the Tutus highlight, our unwillingness to forgive can jeopardize our happiness and fate, a reality Wayne Dyer almost faced. In his memoir *I Can See Clearly Now*, Dyer shares a deeply personal story of forgiveness and its pivotal role in shaping his life's path.

When Dyer was two, his father abandoned the family. Consequently, his mother, who was just 22 and had two other boys (all her sons were under the age of four), had to place them in foster homes. Although his mother later reunited with him, the trauma of separation left a lasting impact.

Burdened with hatred for his father, Dyer searched for him to find out why he had left the family. His search was unsuccessful.

In 1974, during a business trip to Mississippi, Dyer learned from a cousin that his father, who had died a decade earlier in New Orleans, was buried in Biloxi. Knowing his father had passed, Dyer stopped searching, yet his dreams of meeting his father, marked by rage, haunted him. He now had the opportunity to visit his father's grave and possibly gain some closure.

Once he arrived at his father's grave, he stood over it feeling angry, talking with his father and crying aloud, insisting on answers to his questions. After two and a half hours passed, he began to feel an overwhelming calmness and relief, and he felt, almost certainly, the presence of his father.

After wiping his tears and saying goodbyes, he walked away from his father's grave. But an inexplicable force compelled him to return, which he did.[22]

This time, Dyer spoke to his father from a loving and empathetic place: "I somehow feel as if I were sent here today and that you had something to do with it. I don't know what your role is, or even if you have one, but I am certain that the time has come to abandon this anger and hatred that I have carried around so painfully for so long. I want you to know that as of this moment, right now, all of that is gone. I forgive you."[23] He not only forgave his father but also sent him his love from that moment on.

When Dyer finally left, he no longer hated his father and felt a lightness and peace he had never felt before.

Before Dyer went to Biloxi, he was out of shape, drinking too much, and faced a block in his creative writing. Undergoing his transition from hate to love, suffering to peace, he began an eight-mile-a-day running routine lasting 29 years, improved his eating habits, and adopted a more positive outlook.

Upon returning from Biloxi, he stayed in a hotel for 14 days and wrote one of the best-selling nonfiction books of the decade (translated into 47 languages) called *Your Erroneous Zones*.[24]

His whole life transformed because he forgave.

Dyer's story illustrates that forgiving someone who has caused us enormous pain is hard—so hard that it can seem impossible. But when we choose to forgive, our lives can take a new, more empowered direction.

Imagine if Dyer had spent his life in anguish over his father. He might never have achieved the extraordinary contributions he made to humanity.

Forgiving others isn't just something we do for ourselves in the moment; it's something we do for our future selves, so we can open the door to possibility and fulfill our highest potential.

Practice Forgiving Someone

Forgiving someone who has abused or mistreated you or a loved one can be extremely difficult. Writing a letter to that person can help you process your emotions. However, you'll need to want to forgive and feel ready, because forgiving can't be forced.

If you think you are ready, or want to try, sit quietly and comfortably. Visualize the person who hurt you and what you want to say to them. Take a few deep, relaxing breaths. Begin writing the details about how the person offended you, how you felt about what happened, and how it has affected you. Allow the feelings that come up to move through you without judgment.

When trying to understand someone else's behavior, imagining what troubles they may have experienced can be helpful, though this doesn't excuse their actions. Finally, write down your forgiveness statement, such as, "I forgive you for hurting me. I realize that you didn't know any better at the time." Forgiveness can be challenging, so you may need to write and read the letter a few times until you feel you've started healing.

You can mail or email the letter to the person you are forgiving, dispose of it, or keep it. If you do send it, know that reconciliation or a response may not come. You may not want that, anyway, but whether you do or not, you have taken a brave step in giving yourself an extraordinary gift—the gift of spiritual growth and inner peace.

CHAPTER SUMMARY

Forgiveness is letting go of anger, hurt, and resentment over harm to improve well-being and fulfill potential. It's not about condoning someone's actions or seeking reconciliation. Instead, it's about breaking the emotional ties with the one who hurt us. Through forgiving others, asking for forgiveness, and forgiving ourselves, we can free ourselves from the past to move forward in peace.

Complementing virtues: *Empathy, Peace*
Forgiveness transcends: *Anger, Resentment*

Remember this . . .

- People forgive serious offenses by choosing compassion and mercy over hate, anger, and resentment. Although it's not easy and seemingly impossible, we can rid ourselves of the negative emotions that haunt us if we have the will to forgive.

- Forgiveness is not condoning someone's behavior, forgetting what happened, or feeling the need to rejoin the relationship. Instead, it's about acknowledging our feelings and opening our hearts to love.

- Equally important as forgiving others is forgiving ourselves. Healing happens when we apply self-compassion and understand that we are not perfect. We accept responsibility for what happened, express our remorse when possible, and choose to love ourselves.

- Forgiving others takes strength—and it's a gift not just to them, but to ourselves. Through forgiveness, we free ourselves from the past, dissolve negative feelings, reach our potential, and live more peacefully.

CHAPTER 10

Purposefulness

Purposefulness is having a clear aim that brings joy and meaning to life while inspiring, educating, or uplifting others.

We all need a purpose in life. Purpose gives us joy and meaning. Often found in our talents and skills, purpose guides our choices and fuels our motivation to accomplish a worthy endeavor. With a purpose, we can inspire, educate, and uplift others while gaining immense satisfaction.

A single purpose defines many lives. Michael Jordan seemed destined to be a professional basketball player. Jane Goodall advocates for wildlife conservation. J.K. Rowling writes magical stories. We might say they were "called" to do that one thing—it's why they were born. But for many of us, there isn't just one purpose that defines our lives. Instead, we have a variety of purposes like caring for children, pursuing creative projects, or volunteering. Purpose often arises in everyday life when we're simply doing what matters most in the moment.

Over time, purpose can change with life's seasons. While graduating from college might once have been a purpose, now it could be working in our chosen field to support a family. A purpose that was once excelling in a sport might now be mentoring young athletes. We naturally adapt, seeking new ways to find meaning in our lives.

As we grow intellectually and spiritually, our purpose reshapes itself. While we might seek material success in our youth, as we age, our attention may shift to charitable endeavors. What once felt so important may not be as relevant now because of the evolving nature of purpose.

What about you? Do you feel you have a purpose in life? Perhaps you are raising children, caring for a parent, or working at a job you love, yet there's still a lingering feeling that something is missing. You long for a purpose that fully engages your talents and skills but aren't sure where to start.

Alternatively, maybe you've discovered a purpose but feel held back by obligations. Whatever your situation, it's important to remember that finding a purpose or committing fully to one is possible with time and reflection.

The What and Why of Purposefulness

We typically think of purpose as an intended or desired aim or goal. That purpose can drive our decisions and actions, energizing every aspect of our lives. But it's deeper than that because it can go beyond a goal; it can be an endeavor that shapes our futures and be a force for good.

Executive coach and purpose expert Richard J. Leider defines purpose as:

> ... an active expression of the deepest dimension within us—where we have a profound sense of who we are and why we're here. Purpose is the aim around which we structure our lives, a source of direction and energy. Through the lens of purpose, we are able to see ourselves—and our future—more clearly.[1]

Leider says our purpose makes us unique, and is the reason for our existence, and motivates us to get out of bed each morning.[2]

Similarly, in their book *Ikigai: The Japanese Secret to a Long and Happy Life*, Héctor García and Francesc Miralles explore the concept of ikigai, which means "reason for being."[3] They discuss how a defined ikigai contributes to life satisfaction, happiness, and meaning.

The authors observe that while some people have discovered their ikigai, others are still searching for it, though it naturally resides within them. Surprisingly, ikigai is so central to Japanese culture that the idea of retirement is virtually absent in Japan; instead, people continue to engage in their ikigai as long as they are physically able.[4]

Pastor Rick Warren, author of *The Purpose-Driven Life*, defines purpose as God's planned path for us designed for *His* purpose rather than something we find and pursue.[5] He explains that God already has a purpose for us, and we can discover it and our identity through a relationship with Him.

For those who believe in God, his perspective may offer an enlightening way of looking at purpose:

> The purpose of your life is far greater than your own personal fulfillment, your peace of mind, or even your happiness. It's far greater than your family, your career, or even your wildest dreams and ambitions. If you want to know why you were placed on this planet, you must begin with God. You were born *by* his purpose and *for* his purpose.[6]

Victor Strecher, a behavioral scientist at the University of Michigan's School of Public Health and the author of *Life on Purpose,* defines purpose this way:

> It's your fingerprint. Your DNA. It's the statement that separates you from your boss, the street urchin in Mumbai, and your jerk of a brother-in-law. Your 'best purpose' becomes your inner motivator, turning on the ignition switch in your brain to transcend the noise in your life and focus on what matters most.[7]

Whether you feel God placed your purpose inside you, life circumstances led you to it, or you had to work hard to find it, your world cannot be the same once you identify it. You can now make your unique and needed contribution to others. For some of you, your purpose guides all that you do. For others, your purpose may haunt you because time limitations prevent you from fulfilling it. Still, some of you are searching for your higher purpose.

Wherever you stand with your purpose, calling, or gift, it can be a beautiful way to connect with others and leave a lasting legacy.

Why Purpose Matters

In the 1989 movie *Dead Poets Society*, Professor Keating (Robin Williams) is an eccentric English teacher at an all-boys school. On the first day, he asks his students to follow him outside the classroom and into the hallway. With the class gathered around him, he selects a student to read the first stanza of Robert Herrick's poem "To the Virgins, to Make Much of Time," which begins with, "Gather ye rosebuds while ye may."[8] He then explains that the Latin term for this phrase is *carpe diem*, meaning "seize the day."

He directs his students to a glass case displaying an old photo of former students. Referring to the photo, he notes how those boys have the same haircuts, youthful hope, and ambition, just like them. Then he asks, "Did they wait until it was too late to make from their lives even one iota of what they were capable? Because you see, gentlemen, these boys are now fertilizing daffodils."[9]

The boys, now mesmerized, await Keating's next words: "If you listen real close, you can hear them whisper their legacy to you. Go on, lean in. Listen, you hear it? Carpe. Hear it. Carpe. Carpe diem. Seize the day, boys. Make your lives extraordinary."[10]

Keating's message is clear: life passes quickly, and while he never says it outright, he implies that it's up to us to either squander our days or seize them with purpose.

With a meaningful ambition, we can transform a directionless life into an exciting new adventure. Life becomes clear and focused. What matters to us guides our choices and empowers us to leave an impact on others.

Purpose and Life Satisfaction

Having a sense of purpose provides us with significant psychological benefits.

Studies show that people without a purpose are more likely to suffer from depression, anxiety, boredom, and loneliness. Conversely, people with purpose feel more optimistic, hopeful, and satisfied.

But it's even deeper—people with purpose feel better about themselves and their abilities. Consequently, they are more satisfied with life.[11]

Another key to life satisfaction—both in general and in our professional lives—is finding purpose in our work. However, according to one study, how we approach our work matters more than the tasks themselves.

The study found that some hospital cleaning staff saw their work as merely cleaning up after ill patients and, feeling unappreciated, found little enjoyment or meaning in their jobs. In contrast, other cleaning staff performing the same tasks viewed themselves as part of the team that helped heal patients. Working closely with doctors and nurses, they considered their work essential to patient care and, thus, highly meaningful.[12]

Do you find purpose in your job? Some of you may not find meaning in your job, but a new perspective can change that and make your days more fulfilling. Perhaps you can find this meaning in workplace friendships, in the skills and experience you gain, or in the value you bring to your coworkers and customers.

Purpose Improves Health

Not only do we experience positive emotions from having a purpose, but there's also growing evidence that purpose significantly benefits our health.

In 2006, University of Michigan researchers studied nearly 7,000 American adults over 50 to see if a relationship exists between longevity and life purpose. Participants completed psychological questionnaires assessing their sense of purpose.

From 2006 to 2010, the study found that people with a lower sense of purpose were twice as likely to die as compared to those with a stronger sense of purpose. They also found that participants who had a life aim was more strongly linked to longevity than income, relationships, or, surprisingly, even health habits like smoking, drinking, or exercise.[13]

Other studies have found that a strong sense of purpose lowers the risk of Alzheimer's, heart disease, and stroke.[14]

Luckily, creating more purpose in our lives is within our control. As the researchers concluded, if we do not have a strong sense of purpose, we can cultivate that purpose through volunteering in our community, for example. We can also explore our skills, passions, and values and then use them to create more purpose in our lives.

Practice Affirming What's Important

You may have many pursuits that fill you with purpose, but one might stand out as your central focus. If so, explore the questions below to begin shaping that purpose. Knowing what truly matters to you will illuminate your purpose, making it easier to recognize and embrace.

- What makes me truly happy?
- What types of projects or work do I love doing?
- What do I enjoy learning about?
- What needs in the world do I feel drawn to address?
- Have I overcome a setback or trauma and want to help others facing a similar challenge?
- What other career would I choose besides my current one, and why?
- What is the highest vision I have for my life?

Write your answers in your journal to help make your thoughts and feelings more tangible. Once you discover a purpose or mission that resonates with you, you begin aligning your choices to help bring it into reality.

The Ways of Purpose

How does purpose come about in our lives? Certainly, having children gives us the purpose of caring for them. Loving our family and friends also provides us with purpose. Satisfying work gives us purpose. These types of purposes arise naturally as a part of living.

Sometimes, though, purpose happens more unexpectedly, such

as through adversity. Something awful happens, and we turn our pain into purpose. Often times, this purpose not only helps us with feelings of helplessness and grief but also becomes a vehicle of hope for others.

Others find purpose through a quest. They go on an adventure, fight for a cause, or pursue a personal challenge. Through their quest, they gain a deep sense of fulfillment.

Still, others find purpose through self-discovery, taking the time to self-reflect, evaluating their values, skills and passions to arrive at a meaningful pursuit.

Let's explore these ways of purpose and discover how they can shape our lives.

Purpose Through Adversity

At times, an event propels us to take on a cause or pursue a new life direction. The following two stories highlight adversity as a way we gain purpose.

In 2019, a massive fire broke out in a six-story apartment building near the Yonkers-Bronxville border in New York. Flames raged out of the roof and windows while onlookers watched helplessly. Firefighters battled the fire for 12 hours. When the flames finally extinguished, about 150 people had no home. Thankfully, no one had died or was injured.[15]

In the fire's aftermath, caring neighbors from nearby buildings wanted to help, like my sister Stephanie. Because of neighbors' overwhelming generosity, the original drop-off spot became too crowded, so Stephanie coordinated additional locations for pick-up of clothing and other necessities. Then she joined forces with another woman, who opened up an even larger service area at a gym. They worked tirelessly for days in their mini-store, giving out free clothing and vital supplies to those displaced by the fire.

Stephanie said of the experience: "I was laid off from work, so I felt so useful and satisfied spending this quality time helping my community. I also made new friends who I never would have met if I didn't reach out to help."[16]

While Stephanie found purpose in helping others during difficult times, some people experience a devastating event that becomes the foundation for a purpose. One such person is architect Girish Gogia.

Girish was excited about celebrating the new millennium in Goa, India, with his wife, Eesha. He enjoyed deep-sea diving, so they went to his favorite spot.

Girish acrobatically dove off the cliff into the sea, but what he thought was deep water turned out to be shallow. The impact against the bed severely damaged his cervical spinal cord. After that, he remembers only darkness and then waking up in a hospital bed, paralyzed from his neck down. Doctors told him he had little chance of survival and might remain in a vegetative state.

As months passed, Girish said an encouraging, ever-growing voice in his head kept him alive and gave him courage. The voice told him to move forward, fulfill his calling, and uplift billions of others globally.

Defying the doctors' prognosis, Girish continued his career as an architect, completing 15 internationally recognized projects with the support of his wife, Eesha, and family. Still, he felt empty until Eesha helped him realize that what he truly wanted was to inspire others to fight against adversity.[17]

Through his tragedy, he closed his architectural business and became an internationally respected motivational speaker. He dedicated his life to "inspiring all to live out their highest vision."[18]

Although these stories are vastly different, the people in them faced adversity—whether for a season or a lifetime—and discovered purpose by serving others.

While purpose can come through hardship, we can gain it in other ways, such as through a quest, a passion, or self-discovery.

Purpose Through a Quest

Entrepreneur and author Chris Guillebeau says that having a quest brings purpose to life. He defines it as a well-defined goal with measurable steps leading to its completion. A quest also entails overcoming a challenge and making sacrifices. He believes we can feel called to pursue a quest and that this call can lead to an extraordinary accomplishment.[19]

Chris' love for travel led him on a personal quest to visit every country in the world (193 at the time), which he accomplished in 10 years. In his book, *The Happiness of Pursuit*, he tells of other quests: a Boy Scout who earned every merit badge (154 of them), a middle-aged woman who committed the rest of her life to observing every bird species, and a teenager who became the youngest person to sail solo around the world.[20]

Some quests can be obsessive. A person's burning desire for something drives all they do, as in the case of Polish-French physicist and chemist Marie Curie. She relentlessly pursued the isolation of a pure sample of radium to convince the scientific community that the element existed.

In a dimly lit Paris laboratory, Marie set out to extract radium from pitchblende ore, a uranium-rich mineral. After measuring an unlikely amount of radioactivity in the pitchblende, she realized there had to be another element in the mix.

Her discovery was monumental. She not only discovered one, but two new elements: radium and polonium. Despite polonium being more radioactive, radium became the focus of her work because of its availability and potential use in medicine.

Since it was only a theoretical finding, chemists in the scientific community were skeptical. Driven by her desire to prove that radium existed in pure form, she would have to extract it from the pitch-blende ore.

Fascinated by Marie's quest, her husband, Pierre Curie, left his work on crystals to join her efforts. After processing plants in Bohemia removed uranium from pitchblende, the Curies obtained large amounts of the remaining residue.

While Pierre focused elsewhere on the experiment, Marie laboriously boiled and stirred the pitchblende residue with a heavy iron rod. She aimed to break down the ore chemically to maximize radium extraction and purification.

As each day passed, the strenuous job left her increasingly frail, so they hired an assistant. Pierre thought the project seemed unachievable, but Marie persisted in performing countless fractionations and measurements, producing increasing amounts of radium. She often didn't eat and was away from her young daughter for extended periods.

After four grueling years, they isolated about 0.1 grams of radium from several tons of pitchblende, a remarkable feat in chemistry. Their pioneering work revolutionized radioactive isotope purification, laying the foundation for targeted cancer treatments using radiation.

Finally recognized for their collective work on radioactivity, the Curies received the 1903 Nobel Prize in Physics. In 1911, Marie received the Nobel Prize in Chemistry for discovering radium and polonium elements and investigating their properties. Decades later, at the age of 67, Marie succumbed to an illness widely believed was caused by her prolonged exposure to high levels of radiation.[21]

Any worthy pursuit requires obsession to some degree. How can we master anything in life without giving it our all? However, knowing when to place our health, family, or other responsibilities ahead of our pursuit is important, too. Otherwise, we can lose the things we hold most dear. We can even lose our health like Marie Curie. Striking a balance in life is important! Making time for relationships, health and psychological well-being must be a priority, or else we risk losing them.

In the end, a quest can give us a sense of adventure and fulfillment when we reach our goal. A quest can also give us joy as we do what we love. We often grow while pursuing a passion—exponentially! And as we do, we affect others' lives in ways we could never have imagined.

Purpose Through Passion

Most quests involve doing something we feel passionate about, which drives our motivation. Marie Curie felt passionate about identifying the new element radium, which helped her persevere through years of physical and mental hardship. Her moments of bliss and intense devotion to what she sought drove her to an extraordinary discovery that positively affected humanity.

Marie once said to her brother, encouraging him to pass his doctor's thesis: "It seems that life is not easy for any of us. But what of that? We must have perseverance and above all confidence in ourselves. We must believe that we are gifted for something, and that this thing, at whatever cost, must be attained."[22]

Marie's gift and love for science inspired her to pursue a purpose she had to achieve, no matter the cost.

You may feel drawn to fight for something you believe in, to pursue a business, or to take up a creative project. Notice the passion you feel behind this endeavor. What captivates and inspires you about it? Your love for something can lead to a purpose when you commit wholeheartedly to it, even turning it into your life's work.

Purpose Through Self-Discovery

We can also uncover our purpose through self-exploration, a topic we'll discuss in an upcoming section.

Practice Finding the Way of Purpose

Think about how you may have found a purpose through adversity, a quest, or passion. You may have gained purpose from a combination of these areas. If so, write about how your purpose arose, considering the following questions:

- How did the purpose affect your life?
- Did this purpose positively influence others?
- Do you still have this purpose today? Would you like to?
- What challenges did you face with this purpose, and how did you overcome them?

You build a stronger sense of self by understanding the evolution of your purpose, the effort you invested in it, and its role in shaping your life.

Obstacles to Your Purpose

Self-sabotaging behaviors, meeting others' expectations, and fear of our own brilliance can stop us from finding and fulfilling our purpose. Still, we can uncover our true calling through self-awareness and hard work to overcome these limiting patterns.

Scott Harrison is a compelling example of someone caught up in self-sabotaging behaviors like chasing status, wealth, and pleasure—until he chose to redirect his life toward meaningful service.

Self-Sabotaging Behaviors

What would be possible if a person's sole purpose was to help others for one year? Scott found out when he gave up his egocentric life to do just that.

At 18, Scott rebelled against his suburban, Christian upbringing by forgoing college and escaping to New York City to be a famous musician. He played gigs with his band throughout the city, but they eventually broke up.

Scott then landed a lucrative job as a nightclub promoter in the city. Club owners hired him to entertain models, celebrities, and the wealthy. Wearing designer clothing and a Rolex watch, Scott spent his nights drinking, taking drugs, and gambling.

Things began to shift when he was 28. After another vice-filled evening at a club, he had an epiphany—he had become, as he put it, "the worst version of myself."[23] His fast lifestyle was taking its toll on his body and conscience.

In December, Scott traveled to Punta del Este, Uruguay, to vacation with friends over the New Year holiday. After two days of partying, he spent some time alone by the pool reading a book his father gave him called *The Pursuit of God* by A. W. Tozer.

Scott found Tozer's words were speaking directly to him when the author claimed that material objects could never satisfy one's heart. Feeling ashamed of who he had become, Scott knew that if he continued to pursue fancy cars and designer clothing, he would have nothing of meaning to show for his life.

Several months later, with his renewed faith and a desire to change, he took a year off from his lifestyle to pursue one that was its complete opposite.

Scott wanted to serve others, so he applied to multiple charities. After numerous rejections, Mercy Ships, a floating hospital that provides free surgeries in developing countries, offered him a position. They asked him if he would pay them $500 a month for room and board to work as a photojournalist, documenting life-changing surgeries. Scott agreed, stopped all his vices, and boarded a ship to West Africa, first to Benin and then Liberia.

When Scott was taking photos in the rural villages of Liberia, he noticed that people were drinking filthy water, causing diseases like cholera, hepatitis A, and dysentery. Women and girls traveled miles daily to fetch dirty water, carrying 40-pound jerry cans on their heads or backs. His purpose began to form when he learned that half of Liberia's illnesses were from unsafe water and poor sanitation.

Once he completed his time with Mercy Ships, he returned to New York determined to help the people of Africa. He turned to his mentor, Mercy Ships' Chief Medical Officer, Dr. Gary Parker, for advice on which problem to tackle. Dr. Gary suggested Scott focus on one problem intensely. So, Scott reflected on his volunteer experiences, recognizing that access to clean water could significantly improve lives. He committed to concentrate his efforts on this cause.

Scott traveled to Uganda to meet with residents and photograph the most contaminated water he could find. He found that over 30,000 refugees were drinking from a single source of water—contaminated and shared with animals. He returned to New York with a fire in his heart to help them get the water they desperately needed.

Shortly after his return, Scott threw himself a thirty-first birthday party at a New York nightclub. As a nightclub promoter, he leveraged his connections and lured people in with an open bar. Attracting 700 people, they each gave the required $20 donation for entry. Some gave more. Scott raised $15,000 that night! He could now fix three wells and build three more at the refugee camp. His nonprofit, charity: water, had officially launched.

Because he knew that many people didn't trust where their money went when they donated, he boldly committed 100 percent of the donations to clean water projects.[24]

As of this writing, the organization has provided clean water to over 18 million people across 29 countries, funding 154,000 water projects![25]

Just think, if Scott had carried on the way he had been, letting his self-sabotaging behaviors rob him of his purpose, millions would still suffer from the effects of drinking dirty water. He has also made the joy of giving possible for many people who have donated their birthdays and held fundraisers to raise money for charity: water.

Think about how your life is going and ask yourself, "Do I like who I am being? Are self-sabotaging behaviors keeping me from a purpose? Is there meaning in my life? Am I making a difference in the way that I want to?" Your answers can open up new possibilities to help uncover your purpose.

Meeting Others' Expectations

Exploring questions like the above can help us live more authentically, where our choices and behaviors align with our values, passions, and skills. However, our families' expectations can sometimes sway us into making choices that don't align with who we truly are. For example, our parents may not accept our desired career path, but we know it's right for us.

Societal expectations about relationships, work, parenthood, and wealth can further influence our decisions. We may have children before we are ready or pursue a job for the money instead of one we enjoy. Regrettably, it may take years to realize that we should have followed our hearts from the beginning.

Fortunately, you have a choice *now*. You can veer off familial and customary paths to create your own! You can be the great adventurer, the budding artist, the soulful writer, the cupcake maker, the Reiki healer, the bike courier, the veterinarian, the acupuncturist, the environmental lawyer—whatever calls to you.

In your fullest self-expression, you are optimizing your talents, skills, values, and passions to fulfill your purpose and make the best possible contribution. You are pursuing what feels right in your heart and what makes *you* happy.

Fear of Your Brilliance

American author, spiritual leader, and activist Marianne Williamson memorably wrote in her book *A Return to Love*:

> Our deepest fear is not that we are inadequate. Our deepest fear is that we are powerful beyond measure. It is our light, not our darkness, that most frightens us. We can ask ourselves, 'Who am I to be brilliant, gorgeous, talented, fabulous?' Actually, who are you not to be?[26]

We can hide our brilliance—our talents and gifts—because we fear family and friends will feel uncomfortable. While those close to us may be our biggest fans, some might discourage us from making the right choices for ourselves. They have no bad intentions, but their words can stem from fear—the fear of losing the relationship, jealousy, or their own insecurities. This can hurt, but we must stay true to our path; otherwise, we may live with regret.

Imagine you are considering a move to Greece for a year, but a friend says, "You're crazy. How are you going to pay for it?" Although they might have your best interests at heart, what they say shouldn't necessarily derail your plan. It's not that you shouldn't listen, but be mindful of what's behind their concerns. It could be that your friend doesn't want you to move away.

Along with holding back because of the naysayers, we might squash our brilliance because we don't feel worthy. We question ourselves, "Who do I think I am to be doing this?" Self-doubt can stop us from pursuing our aspirations. But our gifts and deepest longings are no accident! Honoring them isn't just our right—it's our responsibility. When we recognize our own brilliance and the value it can bring, holding back can be a disservice not just to ourselves, but to others as well.

Practice Freeing Up Your Purpose

Could self-sabotaging behaviors, the pressure to meet others' expectations, or fear of your own brilliance be holding you back from realizing your purpose? Had Scott Harrison not faced the truth about and addressed his self-destructive behaviors, he might never have discovered his life purpose of ensuring clean water access for all.

When you begin to realize what is preventing your fullest self-expression, you can start the important and hard work to address it—whether on your own, with the support of family and friends, or with the help of a therapist. You might begin by writing about these patterns, exploring what triggers them and the deeper causes beneath them.

By working to release fear and self-sabotaging behaviors, you create space for self-discovery where your purpose can emerge.

Clarifying a Purpose

How often do we take the time to ask ourselves, "Am I happy? Do I feel fulfilled? Am I where I want to be in life?" These questions may come about unintentionally. A breakup, an accident, or recovering from an addictive behavior compels us to reevaluate the choices we've made or didn't make. Or maybe we feel dissatisfied, even a pervasive emptiness, a lingering feeling that we're destined to *do* more, *be* more.

We long for more joy, meaning, or expansion of our world. Self-discovery, whether intentional or not, can be the single most valuable quest of our lives, guiding us to our purpose.

What Is Self-Discovery?

Understanding our purpose begins with the courageous journey of self-discovery—a process of uncovering our values, talents, skills, and desires. It's about finding out what inspires us at our core and identifying the beliefs holding us back from achieving that dream. Through this brave yet vital inquiry into the lovable and not-so-lovable parts of ourselves, we uncover who we are and what we want.

Here are thought-provoking questions to help guide your self-discovery journey:

- What do I value?

- What are my talents and skills?

- What am I passionate about?

- What dream do I want to fulfill?

- What am I willing to struggle for?

- What beliefs or perceptions hold me back from what I want?

- Is a self-sabotaging behavior affecting my life and potential now? (You may need the help of a therapist to help you explore a trauma.)

In the words of the famed writer T.S. Eliot, "We shall not cease from exploration, and the end of all our exploring will be to arrive where we started and know the place for the first time."[27]

We can apply his words to our own journey of self-discovery—when we explore and learn about ourselves, we return to who we are and know ourselves for the first time. We bring the unconscious to light, potentially redirecting our lives toward what truly matters to us and what satisfies our souls.

What Are You Willing to Struggle For?

American self-help author Mark Manson believes that a critical question to ask ourselves is not "What do I want out of life?" but rather "What am I willing to struggle for?"[28] He explains in his insightful article, "The Most Important Question of Your Life," that the answer to the latter question is more significant in determining our success.

Throughout his youth, Manson dreamed about being a rock star but wasn't willing to practice daily, put in the hours or years of hauling gear, finding gigs, and dealing with broken equipment. He wasn't *willing* to struggle for it. He compared his dream to climbing a mountain, where he only desired the view from the top, not the arduous climb itself.[29]

According to Manson, our willingness to struggle for something is a major clue to finding out what we want to do with our lives. If we aren't willing to sacrifice, feel uncomfortable, or be willing to endure the pain, then we know it's not important enough for us to pursue.[30]

Take a moment to reflect on Manson's question: What are you willing to struggle for? What dream are you willing to pursue for months, even years, giving your all while facing rejections and setbacks, just to achieve it? If you have the resilience and fortitude to bear that struggle, then you're on the path to achieving that dream.

What Do You Value?

How does knowing what we value help us find purpose? Typically, what we value is where we place our attention. What we value shapes our lives, for better or worse. If we value creativity, we spend time on creative endeavors. If we value achievement, we set goals and achieve them. If we prioritize social status, we may chase material possessions. Valuing people's opinions of us may mean saying "Yes" to them when we want to say "No," while valuing self-respect means prioritizing our happiness and well-being.

What we value guides our choices and, in turn, the direction of our lives. Think about the ways you'd ideally like to spend your time. Perhaps how you *want* to live your life and how you are *actually* living it are in opposition. Are you going against what you truly value? If so, you can shift to making choices that reflect your values. By doing this, you can uncover the purpose that feels true to who you are.

What Are Your Talents and Skills?

In addition to your values, understanding your unique talents and skills can guide you toward your purpose. You may already be capitalizing on your gifts or you may need to dig deeper to find them. If you're unsure where to begin, life coach and author Talane Miedaner suggests seeking insights on your strengths, weaknesses, talents, or gifts by asking family, friends, and colleagues.[31]

Often, others can see qualities in us that we might easily overlook. They recognize you as an exceptional communicator, natural negotiator, skilled cook, or confident leader. Knowing what you're naturally good at can reveal your authentic self, helping you channel those strengths into meaningful work.

"After coaching thousands of different people," Miedaner says, "I can safely say that people who do work in alignment with their natural talents and their core values are very happy, more likely to be financially successful than those who are unhappy, and they feel personally rewarded and deeply fulfilled."[32]

When we identify and honor our gifts by diligently pursuing them, we unlock our potential, enrich our lives, and positively impact those around us.

What Are You Passionate About?

Passion is often described as a strong feeling or desire for something, whether it's an activity, object, or concept. She has a passion for helping children. He's passionate about art. Her love is gardening. What we feel passionate about helps us discover a purpose. But what exactly is the difference between passion and purpose? Passion is an intense emotion for a person or thing, while purpose is how we steer that passion into meaningful action.

What do you feel passionate about? You know you have a passion when your heart aches for it, when you feel a lift every time you think about it, and when you'd rather being doing that thing than anything else.

If you'd like to find a passion, try things that pique your curiosity. When something captures your interest, consider developing it into a personal project or, if it resonates deeply with you, even your life's mission.

For example, if you're passionate about technology, consider developing an app that solves a common problem you've noticed. If you love fitness, perhaps become a certified trainer and offer classes in your community or online. Maybe designing jewelry or creating greeting cards inspires you. If so, you can open an Etsy storefront.

As you explore, notice what energizes and lifts your spirit. When your values, talents, and passion align, you can make a meaningful contribution to others—and experience true fulfillment and joy.

Practice Clarifying Your Purpose

Let's work on clarifying your purpose. You may already be clear about it or not know it yet. Either way, putting it on paper makes it more tangible. To help uncover your purpose, write down your answers to the questions in this chapter's section, "What is Self-Discovery?"

Next, based on your responses, describe what you think your life purpose might be. Include what talents you intend to use and the specific individual or group of people you will be serving.

Lastly, consolidate what you wrote into one purpose statement. For example, my purpose statement is "to help people create their best lives by practicing virtues (or inner strengths)."

Here are more purpose statement examples:

- To teach children with special needs how to become more independent so they feel happier and more fulfilled [from a special needs teacher]

- To treat each employee with respect, transparency, and appreciation so they enjoy their jobs and are genuinely committed to the organization's success [from a business manager]

- To make delicious and fun specialty cakes and cupcakes that bring people joy [from a specialty cake baker]

- To raise kind, intelligent, and self-reliant children so they live happy, productive lives and make valuable contributions to society [from a parent]

- To prioritize self-care by eating healthy, exercising, getting enough sleep, and engaging in fun activities [from anyone]

Give your life purpose statement your best shot, and try not to judge whether it's noble or significant enough. Your purpose does not have to be grand. It can be whatever speaks to your heart, excites you, and brings out your most authentic self. Remember, it's your purpose—what matters most to you!

Keep your purpose statement handy to fine-tune it as it may evolve.

CHAPTER SUMMARY

Purposefulness is having a clear aim that brings joy and meaning to life while inspiring, educating, or uplifting others. We find purpose through our families, faiths, service, and jobs. We often find our purpose through a combination of our values, talents, skills, and passions. With purpose, our authentic selves shine, and we contribute in ways that are both lasting and valuable.

Complementing virtues: *Authenticity, Integrity*
Purposefulness transcends: *Discontentment, Mediocrity*

Remember this . . .

- Purpose guides our choices, fuels our motivation, and gives us a clear path. When we have a purpose, we enjoy increased mental and physical health.

- Some people seem to be born with a purpose in their hearts. For others, purpose can emerge through adversity, a quest, passion, or self-discovery.

- Self-sabotaging behaviors, meeting others' expectations, and fear of our brilliance can stop us from finding and fulfilling our purpose. What's important is recognizing these patterns and doing the work to move beyond them so we can pursue what truly matters to us.

- Self-discovery is the process of understanding our values, talents, strengths, and weaknesses. Through this brave yet vital inquiry into the lovable and not-so-lovable parts of ourselves, we discover who we truly are. With this awareness, we can channel our strengths into a purpose, fulfilling our potential and positively contributing to others.

CHAPTER 11

Gratitude

Gratitude is the deep appreciation for all that's good in life, from the beauty of nature to the love of family and friends.

As I've grown older, I appreciate nature more. I notice the colorful fall leaves swaying in the wind, the magnificence of a full moon, and the familiar buzz of crickets marking long summer days. The joyful sounds of children playing outside, the morning's first sip of hot coffee, and my mother's calming, supportive voice all reassure me of life's goodness.

Waking up with no pain or illness is something I try not to take for granted. I am deeply grateful for family, friends, and time spent with them. I cherish childhood memories like Sunday dinners with cousins at my grandmother's house, enjoying her delicious lasagna, and playing whiffle ball outside afterward.

I am also thankful for the people I've known for a shorter time. They have each contributed to my life in unique and meaningful ways, whether through their infectious humor, caring gestures, or steady support and encouragement. Together, we've shared life's challenges and joys in the different chapters of our lives.

Simply put, I am more grateful for life now than ever, understanding how precious it is—something time has shown me.

Have you ever noticed how recognizing your blessings can calm and uplift you? I feel this way whenever I think grateful thoughts. Gratitude has that power. We recognize, celebrate, and embrace abundance, if just for a moment. Our negative feelings dissolve and are replaced with positive ones.

Gratitude also has the power to help us see life's interconnectedness. We recognize that plants give off oxygen, which we need to breathe, and we return carbon dioxide, which helps them grow. Our doctors, teachers, daycare workers and transportation drivers support our lives functioning well. People we love support and encourage us as we return the same.

Understanding our mutual dependence deepens our appreciation, making it hard to take anyone or anything for granted.

Gratitude brings many benefits, including better health and greater happiness, and these rewards are so worth its ease of practice.

Gratitude as a New Perspective

How often do you pause for a moment of gratitude? Perhaps you do it occasionally or regularly—gratitude comes more naturally to some. If being thankful is more challenging for you, know that the beauty of gratitude lies in its simplicity. At any moment, you can choose thoughts of appreciation.

That said, it can be challenging to maintain a grateful attitude. Our natural tendency is to focus on what's wrong or lacking in our lives. What's more, given the obligations and fast pace of today's life, we may forget to notice the good things. Instead, we're thinking about the next task or getting somewhere on time. We also may neglect to thank the people who support our success in life, from the coffee barista to our loved ones.

Life's frustrations can also get in the way of feeling grateful. We might complain to our partner about a controlling manager when we come home from work. Of course, venting to others is natural. It feels good! There's nothing wrong with it. But maintaining this negative disposition day after day undermines our happiness.

Tough times can block our gratitude. We might be out of work, living with a chronic illness, or struggling in a relationship. It's harder to see the good that exists amidst our problems. But feeling grateful can turn our minds away from our concerns, worries, and hardships. We now see something to be thankful for, even if that something is small and temporary.

Cultivating a grateful perspective creates a beautiful atmosphere of positivity. We choose what to be thankful for and how much to feel this thankfulness. These choices instill hope and the inner strength to face each day.

The What and Why of Gratitude

Simply defined, gratitude is a feeling of thankfulness and appreciation for favors or benefits received. Favors can be acts of kindness like someone holding the door open for us or offering a compliment. Benefits can include a beautiful sunset, a loving partner, or the pleasure of a delicious meal.

But gratitude goes far beyond an expression of thanks. Harvard Medical School captures gratitude's expansiveness, defining it as:

> "... a thankful appreciation for what an individual receives, whether tangible or intangible. With gratitude, people acknowledge the goodness in their lives. In the process, people usually recognize that the source of that goodness lies at least partially outside themselves. As a result, gratitude also helps people connect to something larger than themselves as individuals—whether to other people, nature, or a higher power."[1]

Experiencing gratitude in the fullest way means we are aware of, and then acknowledge, the good that exists. By doing so, we open ourselves to gratitude's mighty ability to inspire positive emotions and connection. Whether valuing a friend's support or appreciating the warm sun on a beautiful day, we make ordinary moments more special.

Cultural anthropologist and educator Angeles Arrien, author of the beautiful book *Living in Gratitude,* believes gratitude is both a spontaneous emotion and a deliberate choice. She writes, "We can choose to be grateful, or we can choose to be ungrateful—to take our gifts and blessings for granted. As a choice, gratitude is an attitude or a disposition."[2]

Choosing to be grateful not only changes our attitude for the better but also immerses us in the present. We take a moment to enjoy the orange hues of a sunrise, our child's happy face, and the aroma of our favorite meal. When someone does something nice for us, we pause to feel grateful. Because we choose to enjoy and feel thankful for these moments, goodness sweeps over us.

These moments are the building blocks of what Benedictine monk Brother David Steindl-Rast, the visionary behind the Network of Grateful Living, calls grateful living. He describes grateful living as ". . . being fully present to your life so that your perspective can be expanded, your compassion enhanced, and your purpose discovered in this moment."[3]

Br. David invites us to practice gratefulness, which he says is an "inner gesture of giving meaning to our life by receiving it as a gift. The deepest meaning of any given moment lies in the fact that it is given. Gratefulness recognizes, acknowledges, and celebrates this meaning."[4]

We can overlook how life is a precious *gift*, as illustrated by Steve Foran's experience. His story is a testament to gratitude's transformative impact.

> As the oldest of five children, I developed a strong sense of responsibility. I believed people should hold themselves responsible for their lives and the circumstances in which they find themselves. My catchphrase was, "If it's going to be, it's up to me."
>
> With this belief came a strong tendency to judge others. For example, if I came across a panhandler on the street, I'd be the first to pass judgment. I wouldn't give them money (figuring they'd only spend it on liquor). I'd think to myself, "This is my money! If you want money, why don't you get a job and earn it like I did?"
>
> My perspective changed when I realized I wasn't a self-made man. Despite my belief in personal responsibility, I came to understand that my success resulted from my upbringing, my teachers, the people who died for the freedom I enjoy, and the list goes on. I hadn't done anything on my own. With this profound awareness, or "aha!" moment, came an overwhelming sense of gratitude.

At that time, I was finishing a Master's of Business Administration from St. Mary's University in Halifax, Nova Scotia, to complement an electrical engineering degree. Part of the MBA program included a major research project, so I chose to study the relationship between gratitude and philanthropic giving. As part of my research, I was privileged to have deep, meaningful conversations with generous people throughout my community. We talked about what motivated them to give their time and money and why they helped others. Through this research, we built a model of motivations for charitable giving and found that gratitude was at the heart of generosity. Participants felt a deep sense of gratitude for what they had received in life, and because of their gratitude toward others, they wanted to give back.

Captivated by the research results and the impact that gratitude had on me, I knew the study of gratitude would eventually become my life's work. So profound was my motivation that I left a nineteen-year career as an electrical engineer to start a business focused on gratitude as a foundational leadership trait. That was almost two decades ago.

Over this time, my sense of gratitude has continued to grow and reshape how I make sense of the world. I realize that in the ordinariness of my life, I feel truly blessed—like a child in a playground who finds joy in every moment. My dream is that everyone can experience this childlike joy on a regular basis.[5]

Gratitude plays a big part in Steve's life. Yet he admits that feeling grateful is not always easy, given the challenges and busyness of life. Still, he firmly believes that practicing gratitude has the power to address major problems, such as poverty and sustainability, because gratitude shifts mindsets, fosters generosity, and encourages people to care for one another and the world they share.

Since Steve recognized gratitude's impact on his life, he says he now "spends more time thriving and less time surviving." By thriving, Steve means living a life of abundance, joy, and purpose rather than merely surviving day to day. He believes a grateful mindset helps people thrive by shifting their focus from what's missing to what's meaningful and good. Steve inspires others to build this mindset by cultivating daily gratitude.

Practice Gratitude as a New Perspective

Discover how cultivating a grateful mindset can help you thrive—boosting happiness, improving health, and enhancing your overall well-being. Try these simple practices:

- **Make a Gratitude List:**

  In your journal or on a sheet of paper, list the people who have supported you or made sacrifices to help you succeed—such as mentors, family, friends, and colleagues.

  Also, include big and small blessings, like good health, meaningful work, a comfortable home, or even a hot shower.

  Start with at least five entries and add to your list over time. Refer to it often as a reminder of how fortunate you are.

- **Meditate on Gratitude:**

  Spend 5 to 10 minutes each day to sit silently and think about all the good in your life. If your mind wanders, bring your focus back to gratitude. You'll feel more positive while adding the calming practice of meditation to your daily routine.

- **Take a Gratitude Walk:**

  Whether hiking or walking around your neighborhood, pay attention to your surroundings—the flowers' vibrant colors, the crisp, fresh air, the sun's warmth, and the birds' happy chirping. Enjoy each step with thankfulness. Combining gratitude with a walk is a powerful way to ease worries, elevate your mood, and stay fit.

Gratitude Boosts Happiness and Health

Most of us know what makes us happy. It might be life's big moments—getting married, having a baby, or buying a house. Or it could be simple pleasures, like getting lost in a good book, indulging in a creative hobby, taking walks in nature, enjoying a night out with friends, or giving back through volunteer work.

While the source of our happiness differs, we can agree that our happiness fluctuates. Monday morning comes around, and we drag ourselves back to a job we don't like, or we're suffering from a financial hardship, an illness, or a loss. When that happens, happiness plunges. But what if we could find happiness more consistently by recognizing the good around us, even amidst our difficulties?

In 1998, Robert A. Emmons, a leading gratitude science expert and psychology professor at the University of California, Davis, and Michael McCullough, a psychology professor at the University of Miami, conducted a pivotal study on the influence of gratitude on mental and physical health.

The psychologists assigned three randomly chosen groups to write in a journal weekly. The first group listed five things they were grateful for, the second noted five hassles or annoyances, and the third, a control group, recorded five events without any emotional emphasis.

They assessed participants' mood, physical health, and life satisfaction before and after journaling to measure the true impact of gratitude.

After 10 weeks, the psychologists' study revealed that participants who had written down what they were grateful for each week were 25 percent happier than the other two groups. They felt more optimistic and better about life overall. They also exercised more and were healthier.[6]

But even with gratitude's proven benefits on our well-being, our problems can still overshadow our ability to feel thankful. George Bailey (Jimmy Stewart) vividly illustrates this struggle in the 1946 classic film *It's a Wonderful Life*.

George, a small-town building and loan manager at his father's bank, has the respect of his community and always looks after his family and friends.

One snowy Christmas Eve, his Uncle Billy (Thomas Mitchell) accidentally gives $8,000 of the bank's shareholders' money to Mr. Potter (Lionel Barrymore), a greedy local banker who keeps the money. George faces possible financial ruin because of the mistake and falls into despair. He fears he's worth more dead than alive.

As George prepares to jump from a bridge into icy water, an endearing guardian angel, Clarence (Henry Travers), pretends to drown himself, prompting George to save him.

While they both warm up in the tollhouse, George tells Clarence he wishes he had never been born. Clarence grants him his wish.

Taking a journey through time, George sees how different people's lives would have been if he had never existed. For example, without George, Mr. Potter turns the town into a bleak place filled with saloons and nightclubs.

What's more, George's brother, Harry, drowns in a frozen lake as a child because George was not there to save him. As a result, Harry never grows up to become the hero who saves the lives of many soldiers during World War II.

Realizing the true value of his life, George begs Clarence to return him to it, which Clarence does. Grateful for his flawed house, the love of family and friends, and the townspeople's support, George rejoices in his wonderful life![7]

George Bailey's renewed faith and awareness of life's abundance reveal the remarkable potential of gratitude to transform our mindset, from negativity and despair to hope and possibility. Beyond the uplift in spirit as seen in George's story, gratitude also provides these psychological and health benefits:[8]

- **Gratitude improves health:** Research shows that gratitude can lead to healthier blood pressure and heart rate. It also strengthens the immune system, reduces aches and pains, and improves the quality and duration of sleep.

- **Gratitude is a social superpower:** When we are grateful, we naturally become more helpful, generous, and compassionate. Gratitude also fosters forgiveness and connection, reducing feelings of isolation and loneliness.

- **Grateful people handle stress better:** With a thankful disposition, we recover more quickly from trauma, adversity, and suffering.

- **Gratitude boosts workplace productivity:** Employees are over 50 percent more productive when they receive a simple "Thank you!" from a supervisor. In fact, 81 percent of people say they would work harder for a boss who shows appreciation. One of the top reasons people leave their jobs is because they don't feel appreciated.

With such compelling evidence of gratitude's benefits, practicing it is not just a nice idea but a worthwhile pursuit—even a life-changing one!

Practice Writing in a Gratitude Journal

One of the best ways to experience the benefits of gratitude is by keeping a gratitude journal. This simple yet nurturing practice helps shift your focus toward life's goodness Over time, it can deepen your appreciation for people and nature, boosting your well-being.

1. **Start Daily Entries:** Use a notebook or journal to write down three to five things you are grateful for each day. Be specific. Instead of "I am grateful for my mother," write, "I am grateful for my mother's love and how she always supports and encourages me."

2. **Feel Your Emotions:** When writing your gratitude statements, take a moment to feel the emotions associated with your gratitude. Doing so deepens positive feelings and your appreciation.

3. **Make it a Routine:** Consider adding gratitude journaling to your morning or bedtime routine. Commit to this daily habit for at least one month. Research shows it takes 21 days to form a habit. Once it

becomes part of your routine, feeling grateful will come more naturally.

After a month, see if you feel happier, more optimistic, and more grateful overall. Let this positive shift be a source of motivation for you to continue the practice.

Navigating Challenges to Gratitude

The absolute lowest points in our lives make it nearly impossible to feel grateful. Yet, gratitude may be just what helps us get through.

Janice Kaplan, in her inspiring book *The Gratitude Diaries*, shares how dedicating a year to focusing on the bright side changed her life. Her story begins with a resolution made one New Year's Eve. She was at a party, thinking she should be counting her blessings. Instead, her attention was on her aching feet and when she could leave.

Midnight came as she and the other partygoers watched the ball drop in Times Square on a roaring screen. After all the excitement of the New Year had faded, everyone was in a lull, wondering what to do next.

Janice noticed a woman in tears at the bar and asked her if she was okay. The woman confessed that she hated New Year's Eve and nothing would change just because a ball dropped.

That got Janice thinking. She was grateful for her life, which included many blessings: her two wonderful sons, a kind and handsome husband, close friendships, and an intriguing career. But she also knew that she tended to focus on the negative rather than the positive. That night, she resolved to be more grateful in the year ahead.

As a career journalist, Janice approached cultivating a grateful mindset as a project. She consulted books and experts, conducted research, and recorded her findings.

Each month, she focused on an area of her life—marriage, family, money, career, and health—to see how gratitude could bring improvement. She interviewed celebrities like Matt Damon and Daniel Craig to see how gratitude played a role in their lives.

One particular month, she explored how gratitude might ease hardships. She visited people who had experienced personal devastation, from serious health diagnoses to unimaginable tragedies. Despite their heartbreaking situations, she saw a resounding theme: they intentionally and repeatedly found reasons to be grateful, even in painful and sad times. Their consistent practices, such as writing gratitude lists or keeping a gratitude journal, rewarded them by lifting their spirits.

Throughout her yearlong experiment, Janice applied gratitude to different aspects of her life. She recognized that even setbacks in her professional life had led her to meet new people, engage in interesting projects, and embrace exciting opportunities.[9]

"Gratitude was a way of finding good in everything,"[10] she writes.

Experiencing a loss or life-altering health diagnosis can make it hard to see anything positive. However, in time—as in Janice's loss of her job—good can come about. The key lies in actively looking for the good, which can be especially hard when losing a loved one.

How can we possibly feel grateful during our immense grief? Yet, in these sad times, we can shift our focus to gratitude. By choosing to feel thankful, if only for a moment, for the person's love and the time we had with them, we can find comfort and peace.

According to personal change expert M.J. Ryan, gratitude can help us with difficulties by widening our perspective. She explains, "Under depression or stress, we can develop tunnel vision, seeing only this problem, that difficulty. We can get overtaken by a heavy, dark feeling of despair. But when we experience a sense of gratitude, we give ourselves a dose of mental sunshine. Suddenly the world seems brighter, and we have more options."[11]

Think of a time when a loss or difficult situation eventually led to something positive. Perhaps it wasn't right away, but the eventual good was a better relationship, job, or valuable personal growth. Through the lens of gratitude, we can transform our despair into hope. With practice, gratitude becomes a powerful tool, a crutch to lean on in tough times, strengthening our resilience and faith for better days ahead.

Along with life's hardships, challenges like comparing ourselves to others and becoming too caught up in our own lives can undermine our ability to feel grateful.

Comparing Ourselves to Others

How can we handle feelings of envy when a colleague lands the position we've wanted so badly? Or when someone buys their dream home, and we've wanted to buy our own? Or when we think someone is better-looking, thinner, or smarter? Our self-imposed inadequacies seem real.

Certainly, our culture of materialism promises we'll have a better life if we purchase expensive things. Without the latest luxury items, high salaries, or exciting travel experiences, we may envy those who possess them. Even social media woos us into thinking that other people's lives are better than our own. We see friends posting fabulous pictures of their adventures! Our hearts sink because we can't afford the same.

However, gratefulness can combat envy, greed, and materialism by recognizing that we *have* enough and *are* enough. Instead of thinking, "Why can't I be thin like her?" or "How come I'm not further ahead?" we can shift to a grateful perspective, "I'm so lucky to feel healthy and strong" or "I'm right where I need to be."

When you feel the urge to compare yourself to others, think about something good in your life. Replace the disempowering thought with the new grateful one. Shifting our thoughts of wanting more to appreciating what we have is one of the most empowering practices we can do for ourselves. A grateful perspective invites good feelings!

Caught Up in Our Own Lives

At times, we can focus so much on our own wants, needs, and experiences that we lose sight of others. In those moments, we might naturally steer conversations toward ourselves or overlook the thoughts and feelings of those around us.

Fortunately, most of us are also empathetic, generous, and caring. Still, we've all had moments when we've shown frustration for not getting what we wanted, dismissed someone's opinion, or looked for praise and recognition. That's part of human nature! However, excessive self-focus impedes our ability to feel grateful. Unless we look beyond ourselves, we can't appreciate the good things others have done for us. We'd have to be humble to do that.

Steve Foran, whose story was shared earlier in this chapter, was humbled when he realized how much other people had contributed to his success. This awareness deepened his gratitude for them.

In short, too much self-focus can get in the way of gratitude, while humility opens the door to a thankful perspective.

Practice Opening Up to Gratitude

Think about a recent setback or challenge you faced. Now, view the experience from a grateful perspective by asking yourself these questions:

- Did any aspect of the mistake, setback, or failure evolve into a positive outcome?
- How has this situation helped you grow or change for the better?
- Did it take you on a more rewarding path?
- Are comparisons or being caught up in your own life hindering your gratitude?

These questions might not apply to every situation—especially in times of loss, like the passing of a loved one. Under this circumstance, consider finding comfort in the shared memories, their positive influence on your life, and the precious moments spent together.

Reflecting on how good can come from hardship can offer hope and motivates us to keep moving forward.

Expressing Gratefulness

John Thompson served as a U.S. helicopter crew chief during the 1985 Iran-Contra affair, a political scandal where U.S. officials secretly sold weapons to Iran to help free American hostages. The proceeds were then illegally used to fund Contra rebels fighting Nicaragua's Sandinista government.

John was on a relief mission to Honduras, where he and his crew brought supplies to villagers caught in the conflict between the Contra rebels and the Sandinistas, Nicaragua's ruling government.

When John's helicopter landed, a swarm of desperate-looking people—men and women, young and older—ran toward John and his crew. Not knowing if they might encounter armed Sandinistas, John remained on high alert, gripping his gun with one hand while handing out bags of food with the other. Contrary to John's fears of encountering dangerous rebels, the crowd consisted of starving mothers, fathers, children, and an elder woman who desperately wanted his attention.

Here's John's explanation of what happened next:

> A small, elderly woman caught my eye. She was making her way through the crowd, trying to get to the aircraft. I remember being fixated on her for too long. I should have been scanning the crowd. When she got to the edge of the helicopter, our eyes connected as people were moving around. I extended a bag of food to her, thinking that's what she wanted. She didn't reject the bag. She just let someone else take it. What she wanted was my hand. Now I understood she wanted to get to me all along. I held her hand for a moment, and with pure sincerity, she said in broken English, "I thank God above for you."
>
> She wasn't after the food. She wanted to say "Thank you." It was a thank-you so strong that I could feel it; it was not just courtesy or kindness but something much deeper. I said to her in Spanish, "You're welcome."[12]

Looking back on that day, John, now 62, still vividly recalls her face. He feels there was nothing heroic about what he did. He says tearfully, "She was a gift to me, and I wish I could have done more."[13]

Heartfelt appreciation can mean so much to others. As in John's case, the intensity of the elder woman's gratitude and her need to express it profoundly affected him.

People have shown their deep appreciation to strangers who have done a good deed for them. However, it's often the people closest to us whom we might take for granted. We neglect to say how thankful we are for having them in our lives.

It can be as simple as saying, "Thank you for always being there for me," or "Thank you for believing in me when I doubted myself." From strangers to our loved ones, thanking people strengthens our relationships and can create the most memorable moments.

John Kralik discovered how gratitude could transform his life. At 53, he was going through tough times. His law firm was failing. He was 40 pounds overweight, lived in a small, poorly ventilated-apartment, and had drifted apart from two of his children. His girlfriend,

Grace, broke up with him shortly before Christmas. However, she still came to his house on Christmas Eve to exchange gifts.

Before the breakup, John and Grace planned to walk on New Year's Day on the Echo Mountain trail above Pasadena, California. Grace told him she had other plans, so John went alone. Deep into his walk, a voice came to him, seemingly out of nowhere, saying that he wouldn't get what he wanted until he learned to be grateful for what he had. Those vivid words gave John the idea of finding one person to thank each day in the New Year.

The next day, he found a note from Grace in his mailbox, thanking him for the Christmas presents. Her simple yet beautiful note further encouraged him to write daily thank-you notes to those who touched his life.

With 365 notes to write, John needed to think beyond family, friends, and colleagues. He sent thank-you notes to store clerks, repair people, doctors, and neighbors. He thanked anyone who had shown him kindness and support over the years.

During his 15-month journey, John Kralik's practice of gratitude brought him financial stability, closer friendships, weight loss, and a sense of inner peace.[14]

In his book, *365 Thank Yous*, he reflects on the experience, "At the risk of making an unscientific and directly moral statement, I will say that writing thank-you notes is a good thing and makes the world a happier place. It also made me a better man. More than success or material achievement, this is what I sought."[15]

Both John Thompson's experience in Honduras and John Kralik's year of thank-you notes, the expression of gratitude, showed them a more enlightened way of living. Their stories remind us that through gratitude, we expand our hearts with kindness, generosity, and grace.

Consider the people in your life who could use some recognition. Is a frazzled server having a tough day? A friend who is always there for you? A sister who's constantly lending you a hand? Genuinely expressing gratitude can brighten people's day and even leave a lasting impression on their hearts. Additionally, people genuinely appreciate your effort and time in recognizing how their actions made your life better.

As Angeles Arrien memorably said, "When people in great numbers choose to practice, integrate, and embody gratitude, the cumulative force that is generated can help create the kind of world we all hope for and desire, for ourselves and for future generations."[16]

Receiving Gratitude

Equally important as expressing gratitude is our willingness to receive and embrace the gratitude others offer us. If John hadn't accepted the elder woman's gratitude with a simple handshake, he would have kept her from the heartfelt thanks she desired to give; likewise, he may not have felt her gratitude as memorably.

Gracefully receiving gratitude is a gift we give to others! We validate their expression of deep thanks in that moment.

Have you ever noticed that some speakers rush off the stage the moment applause begins? Yet, those who pause to receive the gratitude not only honor others' appreciation but also sustain the positive energy in the room.

Giving and receiving gratitude creates a cycle of positivity that magnifies the goodness in our lives.

Practice Writing a Thank-You Note

Expressing gratitude to others is one of the most generous gifts you can give. Think of someone you'd like to thank—a friend for their steadfast support, a spouse for their love, or a teacher, doctor, mentor, or parent who has made a difference in your life. Choose the person who will receive your heartfelt letter of appreciation.

Begin your letter (or email, though a letter often carries more weight) with the words, "I am writing to thank you for . . ."

When you've finished, send your message, read it aloud to the person, or—if they have passed away—keep it as a meaningful tribute. Your message can be short, just a simple gesture of kindness to let them know how they have influenced your life.

Telling people how much they mean to you will make you feel good, and the receivers of your gratitude will feel valued and appreciated.

CHAPTER SUMMARY

Gratitude is the deep appreciation for all that's good in life, from the beauty of nature to the love of family and friends. Focusing on what we have rather than on what we lack reduces our wants and worries and increases happiness. Feeling grateful helps us to endure dark times and find hope and peace.

Complementing virtues: *Hope, Joy*
Gratitude transcends: *Entitlement, Envy*

Remember this . . .

- Gratitude helps shift our perspective from what's lacking and wrong in life to what's abundant and right. Choosing to be grateful helps acknowledge our interconnectedness and nurtures well-being.

- Gratitude boosts our health and increases our happiness by 25 percent. It also strengthens our social ties, improves sleep, supports productivity at work, and enhances our ability to manage stress.

- When going through tough times, feeling grateful, even momentarily, can lift our spirits and give us hope for a better future.

- Expressing our gratitude is a gift we give to others. As we do, they feel valued, appreciated, and loved. In expressing gratitude, we also lift our own spirits. By practicing gratitude, we contribute to a more positive and harmonious world.

CHAPTER 12

Joyfulness

Joyfulness is a deep sense of pleasure and contentment, often sparked by meaningful experiences, positive relationships, and a deep sense of well-being.

Twelve-year-old John ran to his friend Kevin's house as fast as he could. He was bursting to tell him that his father had completed building the aboveground pool. Kevin quickly got on his bathing suit and grabbed a towel, happily anticipating the first plunge. As they sprinted down John's driveway, Kevin's brightly colored towel waved like a victory flag.

Scurrying up the steps to the pool's deck where John's father sat, Kevin cannonballed into the pool, towel still in hand. John's Dad called out to him, "Why the heck did you jump in with your towel?" With a breathless grin, Kevin said, "I was so excited, I forgot to let go!"[1]

Joy's Expression

Pure joy is when we seemingly "lose ourselves" in the moment. We cannot contain our euphoria, whether through a broad smile, streaming tears, or a boisterous eruption of laughter.

Joy is in the big moments like graduating from college, a marriage proposal, the birth of a baby, and landing a job we desperately want. It's also in the smaller ones: making a fabulous shot on the golf course, receiving a gift we love, and witnessing a moving event. Joy can strike us by surprise or arrive alongside the realization of our good fortune.

However joy emerges, we know the feeling and recognize it in others.

Take, for example, actor Roberto Benigni's ecstatic reaction when he received the 1999 Best Foreign Language Film Oscar for *Life is Beautiful*. When actor Sophia Loren announced his win, Benigni could hardly contain himself. He climbed onto the back of the chair in front of him, barely keeping his balance as he stepped over the man sitting in the chair and onto the back of movie director Steven Spielberg's chair. Spielberg grabbed hold of his hand to steady him.

While straddling both chairs, Benigni raised his arms high in exaltation as the audience clapped and cheered loudly. Then, he ran up to the stage and leaped like a frog up the steps. Benigni's acceptance speech was equally enthusiastic![2]

From Benigni's jubilant reaction at the Oscars to global celebrations, the expression of joy is universal, connecting us all in a shared experience.

Joy Across Cultures

Joyful expressions unite people across cultures. For example, India's Holi Festival, also known as the Festival of Colors and rooted in Hindu tradition, marks the arrival of spring. People gather to throw colorful powders, symbolizing forgiveness, renewal, and the triumph of good over evil.

Brazil's Carnival is a celebration at the beginning of Lent, a few days before Ash Wednesday. Rooted in Catholic tradition with African and Portuguese influences, Carnival is Brazil's most popular holiday. During the street festival, people wear elaborate costumes, dance in the streets, enjoy food, and participate in parades, inviting everyone to share joy, unity, and self-expression.

In the U.S., July 4th commemorates the signing of the Declaration of Independence in 1776. Families and friends gather for fireworks, barbecues, and parades to celebrate freedom and unity.

South Africans embrace Ubuntu, which means, "I am because

we are." They believe one person's well-being is tied to another's, expressing the importance of communal life and joy as a shared experience. Ubuntu reminds us that joy is most fulfilling when shared through collective celebrations, triumphs, or everyday interactions.[3]

These beautiful, sacred traditions—and many others around the world—bind us together through shared joy and positive feelings. Let's explore more of joy's unique characteristics.

The What and Why of Joyfulness

The American Psychological Association (APA) defines joy as "a feeling of extreme gladness, delight, or exultation of the spirit arising from a sense of well-being or satisfaction."[4] This is an intriguing definition, especially when they say that joy is an exultation of the spirit. When we feel joy, it does feel as though our spirit becomes lighter, rising above our typical experiences.

People try to describe joy's transcendent nature, struggling to explain the thrill they felt upon witnessing a moving event. They say, "You had to be there," knowing it's impossible to convey that feeling in a way that allows the other person to experience it, too.

Oprah Winfrey describes joy as:

> "...a sustained sense of well-being and internal peace—a connection to what matters. Real joy, like real power, as Gary Zukav describes it, happens 'when your personality comes to fully serve the energy of your soul.' That's exactly what happened to me during The Color Purple. Playing the character Sofia and being part of the whole production was not just a job for me. In my soul I knew it was something I was meant to do."[5]

Christian theologian and writer C.S. Lewis explores joy in his book *Surprised by Joy*. He describes it as "an unsatisfied desire which is itself more desirable than any other satisfaction."[6]

Unlike happiness or pleasure, joy carries a certain longing, a yearning that feels just beyond our reach as if it belongs to something beyond this world.

Years ago, I was in a manager's meeting listening to the company's president speak. I paused my attention on him and shifted it to my co-workers. We were all sitting around a U-shaped table, so I could see their faces. Looking around at them, I thought about how lucky I was to work with these intelligent, diverse, and fun people. That moment, amid routine corporate business, I felt a surge of joy. It's still a fond memory.

In her book *The Art of Mending*, Elizabeth Berg beautifully describes these kinds of joyful moments often found in unexpected places:

> There are random moments—tossing a salad, coming up the driveway to the house, ironing the seams flat on a quilt square, standing at the kitchen window and looking out at the delphiniums, hearing a burst of laughter from one of my children's rooms—when I feel a wavelike rush of joy. This is my true religion: arbitrary moments of nearly painful happiness for a life I feel privileged to lead.[7]

Unexpectedly, joy can burst within us like a sudden spring of water, reminding us that there is a force for good at work in our lives.

Joy may feel exuberant, but it can also be quiet. The Pope, for example, reflects quiet joy—serene and reserved outwardly, yet joyful inwardly through his devotion to God.

Still, joy can feel elusive. But what if we could invite more of it into our lives? We can do this by recognizing the abundance around us, engaging in meaningful projects, and connecting with others. Reflecting on what brought us joy in the past and what still brings us joy can help bring joy closer.

Joy Versus Happiness

We can better understand joy by exploring how it differs from happiness. Although the two emotions are closely related, happiness, which is a state of contentment and well-being, has been the subject of many more studies and books than joy.

We often seek happiness through external circumstances, such as earning a college degree, undertaking creative work, buying a new car, or getting a dream job. However, happiness isn't always dependent on our achievements—we can be happy without accomplishing or purchasing anything. For instance, we can feel happiness through meditation, gratitude journaling, and religious practices.

In contrast, joy is a more primitive emotion like euphoria or deep contentment. Unexpectedly, we win a hard-earned award and can hardly contain our delight. Exhilaration sweeps over us after we conquer a debilitating fear. Our baby takes his first step, and we cry.

Joy seems to be less dependent on our accomplishments. Surprisingly, out of nowhere, a circumstance or event, elicits joy that typically wouldn't.

George E. Vaillant, psychiatrist and Harvard Medical School professor, scientifically explains the two emotions. He believes happiness comes from the neocortex, which he calls the cognitive part of the brain. Joy, he says, is subconscious, stemming from the limbic system, which seems to control emotions like pleasure.[8]

Joy certainly feels subconscious. We feel calm one minute and then become overwhelmed with excitement or tears the next.

Designer and author Ingrid Fetell Lee helps people find more joy in their surroundings. She writes about how happiness and joy differ: "Happiness is something that measures how good we feel over time. But joy is about feeling good right now, in the moment."[9]

Lee explains that when we reflect on our happiness, we tend to assess how fulfilling our career is, the state of our health, and quality of our relationships. She suggests that sometimes our happiness can be less certain when we continually think it over. However, whether or not we feel joyful is a more straightforward question because joy is an emotion that can be "measured in the moment"[10] without much thought.

Although happiness and joy differ, they work harmoniously to enhance our well-being. Thankfully, we can cultivate both. We can start by asking ourselves, "How can I be happier?" We tend to know what makes us happy, so this question may not be hard to answer.

Joy, on the other hand, can be harder to find in our lives. Since joy is a subconscious emotion, we can't capture it as easily as happiness. Another way to experience more joy is by recognizing the behaviors and feelings that can steal it from us.

Practice Discovering Joy

What comes to mind when you think about joy? Is it a burst of laughter, being out in nature, or the thrill of finishing a cherished project? Does it seem elusive or within reach with more effort? Are you satisfied with the amount of joy in your life? Reflecting on these questions can help you realize what can bring more joy to you.

Take a moment now to write down everything that brings you joy. Some ideas include:

- Working on a beloved creative project
- Listening to a favorite song
- Baking cakes and cookies
- Playing ball outside with your kids
- Reading a captivating book
- Volunteering for a cause you love

Also, cherish the simple moments that bring you joy like savoring your morning coffee, feeling the warmth of sunlight on your face, or listening to rain tapping against the window.

Find ways to add the big and small things you love into daily life, making room for more joy.

Stealers of Your Joy

Feeling joyful can be challenging. We rush through our days, often overwhelmed with everything we must do. Hardships can happen like accidents, illnesses, losses, or financial struggles. How can we possibly feel joyful? Outside stressors are not the only stealers of our joy. Often, unknowingly, we rob ourselves of joy through certain feelings and behaviors such as *perfectionism, envy, not being grateful,* and *lack of purpose.*

By taking a moment to understand these joy stealers below, we can begin to make changes that lead to a more joyful life.

Perfectionism

We squash joy whenever we pressure ourselves to be perfect or to do something perfectly. Striving for flawlessness makes us obsess over things that are not important in the bigger picture. But breaking this perfectionist habit is tricky. Wanting the absolute best is a good thing, right? Yes and no. When perfectionism leads to procrastination, it delays our precious goals. Reaching these goals can bring us joy. Moreover, the constant pursuit of perfection can lead to anxiety and self-doubt, further hindering joy.

We can break free from perfectionism's grip by asking ourselves whether redoing a task or reviewing it again will *actually* improve the outcome. Another way to look at it is to ask ourselves, "Will this extra step or review matter in the big picture?" In some cases, refining something further will make a difference, but posing this question to ourselves prevents unnecessary work when it will not make a difference in the end.

Voltaire, the French philosopher and writer, said, "Perfect is the enemy of the good."[11] In other words, striving for perfection can sometimes get in the way of making meaningful progress.

Envy

Comparing our education, material belongings, or looks to that of others can make us feel inadequate, which undermines joy. But it's not just that. We're also not present to our own positive qualities, talents, skills, and what we've accomplished. We may not have a big house like our cousin, but we have the gift of running a business well.

There is joy in celebrating who we are! Comparing ourselves to others gives power to external circumstances, making it difficult for us to feel joyful. So, when we find ourselves envying others, we can turn our focus to what we have to offer and our successes, which can spark joy.

Not Being Grateful

Thinking about what we lack or what's wrong in life prevents us from feeling joyful. We become blind to the abundance and beauty that surround us.

Feeling grateful puts us in the moment, like when we are soaking in a sunrise, happily playing with our dog, or laughing with friends. We are present and not caught up in our worries and fears. We only feel good. If we aren't aware of our blessings, then joy is lost.

Of course, we won't always be able to think positive thoughts. However, the intentional practice of gratitude does help to open our hearts to let joy in and flourish.

Lack of Purpose

As discussed in the *Purpose* chapter, having a meaningful goal aligns us with what brings us joy. Joy naturally follows when we are true to our values, talents, and passions.

Purpose doesn't have to be a grand mission. We often find it in everyday things like creating art, nurturing relationships, helping a neighbor, or through a career. For example, a woman deeply committed to environmental conservation may make it her life's work. She enjoys personal fulfillment that isn't dependent on societal expectations or material achievements. Through her purpose, she builds confidence and pride—states of mind associated with lasting joy.

But the beauty of purposeful living doesn't stop there. When we pursue what truly matters, we radiate positivity, creating a ripple effect that uplifts those around us.

Cultivating a Joyful Life

Essentially, cultivating a more joyful life involves identifying these stealers of joy and working to lessen their hold on us. Letting go of harmful habits, reframing our thoughts, and engaging in activities that foster joy bring it closer to us.

Joy is about choosing, again and again, to cultivate what gives us purpose and makes us feel alive and connected. As we sow the seeds of joy, we allow one of life's greatest virtues to blossom.

Practice Opening Up to Joy

Think about the ways you may be hindering joy. Are there behaviors or thought patterns, like perfectionism, envy, negative thinking, or a lack of purpose that might be getting in the way? To help open your heart and mind to receiving joy, start by reflecting on what brings you joy. Recall moments or activities that have made you feel happy and fulfilled. Complete the sentences below to help open your heart and mind to receiving joy.

- I feel most joyful when I am _____
  (for example, entertaining the people I love, or
  playing with my dog)
- To bring more joy into my life, I will _____.
- Ways I hinder my joy include _____
  (for example, perfectionism, envy, not being grateful, lack of purpose)
- Ways I can overcome these hindrances include
  _____ (for example, reciting
  positive affirmations, finding a sense of purpose,
  practicing gratitude)

Tackling deeper hindrances to joy may sometimes require profes-sional support, like therapy. However, these questions can offer an initial approach to navigating challenges and opening up to more joy.

Joy and Suffering

When we are suffering, it can be challenging to feel any joy. Unbear-able pain can make even getting out of bed an accomplishment. Grief after loss, a scary diagnosis, a natural disaster, or economic devasta-tion can make joy seem impossible. But is it?

Christina Levasheff's devastating loss offers a heartfelt explora-tion of this question.

> The morning after my 3-year-old son Judson died, I was lying in bed, hardly able to breathe. Tears clouded my eyes as I wondered how I would ever experience joy again. A few seconds later, our 14-month-old daughter Jessie raced into the room and climbed onto the bed, laughing, giggling, and rolling around with delight, oblivious to what had transpired. She was pure joy. At that moment,

it became apparent that joy was and would continue to be present *around* me despite my pain.

We live in a world that holds happiness as the pinnacle value—where good fortune and pleasure are fundamental. Many people consider happiness the highest human condition, and even if we don't deem the pursuit of happiness as life's leading principle, most of us would admit that we want to be happy. Yet happiness, as defined by the world, depends on life's circumstances. Pain exists in opposition to happiness, and misery is its adversary.

When Judson began suffering, we suddenly faced a life that was anything but "happy." Pain and misery had invaded our lives while good fortune and pleasure eluded us. With Judson's death, that pain became pervasive; it permeated even the smallest crevices of my life. And in some of my darkest moments of heartache, staring down a trajectory of brokenness, I wondered if I would ever experience the fullness of joy again.

Over time, I realized that I had been equating joy with happiness and viewing pain in opposition to both. I saw pain as the antithesis not only to happiness but also to my joy. I saw their relationship as antagonistic, as though my heartache purposefully sought to thwart my joy—even crush it!

But pain is not the enemy of joy.

My joy could not eradicate my pain, but neither could pain wipe out or rob me of joy. They are not seeking to conquer one another like hostiles in combat battling to gain full occupation of my heart; pain and joy are not foes.

Judson modeled this.

My little boy, despite having every bodily function stolen from him and experiencing great pain, frustration, and discomfort, exuded indescribable joy. His joy was not conditional to his circumstances. Judson was content, despite his suffering.

Joy, genuine joy, *can* thrive in the midst of pain.

Genuine joy is not a fleeting happiness over life's cir-

cumstances. Genuine joy stems from a deep understanding
that God is present with us, loves us, and has a purpose
for our pain. Therefore, our experience of pain, no matter
how great, cannot thwart joy. God has designed joy and
pain to coexist beautifully together within us.

Living a life of genuine hope means that pain and
joy walk together, hand in hand. Joy cannot diminish my
pain and loss, nor can they imprison it. As I began to
accept and even expect pain and joy to be allies, I began
to experience more of life's fullness. [12]

Christina reminds us that joy and pain are complementary forces
that together help us find meaning and hope in our experiences. She
channeled grief into hope for others by founding Judson's Legacy
Foundation. The foundation stands with families facing Krabbe
disease, the rare genetic disorder that took her beautiful boy, honoring his memory through support and kindness. [13]

Ourselves as a Cause of Suffering

We all experience suffering in different ways, such as through illness,
natural disasters, childhood trauma, substance abuse, financial struggles, or the loss of a loved one. Anger, anxiety, and despair also add
to our suffering. However, the Dalai Lama XIV highlights another,
even more pervasive cause of suffering—how we perceive and react
to life's challenges. [14]

"We create most of our suffering, so it should be logical that we
also have the ability to create more joy. It simply depends on the attitudes, the perspectives, and the reactions we bring to situations and
to our relationships with other people," he writes. "When it comes
to personal happiness there is a lot that we as individuals can do." [15]

The Dalai Lama believes we can alleviate suffering and feel more
joy by developing what he calls "mental immunity." [16] He says just
as good physical health keeps viruses away, so does sound mental
health keep harmful emotions at bay.

To develop mental immunity, he explains, we must learn to
understand the mind and the many thoughts we have—some harmful
and even damaging to our mental well-being, while others can be
healthy and healing. Once we make this distinction for ourselves,

we can engage with the mind more effectively and take preventative measures, such as soothing our emotional reactivity.

For instance, have you ever sat in heavy traffic angrily cursing? Although it's a natural reaction, we often put ourselves into an exaggerated state of suffering.

During this time, we can take certain measures to temper our emotional responses and ease our suffering. So, while sitting in traffic, instead of ruminating on negative feelings, we might consider how fortunate we are that we have plenty of time to reach our destination, or that we're not involved in the accident causing the delay.

Self-kindness can make us feel better when we are upset. Imagine receiving critical feedback on your project at work. It's easy to spiral into feelings of inadequacy, where you question your skills and abilities. But self-kindness can help you understand this was a momentary setback, not a sweeping judgment of your overall worth and talents. You can look at the feedback objectively and perhaps see it as an opportunity to learn and grow professionally.

Lastly, the virtue of hope can help with our exaggerated states of suffering.

A prolonged job search can be a tough one because people can suffer emotionally, financially, and mentally when a constant cycle of applications and interviews yields no success. However, continually reminding ourselves that we will land a job can help us persevere. A hopeful outlook can help us see that each interview gets us closer to a new job.

We open ourselves to more moments of joy when we embrace gratitude, self-kindness, and hopefulness in times of suffering.

Practice Opening to Joy in Suffering

How can you feel more joy amid our suffering? One way is to access other virtues, such as *gratitude*, *kindness*, and *hopefulness*. By doing so, joy becomes present. When you go through tough times, apply the three virtues below to see if they might help.

- **Gratitude** – Even on your saddest days, try to appreciate anything you can, like nature, your favorite music, or the support of your family and friends. Moments of gratitude can bring a glimmer of joy to your day.

- **Kindness** – Be kind to yourself when going through struggles. You can even help someone else to take your mind off your worries and fears. Perhaps write a thank-you note or send a small gift like a book to someone who means a lot to you. Simple acts of kindness can uplift your spirits and those of others, making life more joyful!

- **Hope** – Envisioning a brighter future increases your chances of joy. So, when you feel hopeless, think about how you can nurture hope through actions like creating goals, making peace with the past, doing more of what makes you happy, and believing in yourself.

Remember that you can activate joy in your life with gratitude, kindness, and hope at any time, not just during tough times.

Restoring Joyfulness

Laughter can be the fastest route to joy—when we laugh, we forget everything else. All our anxieties melt away in a moment of hilarity. Laughter is also contagious! Just hearing someone laugh uncontrollably can crack us up, too. The sound of a child's laugh is especially joyous. It's no wonder there are thousands of YouTube views of babies laughing. Laughter truly is the "best medicine" for our woes.

Norman Cousins, editor-in-chief of the *Saturday Review* magazine for many years, personally experienced the healing effects of laughter. Diagnosed in 1964 with a painful and potentially life-threatening connective tissue disease, Cousins spent time watching Marx Brothers films, *Candid Camera,* and having nurses read him humor columns. He found that 10 minutes of belly laughter gave him pain relief and helped him sleep more comfortably.

Along with laughter, generous doses of Vitamin C and medical care, Cousins fully recovered from his condition. He later wrote a groundbreaking book, *Anatomy of an Illness as Perceived by the Patient*, which explored how our mental state affects health.[17]

Along with laughter, *becoming more mindful*, *playing more*, and *creating a beautiful environment* can add joy to our lives.

Becoming More Mindful

In their book *Awakening Joy*, James Baraz and Shoshana Alexander explain that the practice of mindfulness plays a pivotal role in awakening our joy, writing, "Mindfulness has many benefits, but for our purposes, the most important is that it can help you live a happier life. You can't *make* joy or well-being happen, but you can help create the conditions in which those states more naturally arise."[18]

The authors echo what the Dalai Lama describes as developing *mental immunity*, the ability to recognize which thoughts nurture well-being and which cause harm. They explain, "Becoming aware of our habits and the automatic ways we react when we're confused or upset is the first step to free ourselves from their power."[19] How do we do this, though, when our thoughts and behaviors can be so habitual? First, as the authors affirm, mindfulness helps us unravel these patterns, allowing us to respond with greater clarity.

The 1993 comedy *Groundhog Day* vividly illustrates this concept, showing how practicing mindfulness can turn a life of frustration into one of joy. In the film, Phil Connors (Bill Murray), a cynical, self-centered television weatherman, reluctantly travels to Punxsutawney, Pennsylvania, to report on the annual Groundhog Day ceremony. He thinks covering the event is beneath his talents and shows contempt for the town and its people.

The night before the ceremony, Phil stays at a bed and breakfast. Oddly, he wakes up at 6:00 a.m., only to discover that he is stuck in a loop, repeatedly reliving Groundhog Day, February 2. He encounters the same people and situations with each day's repeats, increasing his misery and frustration.

Caught in this endless cycle, Phil begins indulging in reckless behaviors—even crime—because there are no consequences. Feeling depressed and trapped, with seemingly no way out of the time loop, he tries to end his life multiple times by electrocuting himself, stepping in front of a truck, and even driving off a cliff. But the day resets each morning, leaving him right where he began.

Phil eventually tells his producer and potential love interest, Rita (Andie MacDowell) of his plight. Initially skeptical, she believes him after he accurately predicts events throughout the day. She empathetically suggests that the repeating day may be a gift rather than a curse, depending on his perspective.

Over time, Phil sees the truth in Rita's words and begins to accept his fate. The next day, he wakes up with a new approach, choosing to improve himself and be kinder to people. He brings Rita and the cameraman coffee and pastry, takes piano lessons, saves a man choking in a restaurant, and fixes a flat tire for three older women. As Phil becomes a better man, Rita grows more impressed, and he eventually wins her over.

One morning, the alarm wakes Phil at 6:00 a.m. to the song "I Got You Babe" by Sonny and Cher, as it does every day. But this time, to his joy and surprise, Rita is by his side (for the first time since he began reliving the same day). Now curious, Phil goes to the window to see if the same people are outside. Not one person is out there—he only sees fresh snow blanketing the streets.[20]

Phil tells Rita with relief, "Today is tomorrow."[21]

The movie's brilliant lesson unfolds when Phil realizes that he cannot change the day, so he chooses to change himself. With this mindful choice, he breaks free from the habitual loops of his thoughts, behaviors, and emotional reactions, transforming his reality. He begins to experience the world as a kind and caring person, and as he changes, his day improves in surprising and joyful ways, and so does his life.

Playing More

Dancing our hearts out, throwing a Frisbee on the beach, and taking a bike ride or nature walk can elevate our spirits. These joyful moments make us feel alive.

I once met someone who found a beautiful way to bring joy into his life. He told me that he loved to dance but couldn't find any places to go where he could do it. So, he installed a full-size dance floor in his basement and hung a rotating disco ball from the ceiling. Every Saturday night, he and his wife, often joined by friends, transformed their basement into a lively dance party. He brought his joy of dancing into the home!

But play isn't limited to physical activities. Playful curiosity can be just as thrilling. As we explore and discover our unique interests, we uncover boundless sources of joy. For example, investigating a topic of interest, reading a book series, or exploring a religion or historical event can spark joy. Each day, we look forward to plunging ourselves into our meaningful quest.

The upshot is that we must find more time to play. And if we have kids, they'll naturally help us be more playful. However we make space for fun, the mental and physical benefits are undeniable, leading to a more joy-filled life.

Creating a Beautiful Environment

Have you ever walked into a room and felt instantly uplifted? Whatever you loved about that room—the sun glowing over an intriguing painting, a particular statue that triggered a pleasant memory, a comfortable old chair—it gave you joy.

Your home might be filled with objects that reflect your personality, such as a well-worn leather chair, cherished antiques, a prominently displayed guitar, a soccer trophy, a book collection, or treasured souvenirs from your travels.

If you feel your home lacks the joy you desire, explore ways to make changes. If you like festive white lights, string them around a bookcase. Create a cozy, rugged area with a big chair, a lamp, and a small table, complete with a pillow and blanket for added comfort. Think about items that bring you joy and add them to your home.

In her book *Feng Shui for the Soul*, Denise Linn captures the importance of being happy with our environment:

> Our homes have an enormous impact on our state of mind. They can make us feel as though we are plunging into despair, or they can be uplifting havens of beauty and rejuvenation. I believe the soul yearns for places of sanctuary and balance, ones that provide authentic reminders of what is truly important in life."[22]

You don't have to stop with your home. You can create an enchanted garden in your backyard, mastermind a creative project area, or design a Zen-like office space.

Surrounding yourself with what brings out your personality and passions creates an environment where you'll love to be!

Practice Restoring Joyfulness

Take time this week to explore ways you can restore joy through laughter, noticing your surroundings, playing more, or creating a beautiful environment. The key is to approach this as fun, not just another task. Here are some ideas to get you started:

- **Laugh** – Watch a funny sitcom, movie, or comedian. You can also play games like Pictionary, Charades, or Twister with family and friends. Whatever makes you laugh, add it to your week!

- **Notice your surroundings** – Become mindful of how your behavior or thoughts impede your joy. Then, create new habits that can bring more joy into your life.

- **Play more** – Indulge in a fun activity or something new to break your routine. Visit new places, read different types of books, take a fun class, join a club, or start a sport. Playing more introduces you to new people, helps you grow personally, and makes your days more enjoyable.

- **Create a beautiful environment** – Paint your rooms in colors you love, add inspiring artwork, and place meaningful decorations throughout your home. You can make your space more of a sanctuary where you'll love to be.

Are you concerned about time or money? Joy doesn't have to be expensive or time-consuming. Simple practices like taking a relaxing walk, keeping a gratitude list, attending free events, or exploring a local park can offer a quick reset and lift your spirits.

CHAPTER SUMMARY

Joyfulness is a deep sense of pleasure and contentment, often sparked by meaningful experiences, positive relationships, and a deep sense of well-being. It's an inner spring of goodness that transforms ordinary moments into extraordinary ones. When we keep our hearts open, joy becomes accessible—present in both life's small and big moments. Nurturing gratitude, kindness, and hope helps us tap into a deeper sense of joy.

Complementing virtues: *Generosity, Gratitude*
Joy transcends: *Apathy, Sorrow*

Remember this . . .

- Pure joy often comes unexpectedly, immersing us in the moment and brightening our mood. Joy's expression can be loud, with screams and laughter, or quiet through tears and soft smiles.

- Happiness and joy are different. Happiness is typically a response to an external event, such as a promotion or heartfelt compliment. Conversely, joy isn't solely cognitive; it often arises from heartwarming experiences or profound moments of insight.

- Joy and suffering can coexist. Despite our pain, we allow joy into our hearts without reservation. Cultivating gratitude, kindness, and hope can significantly increase our chances of calming our emotional reactions.

- We can intentionally infuse joy into our lives by laughing more, becoming more mindful, playing more, and creating a beautiful environment.

Conclusion

Living Your Best Life

We've reached the end of our journey together! Along the way, we've explored the inner strengths—the virtues—that can help you create your best life. Through stories of people who embodied these virtues and our reflective discussions, I hope you've gained insight, discovered more about yourself, and felt inspired.

Congratulations on completing the practices—whether all of them or just a few! I commend you for stepping outside your comfort zone with the ones you found challenging. Above all, I hope this book has heightened your awareness of the power and value of practicing virtues.

American founding father Thomas Jefferson once advised, "Encourage all your virtuous dispositions, and exercise them whenever an opportunity arises, being assured that they will gain strength by exercise, as a limb of the body does, and that exercise will make them habitual."[1]

The secret to your best life isn't moral perfection but rather the steady practice of virtues. Like exercise for the soul, these small, consistent efforts strengthen your character over time and bring meaningful rewards.

As you embark on the path of virtue, it's natural to encounter obstacles. But with virtues, you have what you need to face any life circumstance. Whether you're choosing to respond to a partner with love instead of anger, practicing self-compassion to overcome personal struggles, finding the courage to pursue your dreams, or offering forgiveness to heal old wounds, virtues can help you navigate life more effectively.

Through love, compassion, courage, and forgiveness, you not only transform your own experiences but also radiate positivity to those around you. Just as a stone cast into a lake creates ripples that reach far beyond what you can see, so do your virtuous actions.

Your stone could be a simple act of kindness, like sending a helpful book to a friend going through a tough time. She may connect with its wisdom and feel inspired to make a bold change. That change could motivate another friend—or even an entire community—to rally behind her cause. And so, the ripple continues.

Or perhaps you choose to forgive a family member after years of estrangement. That act of forgiveness might reunite the family and safeguard relationships for generations to come. It's truly remarkable what one virtuous act can set into motion!

Commitment, love, perseverance, hope, integrity, creativity, compassion, courage, forgiveness, purposefulness, gratitude, and joyfulness—these are the inner strengths in your life's toolbox. Bring them out when you need them. When you do, life will return beautiful, meaningful things to you! And if it doesn't, take heart in knowing you did your best and were at your best. More often than not, the good you put into the world creates more goodness.

What strengthens our own lives can also strengthen the world. Now more than ever, we need virtue. Amid today's social, economic, and environmental challenges, the world is longing for renewal shaped by empathy, fairness, and respect. Our moral intelligence is the antidote for creating a healthier world, one we'll be proud to leave to future generations. We can make it happen, one virtuous act at a time!

Committing to these acts strengthens our character, earning the trust and respect of our friends, families, colleagues, and neighbors. They will seek our guidance and feel inspired to improve themselves.

So I invite you to consciously seek out and cultivate your twelve inner strengths. As you do, you'll begin to thrive, live with greater purpose and joy, and ultimately create your best life.

Acknowledgments

In the spirit of gratitude—a beautiful virtue—I extend my heartfelt thanks to the many individuals whose inspiring stories of virtue are featured throughout this book. You have brought to light the incredible power of drawing on inner strengths to enrich your lives and uplift others.

I am immensely grateful to those who allowed me to share their personal stories of virtue: Steve Foran (Gratitude), Linda Lochridge Hoenigsberg (Perseverance), Trevor McDonald (Self-Compassion), and Christina Levasheff (Joy).

Thank you to the spiritual and personal growth experts whose wisdom I highlight throughout the book. I am especially grateful for Dr. Wayne Dyer, who has been my mentor from afar—sparking my love for personal development—even though we never met. His extraordinary work during his time on this planet has profoundly affected my life and the lives of countless others.

To my talented editors: Jennifer Holder, Matthew Hickey, and Lisa Howard—your dedication to my book's message shone brightly. Your insightful input, brilliant feedback, and, most of all, your encouragement were indispensable. Working with you was a pleasure and a privilege. Thank you as well to my proofreader, Stephanie Scott, for your careful eye and attention to detail.

Thank you to my mother-in-law, Phyllis Thompson, who was the first to read my draft. Your keen eye for detail and grammar expertise were invaluable in the early stages of this manuscript. Your contributions have helped make this book the best it could be.

To Michelle Argyle Park: Your talent for cover and interior book design is remarkable. Your positive energy and excellence in your work were truly inspiring. I loved working with you!

To my Mom: What a blessing to have you as my mother! Your love, encouragement, and support have deeply touched my life. I can't thank you enough for all you've done for me. My gratitude and love for you are beyond words.

To my Dad: Your fun-loving, generous spirit has always inspired me to be the same way. I am forever grateful for your love and support. I hope you know how much I appreciate and love you.

To my sister: You generously listened to me talk about this book for hours on end and gave me excellent advice. Thank you for being the extraordinary person and sister you are and for always cheering me on!

To my husband, John D. Thompson: Your steadfast encouragement helped bring this book to life. Thank you for your patience as I slipped away to write for so many hours, night after night. I am also grateful for your contributions to the book, especially your story about your relief mission in Honduras, where you met a grateful woman who touched your life through her sincere expression of gratitude. You are my rock, my best friend, and my loving partner.

I hold in my heart my beloved friend Kathie Heckler, Uncle Robert May, and Aunt Ann Rice, to whom I dedicate this book in loving memory. Your love continues to live on in my life and in the lives of your families.

List of Virtues

Virtues are timeless qualities that reflect the best of who we are and who we can become. Based on *Merriam-Webster Online* definitions, each of these 50 qualities is defined to support your self-awareness and personal growth as you work to apply them in creating your best life.

Acceptance
Accepting others and situations willingly and with a positive attitude

Authenticity
Staying true to one's personality, values, and spirit

Beauty
Appreciating characteristics in others or things that delight the senses

Commitment
Devoting oneself to an endeavor, promising to act on its behalf

Compassion
Recognizing others' suffering with a desire to alleviate it

Confidence
Believing in one's judgment, abilities, and decisions

Courage
Facing physical, moral, and emotional challenges with strength and resolve

Creativity
Turning ideas into reality, solving problems with unconventional thinking, or making unique connections

Determination
....
Persisting in pursuit of a goal despite obstacles

Dignity
....
Maintaining self-control and respectfulness in behavior

Encouragement
....
Motivating others through uplifting words or actions

Excellence
....
Achieving exceptional performance in various pursuits

Fairness
....
Treating people equally, without bias, self-interest, or favoritism

Faith
....
Believing in something without tangible proof

Forgiveness
....
Releasing anger, hurt, and resentment to achieve well-being and full potential

Generosity
....
Sharing time and resources to help others

Gentleness
....
Being kind and tender in words and actions

Grace
....
Radiating beauty and inner strength in one's character and deeds

Gratitude
....
Feeling and expressing deep appreciation for all the good in life

Honesty
....
Being fair and truthful in words and actions

Honor
....
Respecting and upholding strong moral values

Hope
....
Wishing for something good and taking action to make it a reality

Humility
....
Displaying modesty about one's accomplishments

Idealism
....
Pursuing high ideals and shaping life through their influence

Integrity
....
Aligning words and actions with moral and ethical principles

Joyfulness
....
Exuding profound pleasure from good fortune, meaningful experiences, positive relationships, and well-being

Justice
....
Treating others with fairness and moral rightness

Kindness
....
Showing friendliness, generosity, and consideration to others

Love
....
Abiding, deep affection shown through words and actions

Loyalty
....
Being faithful and dedicated to others and commitments

Modesty
....
Avoiding excessive pride or self-promotion

Orderliness
....
Keeping things tidy and organized

Patience

Enduring delays and hardships calmly and without complaint

Peacefulness

Maintaining tranquility and inner calmness

Perseverance

Willingness to see things through despite fear, obstacles, discouragement, and opposition

Prudence

Exercising self-discipline, caution, and sound judgment in both decisions and actions

Purposefulness

Having a clear aim that gives life meaning and can inspire, educate, and uplift others

Respect

Valuing others based on their skills, qualities, or achievements

Responsibility

Taking accountability for one's words and actions

Reverence

Showing deep respect, admiration, and awe

Service

Helping others with a kind and giving spirit

Tact

Communicating sensitively to avoid offense and foster respect

Temperance

Practicing moderation and self-restraint in one's appetites or passions

Tenacity

Staying firmly committed to values and goals despite challenges

Tolerance
....
Enduring hardship and respecting differing beliefs or behaviors

Trust
....
Relying on others' integrity and abilities with confidence

Understanding
....
Comprehending situations or people with clarity and compassion

Unity
....
Achieving harmony and oneness with others through collective effort and shared purpose

Wisdom
....
Applying knowledge, experience, and sound judgment

Wonder
....
Encountering awe and admiration for the unexpected or beautiful

Notes

Introduction

1. Henry Ward Beecher, *Proverbs From Plymouth Pulpit* (France: Ulan Press, 2012), 216.

2. Carl Gustav Jung, *Psychology & Religion* (New Haven, CT: Yale University Press, 1938), 92.

Chapter 1: Commitment

1. Andrew Binner, "From Siberia to Swimming Stardom: This is Paralympic Star Jessica Long's Amazing Story," Olympics.com, March 30, 2021, https://olympics.com/en/featured-news/siberia-to-swimming-stardom-paralympic-jessica-long-amazing-story; Alex Azzi, "Jessica Long Wins 29th Medal, Calls Tokyo 'Total Success,'" NBC Sports, September 4, 2021, https://www.nbcsports.com/on-her-turf/news/jessica-long-swimming-tokyo-paralympics-29-medals.

2. World Para Swimming, "Paris 2024: Jessica Long Rewrites History Books with 17th Paralympic Gold," World Para Swimming, September 4, 2024, https://www.paralympic.org/news/paris-2024-jessica-long-seventeenth-paralympic-gold.

3. Carlo Lucatino, in discussion with the author, August 15, 2024.

4. Ken Blanchard and Jesse Lyn Stoner, *Full Steam Ahead! Unleash the Power of Vision in Your Work and Your Life*, 2nd ed. (San Francisco, CA: Berrett-Koehler, 2011), 169.

5. Blanchard and Stoner, *Full Steam Ahead!*, 172-173.

6. Chris Widener, *The Angel Inside: Michelangelo's Secrets for Following Your Passion and Finding the Work You Love* (New York: Broadway Books, 2004), 10–14.

7. U.S. Declaration of Independence, 1776.

8. History.com Editors, "Martin Luther King Jr. Delivers 'I Have a Dream' Speech at the March on Washington," HISTORY, A&E Networks, last updated August 26, 2004, https://www.history.com/this-day-in-history/august-28/king-speaks-to-march-on-washington.

9. Karen Armstrong, "My Wish: The Charter for Compassion," TED Talk, February 2008, 21:14, https://www.ted.com/talks/karen_armstrong_my_wish_the_charter_for_compassion.

10. "Build Compassion Communities, Affirmed Cities," Charter for Compassion, https://charterforcompassion.org/what-we-do/build-compassionate-communities/affirmed-cities/affirmed-cities.html.

11. "Meet Our Founder: Alexandra Scott," Alex's Lemonade Stand Foundation for Childhood Cancer, https://www.alexslemonade.org/about/meet-alex.

12. "Our Mission & History," Alex's Lemonade Stand Foundation for Childhood Cancer, https://www.alexslemonade.org/about/our-mission-history.

13. Phillip Moffitt, *Emotional Chaos to Clarity: Move from the Chaos of the Reactive Mind to the Clarity of the Responsive Mind* (New York: Plume, 2013), 77–78.

14. Moffitt, *Emotional Chaos to Clarity,* 78.

15. Often attributed to Patanjali, "Patanjali Quotes," as cited in Goodreads, https://www.goodreads.com/quotes/337352-when-you-are-inspired-by-some-great-purpose-some-extraordinary.

16. Enya, "Hope Has a Place," *The Memory of Trees*, Warner Bros., 1995.

17. The Editors of *Encyclopaedia Britannica*, "Nelson Mandela," *Encyclopaedia Britannica*, last updated March 15, 2025, https://www.britannica.com/biography/Nelson-Mandela.

18. "Biography of Nelson Mandela," Nelson Mandela Foundation, https://www.nelsonmandela.org/content/page/biography.

19. Zero Dean, *Lessons Learned from The Path Less Traveled Volume 1: Get Motivated & Overcome Obstacles with Courage, Confidence & Self-discipline* (From The Path Less Traveled Publishing, 2018), 261.

Chapter 2: Love

1. E. E. Cummings, "[i carry your heart with me(i carry it in]," Poetry Foundation, https://www.poetryfoundation.org/poetrymagazine/poems/49493/i-carry-your-heart-with-mei-carry-it-in.

2. Rabbi David Wolpe, "We Are Defining Love the Wrong Way," *Time*, February 16, 2016, https://time.com/4225777/meaning-of-love.

3. Wolpe, "We Are Defining Love the Wrong Way."

4. *Forrest Gump*, directed by Robert Zemeckis (Hollywood, CA: Paramount Pictures, 1994), 1:49:06, Amazon Prime Video.

5. Zemeckis, *Forrest Gump*, 1:49:19.

6. Zemeckis, *Forrest Gump*.

7. Barbara Frederickson, *Love 2.0: Creating Happiness and Health in Moments of Connection*, 2nd ed. (New York: Plume, 2013), 17.

8. Frederickson, *Love 2.0.*, 17–18.

9. Brené Brown, *Daring Greatly: How the Courage to Be Vulnerable Transforms the Way We Live, Love, Parent, and Lead* (New York: Avery, 2012), 34.

10. Brown, *Daring Greatly*, 37.

11. Often attributed to Rumi (Jalal ad-Din Muhammad Rumi), Goodreads, https://www.goodreads.com/quotes/9726-your-task-is-not-to-seek-for-love-but-merely.

12. Tamsen Firestone with Robert W. Firestone, *Daring to Love: Move Beyond Fear of Intimacy, Embrace Vulnerability, and Create Lasting Connection* (Oakland, CA: New Harbinger Publications, 2018), 73.

13. Firestone with Firestone, *Daring to Love*, 73.

14. Neale Donald Walsch, *Conversations with God: An Uncommon Dialogue, Book 1* (Charlottesville, VA: Hampton Roads Publishing, 1995), 130.

15. Elaine Murray Stone, *Maximilian Kolbe: Saint of Auschwitz* (Mahwah, NJ: Paulist Press, 1997).

16. Emily Esfahani Smith, "Masters of Love," *The Atlantic*, June 12, 2014, https://www.theatlantic.com/health/archive/2014/06/happily-ever-after/372573.

17. Smith, "Masters of Love."

18. Plato, *Apology*, trans. G. M. A. Grube (Indianapolis: Hackett, 2002), 38a.

19. Shannon Kaiser, *The Self-Love Experiment: 15 Principles for Becoming More Kind, Compassionate, and Accepting of Yourself* (New York: TarcherPerigee, 2017), xxii–xxv.

20. Kaiser, *The Self-Love Experiment*, xxv.

Chapter 3: Perseverance

1. "Turning Trash into Liquid Assets," CBS News, January 30, 2009, https://www.cbsnews.com/news/turning-trash-into-liquid-assets.

2. CBS News, "Turning Trash into Liquid Assets."

3. "Maisie's Pool," YouTube video, 4:36, posted by TheHardestYear.com, August 3, 2009, https://www.youtube.com/watch?v=wtSBw6xw_I0.

4. TheHardestYear.com, "Maisie's Pool," 4:03.

5. Elizabeth Drake, "Harriet Beecher Stowe: 10 Memorable Quotes on Her Birthday," *The Christian Science Monitor*, June 13, 2012, https://www.csmonitor.com/Books/2012/0613/Harriet-Beecher-Stowe-10-memorable-quotes-on-her-birthday/Persistence.

6. "17 Renowned Writers on Overcoming Rejection," Writing Routines, https://www.writingroutines.com/renowned-writers-on-overcoming-rejection; Wikipedia, "Lady Gaga," last updated March 9, 2025, https://en.wikipedia.org/wiki/Lady_Gaga; "A Motivational Video – Edison, The Beatles, Michael Jordan, Walt Disney, Lincoln," YouTube video, 1:16, posted by Leo Morales, March 28, 2013, https://www.youtube.com/watch?v=X-MpSjB7LErs.

7. Angela Lee Duckworth, "Grit: The Power of Passion and Perseverance," TED Talk, April 2013, 6:00, https://www.ted.com/talks/angela_lee_duckworth_grit_the_power_of_passion_and_perseverance.

8. Duckworth, "Grit: The Power of Passion and Perseverance."

9. Chris Gardner with Quincy Troupe, *The Pursuit of Happyness* (New York: Amistad, 2006).

10. Gardner, *The Pursuit of Happyness*, 6.

11. "Chris Gardner," Wikipedia, last updated March 1, 2025, https://en.wikipedia.org/wiki/Chris_Gardner.

12. Rachel Thompson, "Wilma Rudolph, Once Told She Would Not Walk, Became the World's Fastest Woman 60 Years Ago," NBC Sports, September 8, 2020, https://olympics.nbcsports.com/2020/09/08/wilma-rudolph-rome-olympics.

13. "Wilma Rudolph Quotes," BrainyQuote, https://www.brainyquote.com/quotes/wilma_rudolph_184352.

14. Brad Aronson, "Famous Failures: 23 Stories to Inspire You to Succeed," Brad Aronson, https://www.bradaronson.com/famous-failures.

15. "Biography," Andy Andrews, https://www.andyandrews.com/about.

16. Andy Andrews, "The Worst Rejections I Ever Received," Andy Andrews (blog), April 25, 2013, https://www.andyandrews.com/the-worst-rejections-i-ever-received.

17. Andrews, "The Worst Rejections."

18. Lawrence W. Reed, "Failure Made Disney Great," Foundation for Economic Education, April 15, 2016, https://fee.org/articles/failure-made-disney-great.

19. Amethyst Tate, "Celebs Who Went from Failures to Success Stories," CBS News, July 19, 2012, https://www.cbsnews.com/pictures/celebs-who-went-from-failures-to-success-stories.

20. "About Temple Grandin," Temple Grandin, Ph.D., http://www.templegrandin.com.

21. "About Dr. Wayne Dyer," Dr. Wayne W. Dyer, https://www.drwaynedyer.com/about-dr-wayne-dyer.

22. Linda Lochridge Hoenigsberg, "It's Never Too Late,"

Virtues for Life, https://www.virtuesforlife.com/its-never-too-late.

23. Charles Hunt, "What Trauma Taught Me About Resilience," YouTube video, 14:21, posted by TEDx Talks, November 18, 2016, https://www.youtube.com/watch?v=3qELiw_1Ddg.

24. "About" The Audacity Firm, https://www.audacityfirm.com/aboutcharles.

25. Hunt, "What Trauma Taught Me About Resilience," 12:14.

26. "Erik Weihenmayer," Erik Weihenmayer, https://erikweihenmayer.com/about-erik.

Chapter 4: Hope

1. *The Shawshank Redemption*, directed by Frank Darabont (Beverly Hills, CA: Castle Rock Entertainment, 1994), Amazon Prime Video.

2. Darabont, *The Shawshank Redemption*, 2:15:44.

3. "Biography," Amelia Earhart, https://www.ameliaearhart.com/biography.

4. The Editors of *Encyclopaedia Britannica*, "Edmund Hillary," *Encyclopaedia Britannica*, last updated February 20, 2025, https://www.britannica.com/biography/Edmund-Hillary.

5. Charles R. Snyder, "Hope Theory: Rainbows in the Mind," *Psychological Inquiry* 13, no. 4 (2002): 249 - 275.

6. Snyder, "Hope Theory," 258.

7. Snyder, "Hope Theory," 259.

8. Snyder, "Hope Theory," 260.

9. Snyder, "Hope Theory," 263–264.

10. Casey Gwinn and Chan Hellman, *Hope Rising: How the Science of Hope Can Change Your Life* (New York: Morgan James Publishing, 2002), 8.

11. Gwinn and Hellman, *Hope Rising*, 9.

12. Gwinn and Hellman, *Hope Rising*, 9–12.

13. Darabont, *The Shawshank Redemption*, 1:45:44.

14. Jerome Groopman, *The Anatomy of Hope: How People Prevail in the Face of Illness* (New York: Random House Trade Paperbacks, 2005), xiii.

15. Groopman, *The Anatomy of Hope*, 121–146.

16. Groopman, *The Anatomy of Hope*, 144.

17. Viktor E. Frankl, *Man's Search for Meaning* (Boston, MA: Beacon Press, 2006).

18. Frankl, *Man's Search for Meaning*, 115.

19. Frankl, *Man's Search for Meaning*, 75.

20. Frankl, *Man's Search for Meaning*, 117.

21. Christopher Reeve, *Still Me* (New York: Ballantine Books, 1999), 28.

22. Reeve, *Still Me*, 28.

23. Reeve, *Still Me*, 124–132.

24. "Our History," Christopher & Dana Reeve Foundation, https://www.christopherreeve.org/community/about-us/history-of-the-reeve-foundation.

25. "Our Research Priorities," Christopher & Dana Reeve Foundation, https://www.christopherreeve.org/tomorrows-cure/approach-to-research/research-priorities.

Chapter 5: Integrity

1. So-Young Kang, "So-Young Kang: Global Leadership – True Meaning of Integrity (updated)," YouTube video, 5:50, posted by Awaken Group, September 24, 2015, https://www.youtube.com/watch?v=KOeB-_B1bPY&t=2s.

2. Kang, "So-Young Kang: Global Leadership – True Meaning of Integrity (updated)."

3. Henry Cloud, *Integrity: The Courage to Meet the Demands of Reality* (New York: HarperCollins Publishers, 2006), 31.

4. Cloud, *Integrity*, 33–35.

5. Cloud, *Integrity*, 34–37.

6. *Willy Wonka & the Chocolate Factory*, directed by Mel Stuart (Burbank, CA: Warner Brothers, 1971), 1:34:41, Amazon Streaming Video.

7. Stuart, *Willy Wonka*.

8. Kelley Kosow, *The Integrity Advantage: Step into Your Truth, Love Your Life, and Claim Your Magnificence* (Boulder, CO: Sounds True, 2017), 14.

9. Kosow, *The Integrity Advantage*, 14.

10. Kosow, *The Integrity Advantage*, 14.

11. "Rescuing Yourself – Lisa Nichols | Inside Quest #66," YouTube video, 55:14, posted by Tom Bilyeu Classics, May 14, 2017, https://www.youtube.com/watch?v=-_JMP-wGjZLo.

12. Lisa Nichols, *"Rescuing Yourself,"* 2017.

13. "Lisa Nichols," Motivating the Masses, https://www.motivatingthemasses.com/about/lisa-nichols.

14. Michael Martel, *Improvise, Adapt, Overcome – Achieve*

the Green Beret Way (self-published, 2012), chap. 3, Kindle.

15. TODAY books, "Former eBay CEO on Success in Career and Life," *TODAY*, January 25, 2010, https://www.today.com/popculture/former-ebay-ceo-success-career-life-wbna35062659.

16. TODAY books, "Former eBay CEO."

17. Don Miguel Ruiz, *The Four Agreements: A Practical Guide to Personal Freedom* (San Rafael, CA: Amber-Allen Publishing, 1997), 25.

18. Ruiz, *The Four Agreements*, 26–27.

19. Steve Hartman, "La. Principal's Success is a Lesson in Perseverance," CBS News, February 7, 2014, https://www.cbsnews.com/news/louisiana-principals-success-is-a-lesson-in-perseverance.

20. Hartman, "La. Principal's Success."

Chapter 6: Creativity

1. Neville Goddard, *The Power of Awareness: Ideas that Shape the World* (Seattle, WA: Pacific Publishing Studio, 2010), 14.

2. Rollo May, *The Courage to Create* (New York: W. W. Norton & Company, 1975), 61–62.

3. Osho, *Creativity: Unleashing the Forces Within* (New York: St. Martin's Griffin, 1999), 146.

4. Mihaly Csikszentmihalyi, *Flow: The Psychology of Optimal Experience* (New York: Harper & Row, Publishers, 1990), 4.

5. A.H. Maslow, *Motivation and Personality* (New York: Harper & Row, Publishers, 1954), 46.

6. Rebecca Tuhus-Dubrow, "4 Fascinating Stories of Creative Inspiration," Oprah.com, https://www.oprah.com/spirit/fascinating-stories-of-creative-inspiration.

7. "About," Biomason, https://biomason.com/about.

8. Bob Granath, "Apollo 13 Mission Remembered as 'NASA's Finest Hour'," *SpaceAgeChronicle*, April 11, 2020, https://spaceagechronicle.com/apollo-13-mission-remembered-as-nasas-finest-hour. *(Originally published April 17, 2015, on NASA.gov.)*

9. Granath, "Apollo 13 Mission Remembered."

10. Sylvia Duckworth, "12 Benefits of Creativity," Sylvia-Duckworth.shop, https://sylviaduckworth.shop/product/12-benefits-of-creativity.

11. Betsy Schwarm, "Piano Concerto No. 2 in C Minor, Op. 18," *Encyclopaedia Britannica*, last updated April 5, 2024, https://www.britannica.com/topic/Piano-Concerto-No-2-Rachmaninoff.

12. Steven Pressfield, *The War of Art: Break Through the Blocks and Win Your Inner Creative Battles* (New York: Black Irish Entertainment LLC, 2002), chap. "The Unlived Life."

13. Pressfield, *The War of Art*, 40.

14. Sir Ken Robinson, *Out of Our Minds: Learning to Be Creative*, 2nd ed. (North Mankato, MN: Capstone Publishing Ltd., 2011), 3.

15. Robinson, *Out of Our Minds*, 4.

16. Amy Novotney, "The Science of Creativity," American Psychological Association, https://www.apa.org/gradpsych/2009/01/creativity.

17. Novotney, "The Science of Creativity."

18. Heinrich L. Heydenreich, "Leonardo da Vinci," *Encyclopaedia Britannica*, last updated April 30, 2024, https://www.britannica.com/biography/Leonardo-da-Vinci.

19. Michael J. Gelb, *How to Think Like Leonardo da Vinci: Seven Steps to Genius Every Day* (New York: Dell, 2000).

20. David Brooks, "What is Inspiration?" *The New York Times*, April 15, 2016, https://www.nytimes.com/2016/04/15/opinion/what-is-inspiration.html.

21. "Giacomo Puccini," AZ Quotes, https://www.azquotes.com/quote/810824.

22. "Behind The Song: The Beatles, 'Let It Be'," American Songwriter, https://americansongwriter.com/let-it-be-by-the-beatles-behind-the-song.

23. Tom Kelley and David Kelley, *Creative Confidence: Unleashing the Creative Potential Within Us All* (New York: Currency, 2013), 78.

24. Kelley and Kelley, *Creative Confidence*, 78.

25. Kelley and Kelley, *Creative Confidence*, 79.

26. Julia Cameron, *The Artist's Way: A Spiritual Path to Higher Creativity* (New York: Penguin Putnam, Inc., 1992), 9–11.

Chapter 7: Compassion

1. Steve Hartman, "Bachelor Detective Takes on Case of Two Pittsburgh Boys," CBS Evening News, December 25, 2015, https://www.cbsnews.com/news/bachelor-detective-takes-on-case-of-two-pittsburgh-boys. *(Originally aired on September 19th, 2014.)*

2. Hartman, "Bachelor Detective Takes on Case of Two Pittsburgh Boys."

3. The Dalai Lama, *An Open Heart: Practicing Compassion*

in Everyday Life (New York: Little, Brown and Company, 2001), 110–114.

4. Pema Chödrön, *The Places That Scare You: A Guide to Fearlessness in Difficult Times* (Boulder, CO: Shambhala, 2018), 50.

5. Oriah Mountain Dreamer, *The Dance: Moving to the Deep Rhythms of Your Life* (New York: HarperOne, 2006), 42.

6. Sharon Salzberg, *LovingKindness: The Revolutionary Art of Happiness* (Boston, MA: Shambhala Publications, 1995), 29-32.

7. Maria Mazziotti Gillan and Jennifer Gillan, eds., *Unsettling America: An Anthology of Contemporary Multicultural Poetry* (New York: Penguin Books, 1994), 266–267.

8. Tara Cousineau, "Q&A on Kindness with Tara Cousineau, PhD," interview by Stacey Thompson, Virtues for Life, February 1, 2018, https://www.virtuesforlife.com/qa-on-kindness-with-tara-cousineau-phd.

9. Cousineau, "Q&A on Kindness."

10. Shankar Vedantam, "Feeling Good to Be Good May Be Only Natural," NBC News, May 28, 2007, https://www.nbcnews.com/id/wbna18899688.

11. "Allan Luks' Helper's High: The Healing Power of Helping Others," Allan Luks, http://allanluks.com/helpers_high.

12. Jill Suttie, "A Healthier Kind of Happiness," *Greater Good Magazine*, September 10, 2013, https://greatergood.berkeley.edu/article/item/a_healthier_kind_of_happiness.

13. Suttie, "A Healthier Kind of Happiness."

14. Marcus Engel, *I'm Here: Compassionate Communication in Patient Care* (Ella Press, Third Edition, 2010).

15. Grahame Winters Slogesky, "Compassionate Care Subject of 'I'm Here' Talk by Marcus Engel," *Hartford Courant*, November 5, 2014, https://www.courant.com/community/rnw-eh-1113-engel-at-goodwin-college-20141105-story.html.

16. A tale from India retold by Mary Dessein, "The Cracked Pot," National Storytelling Network (NSN), https://storynet.org/the-cracked-pot. Mary Dessein's version of the tale was excerpted by NSN from the book, *The Healing Heart ~ Communities*, Allison M. Cox (editor) and David H. Albert (editor), (Gabriola Island, BC, Canada: New Society Publishers, 2003), 96.

17. Trevor McDonald, "How Self-Compassion Helped Heal My Life," Virtues for Life, August 10, 2017, https://www.virtuesforlife.com/how-self-compassion-helped-heal-my-life.

18. Kristin Neff, *Self-Compassion: The Proven Power of Being Kind to Yourself*, (New York: William Morrow, 2011), 41–106.

Chapter 8: Courage

1. Cara Buckley, "Man is Rescued by Stranger on Subway Tracks," *The New York Times*, January 3, 2007, https://www.nytimes.com/2007/01/03/nyregion/03life.html; Maurice DuBois, "5 Years Later, New York City Subway Hero Wesley Autrey Is Still The Man," CBS New York, February 21, 2012, https://newyork.cbslocal.com/2012/02/21/5-years-later-new-york-city-subway-hero-wesley-autrey-is-still-the-man.

2. Buckley, "Man is Rescued."

3. "Anais Nin Quotes," Goodreads, https://www.goodreads.com/quotes/2061.

4. The Editors of *Encyclopaedia Britannica*, "Neil Arm-

strong," *Encyclopaedia Britannica*, last updated April 19, 2024, https://www.britannica.com/biography/Neil-Armstrong; The Editors of *Encyclopaedia Britannica*, "Harriet Tubman," *Encyclopaedia Britannica*, last updated May 10, 2024, https://www.britannica.com/biography/Harriet-Tubman; B.R. Nanda, "Mahatma Gandhi," *Encyclopaedia Britannica*, last updated May 13, 2024, https://www.britannica.com/biography/Mahatma-Gandhi.

5. "Addison, Wendy," Giraffe Heroes Project, https://giraffeheroes.org/1266/WendyAddison.

6. "About," Speakout Speakup, https://speakout-speakup.org/about.

7. Brené Brown, *The Gifts of Imperfection: Let Go of Who You Think You're Supposed to Be and Embrace Who You Are* (Center City, MN: Hazelden Publishing, 2010), 12.

8. Brown, *The Gifts of Imperfection*, 12–13.

9. Helen Kantilaftis, "Stage Fright: Examples & Lessons from Famous Sufferers," New York Film Academy, July 1, 2014, https://www.nyfa.edu/student-resources/stage-fright-examples-lessons-famous-sufferers.

10. Mark Twain, *Pudd'nhead Wilson* (Bulgaria: Demetra Publishing, 2019), 62.

11. Thich Nhat Hanh, *Fear: Essential Wisdom for Getting Through the Storm* (New York: HarperOne, 2014), 2–4.

12. Hanh, *Fear*, 2.

13. *The Wizard of Oz*, directed by Victor Fleming (Culver City: Metro-Goldwyn-Mayer, 1939), DVD.

14. Robert Biswas-Diener, *The Courage Quotient: How Science Can Make You Braver* (San Francisco, CA: Jossey-Bass, 2012), 14.

15. Biswas-Diener, *The Courage Quotient*, 15.

16. Amy Tikkanen, "US Airways Flight 1549," *Encyclopaedia Britannica*, January 20, 2024, https://www.britannica.com/topic/US-Airways-Flight-1549-incident.

17. Tilar J. Mazzeo, *Irena's Children: A True Story of Courage* (New York: Gallery Books, 2016).

18. "Terry's Story," The Terry Fox Foundation, https://terryfox.org/terrys-story.

19. John Bacon, "Report: Teacher Tried to Divert Shooter," *USA Today*, December 16, 2012, https://www.usatoday.com/story/news/nation/2012/12/16/newtown-shootings-gunman-soto-details/1772791.

20. "Mary W. Jackson," NASA, May 25, 2017, https://www.nasa.gov/history/mary-w-jackson.

21. CNN Editorial Research, "Tiananmen Square Fast Facts," CNN, last updated May 21, 2024, https://www.cnn.com/2013/09/15/world/asia/tiananmen-square-fast-facts/index.html.

Chapter 9: Forgiveness

1. Immaculée Ilibagiza with Steve Erwin, *Left to Tell: Discovering God Amidst the Rwandan Holocaust* (New York: Hay House, 2006).

2. Ilibagiza with Erwin, *Left to Tell*, 94.

3. Ilibagiza with Erwin, 94.

4. Sylvie Lubow and Mitra Bonshahi, "'Worth Being Forgiven': A Father And His Son's Killer Bring Past and Present Together," NPR (StoryCorps), February 26, 2021, https://www.npr.org/2021/02/26/971327506/worth-being-forgiven-a-father-and-his-sons-killer-bring-past-and-present-together.

5. Lubow and Bonshahi, "'Worth Being Forgiven.'"

6. Teri Figueroa, "Newly Free from Prison, a Man Who Killed at Age 14 Atones for His Past and Looks to His Future," *The San Diego Union-Tribune*, January 12, 2020, https://www.sandiegouniontribune.com/news/public-safety/story/2020-01-12/newly-free-from-prison-a-man-who-killed-at-age-14-looks.

7. Fred Luskin, *Forgive for Good: A Proven Prescription for Health and Happiness* (New York: HarperOne, 2003), 68.

8. Fred Luskin, "Q&A on Forgiveness with Dr. Fred Luskin," interview by Stacey A. Thompson, Virtues for Life, September 27, 2010, https://www.virtuesforlife.com/qa-on-forgiveness-with-dr-fred-luskin.

9. Luskin, "Q&A on Forgiveness."

10. Joan Borysenko, *Fire in the Soul: A New Psychology of Spiritual Optimism* (New York: Warner Books, 1993), 128.

11. Susyn Reeve, *Heart Healing: The Power of Forgiveness to Heal a Broken Heart* (Coral Gables, FL: Mango Publishing Group, 2018), 66.

12. Susyn Reeve, "Q&A on Healing Our Hearts through Forgiveness with Susyn Reeve," interview by Stacey A. Thompson, Virtues for Life, February 2019, https://www.virtuesforlife.com/qa-on-healing-our-hearts-through-forgiveness-with-susyn-reeve.

13. Reeve, *Heart Healing*, 82–83.

14. Reeve, *Heart Healing*, 88 (from the "When to Forgive Checklist").

15. "Mahatma Gandhi Quotes," BrainyQuote, https://www.brainyquote.com/quotes/mahatma_gandhi_121411.

16. Rick Hanson, "Just One Thing: Forgive Yourself," *Greater Good Magazine*, June 25, 2015, https://greater-

good.berkeley.edu/article/item/just_one_thing_forgive_ yourself.

17. Kelly Connor, "Kelly Connor," The Forgiveness Project, https://www.theforgivenessproject.com/stories/kelly-con- nor.

18. Connor, "Kelly Connor."

19. Connor, "Kelly Connor."

20. Often attributed to Rumi (Jalal ad-Din Muham- mad Rumi), Goodreads, https://www.goodreads.com/ quotes/1299504-i-said-what-about-my-eyes-he-said-keep- them.

21. Desmond Tutu and Mpho Tutu, *The Book of Forgiving: The Fourfold Path for Healing Ourselves and Our World* (New York: HarperOne, 2014), 16.

22. Wayne W. Dyer, *I Can See Clearly Now* (New York: Hay House, 2014), 144–152.

23. Dyer, *I Can See Clearly Now*, 147.

24. Dyer, *I Can See Clearly Now*, 149–151.

Chapter 10: Purposefulness

1. Richard J. Leider, *The Power of Purpose: Find Meaning, Live Longer, Better* (Oakland, CA: Berrett-Koehler Pub- lishers, 2015), vii–viii.

2. Leider, *The Power of Purpose*, vii.

3. Héctor García and Francesc Miralles, *Ikigai: The Japanese Secret to a Long and Happy Life* (New York: Penguin Books, 2016), 9.

4. García and Miralles, *Ikigai*, 10.

5. Rick Warren, *The Purpose Driven Life: What on Earth*

Am I Here For? (Grand Rapids, MI: Zondervan, 2002), 17.

6. Warren, *The Purpose Driven Life,* 17.

7. Victor J. Strecher, *Life on Purpose: How Living For What Matters Most Changes Everything* (New York: Harper-One, 2016), 58.

8. Robert Herrick, *"To the Virgins, to Make Much of Time,"* Poetry Foundation, https://www.poetryfoundation.org/poems/46546/to-the-virgins-to-make-much-of-time.

9. *Dead Poets Society,* directed by Peter Weir (Burbank, CA: Touchstone Pictures, 1989), 15:32, Amazon Streaming Video.

10. Weir, *Dead Poets Society,* 15:45.

11. Members of Adolescent Moral Development Lab, "The Psychology of Purpose," created for Prosocial Consulting and the John Templeton Foundation (Claremont, CA: John Templeton Foundation, 2018), https://www.templeton.org/wp-content/uploads/2020/02/Psychology-of-Purpose.pdf, 10–11.

12. Members of Adolescent Moral Development Lab, *The Psychology of Purpose,* 15–16.

13. A. Alimujiang, A. Wiensch, J. Boss, et al., "Association Between Life Purpose and Mortality Among US Adults Older Than 50 Years," *JAMA Network Open* 2, no. 5 (2019): e194270, https://doi.org/10.1001/jamanetworkopen.2019.4270.

14. A. Kaplin and L. Anzaldi, "New Movement in Neuroscience: A Purpose-Driven Life," *Cerebrum: The Dana Forum on Brain Science* (2015): 7.

15. Yaron Steinbuch, "Massive Yonkers Fire Displaces More Than 150 Residents," *New York Post,* March 13, 2019,

https://nypost.com/2019/03/13/massive-yonkers-fire-dis-places-more-than-150-residents.

16. Stephanie Porto, in discussion with the author, September 10, 2020.

17. Girish Gogia, "Living Limitless – An Inspiring Story of Ultimate Human Potential," The Good Men Project, January 30, 2016, https://goodmenproject.com/fea-tured-content/living-limitless-an-inspiring-true-story-of-ul-timate-human-potential-bbab.

18. Gogia, "Living Limitless."

19. Chris Guillebeau, *The Happiness of Pursuit: Finding the Quest That Will Bring Purpose to Your Life* (New York: Harmony Books, 2014), 15–16.

20. Guillebeau, *The Happiness of Pursuit*, 6–10.

21. Barbara Goldsmith, *Obsessive Genius: The Inner World of Marie Curie* (New York: W.W. Norton & Company, 2005).

22. Eve Curie, *Madame Curie: A Biography*, trans. Vincent Sheean (Boston, MA: Da Capo Press, 2001), 116.

23. Scott Harrison with Lisa Sweetingham, *Thirst: A Story of Redemption, Compassion, and a Mission to Bring Clean Water to the World* (New York: Currency, 2018), 47.

24. Harrison with Sweetingham, *Thirst*.

25. "charity: water," https://www.charitywater.org.

26. Marianne Williamson, *A Return to Love: Reflections on the Principles of "A Course of Miracles"* (New York: HarperOne, 1996), 190.

27. T.S. Eliot, *Four Quartets* (Boston, MA: Mariner Books, 1968), 59.

28. Mark Manson, "The Most Important Question of Your

Life," Mark Manson (blog), https://markmanson.net/question.

29. Manson, "The Most Important Question."

30. Manson, "The Most Important Question."

31. Talane Miedaner, *Coach Yourself to Success: 101 Tips to Accomplish Your Personal and Professional Goals* (New York: McGraw-Hill Education, 2015), 156.

32. Miedaner, *Coach Yourself to Success*, 158.

Chapter 11: Gratitude

1. Harvard Health Publishing, "Giving Thanks Can Make You Happier," August 14, 2021, https://www.health.harvard.edu/healthbeat/giving-thanks-can-make-you-happier.

2. Angeles Arrien, *Living in Gratitude: A Journey That Will Change Your Life* (Boulder, CO: Sounds True, 2011), 3.

3. "Welcome," Network for Grateful Living, https://grateful.org/welcome.

4. Brother David Steindl-Rast, *Gratefulness, the Heart of Prayer: An Approach to Life in Fullness* (New York: Paulist Press, 1984), 207.

5. Steven Foran, email message to author, March 12, 2019. For further reference, Steve wrote an insightful book on grateful leadership called, *Surviving to Thriving: The 10 Laws of Grateful Leadership.*

6. Robert A. Emmons, *Thanks! How Practicing Gratitude Can Make You Happier* (New York: Houghton Mifflin Company, 2007), 27–30.

7. *It's a Wonderful Life*, directed by Frank Capra (Culver City, California: Liberty Films, 1946), Amazon Streaming Video.

8. Robert A. Emmons, "Why Gratitude is Good," *Greater Good Magazine*, November 16, 2010, https://greater-good.berkeley.edu/article/item/why_gratitude_is_good; Emmons, "Why Gratitude is Good"; Emmons, "Why Gratitude is Good"; Steve Foran, Gratitude at Work, https://www.gratitudeatwork.ca/#home-1.

9. Janice Kaplan, *The Gratitude Diaries: How a Year Looking on the Bright Side Can Transform Your Life* (New York: Dutton, 2016).

10. Kaplan, *Gratitude Diaries*, 253.

11. M.J. Ryan, *Attitudes of Gratitude: How to Give and Receive Joy Every Day of Your Life* (Coral Gables, FL: Mango Publishing Group, 2020), 18.

12. John D. Thompson (former Helicopter Crew Chief for United States Army Special Operations), in discussion with the author, May 18, 2020.

13. Thompson, in discussion with the author.

14. John Kralik, *365 Thank Yous: The Year a Simple Act of Daily Gratitude Changed My Life* (New York: Hachette Books, 2010).

15. Kralik, *365 Thank Yous*, 218.

16. Arrien, *Living in Gratitude*, 2–3.

Chapter 12: Joyfulness

1. David E. Thompson (father of John D. Thompson), in discussion with the author, March 5, 2016.

2. "'Life Is Beautiful' Wins Foreign Language Film: 1999 Oscars," YouTube video, 3:33, posted by the Oscars, February 19, 2008, https://www.youtube.com/watch?v=8c-TR6fk8frs&t=1s.

3. Charles Preston and Shabnam Dohutia, "Holi," *Ency-*

clopaedia Britannica, last updated June 17, 2024, https://www.britannica.com/topic/Holi; Ronald Milton Schneider and Richard P. Momsen, "Carnival," *Encyclopaedia Britannica*, last updated March 14, 2025, https://www.britannica.com/place/Brazil/Performing-arts; David L. Waldstreicher, "Independence Day (United States)," *Encyclopaedia Britannica*, last updated March 3, 2024, https://www.britannica.com/topic/Independence-Day-United-States-holiday; "Ubuntu Philosophy," Wikipedia, https://en.wikipedia.org/wiki/Ubuntu_philosophy.

4. "APA Dictionary of Psychology," American Psychological Association, https://dictionary.apa.org/joy.

5. Oprah Winfrey, "What Oprah Knows for Sure About Growing Up," Oprah.com, https://www.oprah.com/spirit/oprahs-lessons-about-growing-up.

6. C.S. Lewis, *Letters to Malcolm: Chiefly on Prayer* (San Francisco, CA: HarperOne, 2017), 125.

7. Elizabeth Berg, *The Art of Mending* (New York: Random House, 2004), 213–214.

8. Jessica Cerretani, "The Contagion of Happiness," *Harvard Medicine*, Summer 2011, https://hms.harvard.edu/magazine/science-emotion/contagion-happiness.

9. Ingrid Fetell Lee, "Why the Secret to Happiness Might Be Joy," The Aesthetics of Joy, https://aestheticsofjoy.com/2018/05/14/why-the-secret-to-happiness-might-be-joy.

10. Lee, "Why the Secret to Happiness."

11. "Voltaire," Goodreads, https://www.goodreads.com/quotes/108491-perfect-is-the-enemy-of-good.

12. Christina Levasheff (Judson's Mother), "Joy in Heartache," Judson's Legacy, https://judsonslegacy.org/finding-hope-in-suffering/joy-in-suffering.

13. "Our Mission," Judson's Legacy, https://judsonslegacy.org/our-mission.

14. Dalai Lama and Desmond Tutu, *The Book of Joy: Lasting Happiness in a Changing World* (New York: Avery, 2016), 14.

15. Lama and Tutu, *The Book of Joy*, 14.

16. Lama and Tutu, *The Book of Joy*, 83.

17. Don Colburn, "Norman Cousins, Still Laughing," *The Washington Post*, October 21, 1986, https://www.washingtonpost.com/archive/lifestyle/wellness/1986/10/21/norman-cousins-still-laughing/e17f23cb-3e8c-4f58-b907-2dcd00326e22.

18. James Baraz and Shoshana Alexander, *Awakening Joy: 10 Steps to Happiness* (Berkeley, CA: Parallax Press, 2012), 32.

19. Baraz and Alexander, *Awakening Joy*, 35.

20. *Groundhog Day*, directed by Harold Ramis (Culver City, CA: Columbia Pictures, 1993), Amazon Streaming Video.

21. Ramis, *Groundhog Day*, 1:36:23.

22. Denise Linn, *Feng Shui for the Soul: How to Create a Harmonious Environment That Will Nurture and Sustain You* (Carlsbad, CA: Hay House, 2000), 14.

Conclusion: Living Your Best Life

1. Thomas Jefferson to Peter Carr, August 19, 1785, *Founders Online*, National Archives, https://founders.archives.gov/documents/Jefferson/01-08-02-0319.

About the Author

Stacey Thompson is a certified life coach and the founder of Virtues for Life, a website dedicated to helping people live their best lives by exploring and practicing virtues. She is passionate about personal development and fascinated by stories of people who have triumphed over adversity, achieved a dream, or developed a stronger sense of self.

Through studying these stories, she noticed a common thread: these individuals consistently embodied an inner strength or virtue, such as courage, perseverance, or purposefulness, on their path to success. Inspired by this insight, Stacey combined her love of personal growth and virtue-centered hero stories to create Virtues for Life and write this book.

Her vision is to inspire others to cultivate their virtues, or inner strengths, so they can lead thriving, purposeful lives. She lives in Connecticut with her husband.

Connect with Stacey:

Facebook: @VirtuesforLife
Instagram: @VirtuesforLife
X: @VirtuesforLife
E-mail: stacey@virtuesforlife.com
Website: virtuesforlife.com

Join Our Community

Subscribe to Stacey's newsletter for inspiring blog posts, tips on practicing virtues and exclusive updates at virtuesforlife.com.